SAGE was founded in 1965 by Sara Miller McCune to support the dissemination of usable knowledge by publishing innovative and high-quality research and teaching content. Today, we publish more than 750 journals, including those of more than 300 learned societies, more than 800 new books per year, and a growing range of library products including archives, data, case studies, reports, conference highlights, and video. SAGE remains majority-owned by our founder, and on her passing will become owned by a charitable trust that secures our continued independence.

Los Angeles | London | Washington DC | New Delhi | Singapore

A Governors' Raj

A Governors' Raj

British Administration during Lord Irwin's Viceroyalty, 1926–1931

Michael Fenwick Macnamara

www.sagepublications.com
Los Angeles • London • New Delhi • Singapore • Washington DC

First published in 2015 by

SAGE Publications India Pvt Ltd
B1/I-1 Mohan Cooperative Industrial Area
Mathura Road, New Delhi 110 044, India
www.sagepub.in

SAGE Publications Inc
2455 Teller Road
Thousand Oaks, California 91320, USA

SAGE Publications Ltd
1 Oliver's Yard, 55 City Road
London EC1Y 1SP, United Kingdom

SAGE Publications Asia-Pacific Pte Ltd
3 Church Street
#10-04 Samsung Hub
Singapore 049483

Published by Vivek Mehra for SAGE Publications India Pvt Ltd, typeset in 10/12 Adobe Garamond Pro by Diligent Typesetter, Delhi and printed at Saurabh Printers Pvt Ltd, New Delhi.

Library of Congress Cataloging-in-Publication Data Available

ISBN: 978-93-515-0044-5 (HB)

The SAGE Team: N. Unni Nair, Saima Ghaffar, Rajib Chatterjee and Vinitha Nair

This work is dedicated to my dear wife Bronwen and our three wonderful daughters, Janet, Evelyn and Gwenyth—scholars all

Thank you for choosing a SAGE product! If you have any comment, observation or feedback, I would like to personally hear from you. Please write to me at contactceo@sagepub.in

—Vivek Mehra, Managing Director and CEO,
SAGE Publications India Pvt Ltd, New Delhi

Bulk Sales

SAGE India offers special discounts for purchase of books in bulk. We also make available special imprints and excerpts from our books on demand.

For orders and enquiries, write to us at

Marketing Department
SAGE Publications India Pvt Ltd
B1/I-1, Mohan Cooperative Industrial Area
Mathura Road, Post Bag 7
New Delhi 110044, India
E-mail us at marketing@sagepub.in

Get to know more about SAGE, be invited to SAGE events, get on our mailing list. Write today to marketing@sagepub.in

This book is also available as an e-book.

Contents

Contents

Governors' Conference In Simla (July 1930)

Left to right: Sir Montague Butler (Central Provinces), Sir Charles Innes (Burma), Sir George Stanley (Madras), Sir Geoffrey de Montmorency (Punjab), The Viceroy, Lord Irwin, Sir Fredrick Sykes (Bombay), Sir Hugh Stephenson (Acting Governor of Bengal), Sir Malcolm Hailey (United Provinces), Sir James Sefton (Acting Governor of Bihar and Orissa), Sir Laurie Hammond (Assam).

Source: Government of India, Simla, 1930.

The Governors of British India: 1926–1931

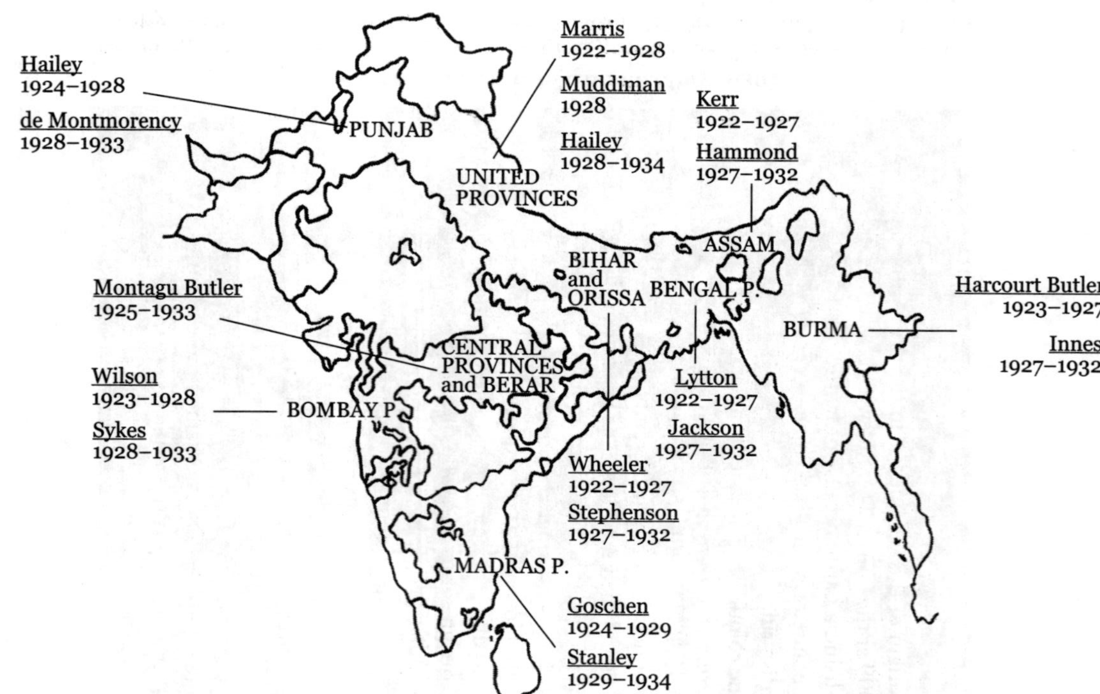

Source: Author's illustration.

Preface

The origin of this volume lies in the work done to complete a PhD thesis[1] in 2009 at the University of New England. I had always been fascinated by British India partly because of family connections, as well as Kipling, and also because of what I had come to regard as the 'phenomenon' of the fact of British rule.

The colour and pageant of India, the adventures of Britons therein, the soldiering and triumph of British arms. The creation of the Indian political entity itself. The skill and efficiency of an administration that ruled a huge subcontinent. The adventures and tribulations of the administrators and their families and their sacrifices. The benefits of this administration include: the railways, canals and improved agriculture; the language, the law and sport. These Anglophilic perceptions were perhaps derived from earlier selective readings. However, as my explorations became wider and deeper I became aware of different perceptions. These included main views that the British were foreign conquerors who ruled India mainly for their benefit at the cost of the Indian people and had no real wish to alter their advantage; that foreign domination was an abomination to be thrown off at the earliest opportunity; and that the British used identifiable techniques, apart from military subjugation, such as subversive collaboration and the division of religious groups to ensure their continuing rule, and indeed, that they were even perfidious in the face of, for example, the Montagu–Chelmsford Reforms,[2] the construct of the 1919 *Government of India Act* and the implied promise of Indian independence contained therein, but which failed to identify an actual end point for British rule.[3]

Having positive views of the British principle and ethics, these perceptions intrigued me and I determined to explore their truth or otherwise. But the question was how to do so in the most effective, accurate and incontrovertible way? In my explorations of material for this work, I discovered the complete papers of Lord Irwin, compiled during his viceroyalty of India 1926–1931, in the British Library in London.[4] This set contains all private communication to Irwin and from Irwin, including all communication to and from the British governors of India, during their rule. Also available are the papers of secretaries of state and a limited number of governors. Relevant information is also preserved in the National Archives of India in New Delhi.[5] This original source material gave me the opportunity to explore the fact of British intent and ethics towards India through these original papers. If the British were indeed perfidious and unethical surely it would be reflected here?

This also opened an opportunity and interest to consider further, and more widely, the relationship between the governors of British India, the Viceroy and the Secretary of State in general, and the governors' influence on Central decision making and outcomes in particular. This work revealed some interesting information. Wherever the governors are mentioned in the historical literature, their reference is largely incidental to the main story. This opened up the main field of research—the influence of the Governor cadre on British Indian policy which became the overarching theme of this book.

Endnotes

1. Macnamara, 'The Governors of British India during Lord Irwin's Viceroyalty: 1926–1931'.
2. The progressive Montagu–Chelmsford Reforms (hereafter Montford Reforms) were encapsulated in the Montagu Declaration of August 1917 and in the 1919 *Government of India Act.* The first paragraph of the Preamble read: '... the increasing association of Indians in every branch of Indian administration and for the gradual development of self-governing institutions with a view to the progressive realisation of responsible government in British India as part of the empire'. The Reform proposals were developed by Edwin Montagu, the Secretary of State (1917–1922) and Lord Chelmsford, the Viceroy (1916–1921).
3. See Low, *Britain and Indian Nationalism,* 1–40; Moore, *Endgames of Empire,* 37–85; Hyam, *Britain's Declining Empire,* 59–69. These studies set out the complexity and ambiguity of Britain's approach towards the Indian demand for their independence.
4. India Office Library (IOL), (British Library, London). MSS EUR C152—Halifax Papers. These files contain the private and personal papers of Lord Irwin, later Lord Halifax. They include all the correspondence between Irwin and his interlocutors, including secretaries of state and governors, during his Viceroyalty. The papers contain working communications, which the Viceroy wished to keep private and confidential, as well as strictly personal material written to his father and friends. The *Halifax Papers* are a separate source to the official communications of the various governments in India to which the viceroy and governors also contributed. This latter material is held in the IOL, the National Archives of India (NAI) (New Delhi), and the various Indian State Archives.

5. IOL. MSS EUR D703—*Birkenhead Papers*; MSS EUR F116—*Harcourt Butler Papers*; MSS EUR F225 and MSS EUR C286—*Montagu Butler Papers*; MSS EUR E252—*Clague Papers* (reference to *H. Butler* and *Innes*); MSS EUR C359—*Gandhi Papers*; MSS EUR D595—*Goschen Papers*; MSS EUR F115—*Haig Papers*; MSS EUR E220—*Hailey Papers*; MSS EUR F160—*Lytton Papers*; MSS EUR C729—*Marris Papers*; MSS EUR F226—*Memoirs of Indian Political Officers*; MSS EUR D714—*Papers of Permanent Under-Secretaries of State*; MSS D528—*Peel Papers*; MSS EUR E238—*Reading Papers*; MSS EUR 961—*Royal Empire Society* (reference to *Kerr*); MSS EUR F77—*Simon Papers* (as chair of Statutory Commission); MSS EUR F150—*Sykes Papers*; MSS EUR F93—*Willingdon Papers*; MSS EUR D601 (b)—*Wilson Papers.*

   NAI: British Indian Government files indexed in: *Proceedings of the Home and Political Departments for the Years 1926–1931*, New Delhi, Government of India Press.

Introduction

An examination of the relevant and available secondary sources reveals a surprising lack of academic research and analysis of the role and influence of the governors of British India on viceregal and metropolitan policy decisions.[1] In the context of the narrative of British Indian history, scholars have concentrated much more on actions at the viceregal and Secretary of State levels, without looking closely at the processes leading to decision making. There has been less motivation to explore below into the influence of the other layers of British Indian Government, because the significant and politically important decisions affecting the Indian Empire were, on the face of it, made at the more senior level. The role of the governors within this command framework has largely not been explored. The popular story of Indian nationalism, for example, is mostly an account of the political relationship between the indigenous leaders and the viceroys.

Lord Irwin's viceroyalty was one in which many British initiatives of consequence and important policy changes were discussed, developed and determined. It was a vital and pivotal period which defined critical British responses to major nationalist challenges such as Gandhi's Salt March and Bardoli and their devolutionary pressures. The Simon Commission,[2] the Irwin Declaration and the first Round Table Conference constituted key landmarks in Britain's attempt to deal with India's call for independence, expressed most stridently through Gandhi,[3] the Indian National Congress[4] and the Non-cooperation Movement. Irwin's viceroyalty provides an ideal framework for an examination of the governors at work in relation to these matters, the degree of their influence on an important Viceroy and of underlying British intent towards India. This study of the Irwin period shows the degree to which even a seminal figure like Irwin relied on local advice, especially that of a couple of favourite governors.

The Montford Reforms had introduced an inevitability of Indian independence. What continues to be debated is whether Britain had a genuine timetable and an identifiable end-point to the process. Did the qualification contained in the preamble to the 1919 *Government of India Act*, of advancing by steps satisfactory to Britain's assessment of Indian political maturity, really reflect a genuine British intent to grant independence to India, albeit by as yet some undefined time? This study answers this question by examining the governors' influence on and input to the decision-making process affecting British India. It identifies the policy issues which the governors were influencing at the provincial and all-India levels, and the level and nature of their advice to Irwin and the secretaries of state, and the degree to which it was sought. The period 1926–1931 provides a convenient and highly pertinent time frame, particularly given the ability to contrast what is recognised as the liberal attitude of Lord Irwin towards the issues being faced by his administration, and what might be assumed to be the more reactionary and conservative gubernatorial attitudes to these matters. It is also of relevance to this approach that the governors who served under Irwin, as is normal in human affairs performed to different competencies. Lord Irwin's personal, private and confidential correspondence with the governors reveals a variation, in both the quality and quantity, of contribution from his colleagues on important matters. A number of governors were located in particularly sensitive locations which required special skills and application, and these governors had the most demanding jobs. Other governors worked from more benign environments and will be seen to tend not to make as substantial a contribution to all-India affairs.

The governors were a cadre which, within a constitutional framework, administered the three presidencies and the six provinces of British India,[5] synchronised as appropriate by the government in New Delhi. The governors were not mere ciphers under the immediate direction and active control of the Viceroy. They governed their provinces with a high degree of independence of action and authority. These men had the opportunity to interact with the central authority to a very high degree in contributing to the decision-making process effecting important all-India matters. In this context the governing style of Lord Irwin must be taken into account. An examination of the *Halifax Papers* indicates that he was by nature not autocratic, but a ruler who did seek counsel and advice from those who were willing to contribute and engage beyond a provincial level.[6] Where he gave instructions to his governors they were not peremptory, and were nearly always open to further mutual and constructive consideration. It is very rare that one detects even the smallest level of impatience in his analysis of advice received. Without unanimity of view, Irwin very often deferred or altered his decisions. In those areas which were fully recognised as provincial he offered his advice and consistently conceded to the governors' experience and authority. The governors, with some exceptions, reciprocated in not only working within their levels of authority but also proactively working towards mutually identified and agreed objectives. As will be seen later, the essence of Irwin's approach was teamwork and hence, most governors reciprocated in participating with him.

Where there is reference in the literature to the governors, it is largely only a peripheral part of the narrative and does not attempt to identify and analyse their role in Indian history. In terms of transfer of power and policy of devolution, the standard histories are rather cynical of the British buying time by offering, at intervals, constitutional concessions. Within this framework, the governors and what they did can be interpreted as somewhat irrelevant. This volume defines the standing of the governors in British India, the nature of their relationship with the Viceroy and the secretaries of state and the degree and nature of their influence on Indian affairs, including nationalism. In fact, the governors were vital components of the structure of the administration of the Raj, crucial to the process of devolution to independence and instrumental in maintaining a non-violent relationship between the metropolis and colony. To a significant degree, British India was a governors' Raj.[7] One can examine the various Irwin biographies and his autobiography to identify Irwin's ostensible reform policy in India but it is through an examination of the governors' role that the inner working of the official mind of imperialism is established. This study offers this perspective.

During the period 1926–1931, Lord Irwin worked with 17 governors, excluding those in an acting capacity, and 3 secretaries of state.[8] References to Irwin,[9] Hailey,[10] Lytton,[11] Sykes,[12] Marris,[13] De Montmorency,[14] Harcourt Butler,[15] Kerr, Muddiman and Wheeler can be found in the literature.[16] The other governors of the period, as well as acting governors, remain unpublished.

Given the expertise and experience available to Irwin, within the circle of the governors, it would be surprising if he had not drawn upon it. Yet with small exception, the available published material, including journal articles, would seem to indicate otherwise. This is a consistent theme in the literature. The governors are kept in the background. As a prime example, in Irwin's major biography by Birkenhead, it is argued that as the Indian constitutional arrangements of the time did not provide for a cabinet, 'the Viceroy himself was the true ruler of India. It was he who laid down the policy which would be carried out both at the centre in Delhi and in all the Provinces of his vast domain'.[17] Campbell Johnson, in his biography of Irwin, hardly mentions the governors but does make some reference to the influence of both Hailey and Sykes on Irwin's decisions in relation to reconciliation[18] and resistance[19] to the nationalists. In recording his view of the contribution of Irwin to Indian history, Hodgson makes only one direct reference to a governor, namely in relation to the Harcourt Butler Report on the Indian States.[20] In the same vein, Roberts makes no real reference to the governors or their role in policy advice. For example, he writes that it was 'he [Irwin who] conceived a plan so bold that it would leapfrog the [Simon] Commission'.[21] It was in fact Governor Stephenson who put forward the Dominion Status Declaration initiative to Irwin, as shall be seen in Chapter 4. Also, Gopal, in his standard work on Irwin's viceroyalty, provides little analysis of the governors' contribution to or influence on the governing of all-India affairs. While acknowledging the skilful technicians who advised Irwin, Gopal believes that 'on the political and constitutional issues, which dominated British Indian history in the twentieth century, almost every decision was taken by Irwin'.[22]

Cell in his comprehensive biography of Hailey records the functions and role of a key governor in all-India affairs, and provides an account of his influence as a key adviser to five viceroys. However, given the focus of his work, understandably, Cell makes scant reference to Hailey's gubernatorial colleagues. The *Halifax Papers* reveal that it was not only Hailey to whom Irwin and other viceroys had turned to for advice and support on important matters, and that Hailey's relationship with the viceroys may have not been entirely unique and special. An examination of the secondary sources and of the published material written by the governors and Viceroy does not really answer the question: What did the governors, of the Irwin era, actually do and achieve within the Raj?

What were British goals in India in the 1920s and early 1930s and what were the overriding strategies they employed in governing India? Faced with the complexity of India, the nationalist movement and its own democratic tradition, Britain had a conundrum about how to devolve a truly representative democracy, and to keep India within the empire. Irwin and the governors wrestled with this problem at a number of significant levels. They tried to deliver government through dyarchy ostensibly demonstrating the genuineness of British constitutional intentions, which included imparting the necessary administrative and political experience to Indians. They also developed strategies to deal with the nationalist movement. At the same time, they continued to provide, to the population of India, government and administration, including civic, social and economic works and the infrastructure, particularly in relation to agriculture, necessary to the welfare of the population, which governments were expected to deliver.

While Lord Irwin had been sent to India to rule and administer, with the support of the Indian Civil Service (ICS) and governors, what were the major overarching imperatives influencing the policies formulated for India by London, Irwin and the governors? Foremost amongst these was that of imperial decline precipitated by the First World War, which impacted, in various ways, not only on their administration of India but also on the whole British Empire and the British position globally. '...historians have sometimes tended to regard the outbreak of the First World War as the decisive turning point in Britain's imperial existence, separating the era of strength and success from the era of decline and dissolution'.[23] In fact, the Great War had not only significantly affected and weakened British global power and authority but also more broadly that of all European colonial powers in Africa and Asia. British policymakers were not only dealing with the Indian Empire but also with a world empire, and the whole was linked to the framework of the British treatment of colonial policy.[24] Certainly in 1919, the India Office, in London, knew the implications of a rising new world order and the international environment of post-war weakness for Britain and India which impacted on British imperial policy.[25] (And, of course, it was not only the ICS which knew Britain's real position in India and the world but also the Indian nationalists.) Britain's 'fundamental imperial problem was defence'[26] of its world empire and, of course, India and its manpower were critical in protection of Britain's world interests as had been proved in the First World War. Thus Britain needed 'special links and ties with India'.[27] What form would they take in this new world formed after the Great War and what strategies would be employed to achieve them? This was the overarching question proffered to Irwin and his administration.

At the beginning of his viceroyalty, at least, Irwin could not be expected to have absorbed the information necessary to deal with the complex matters which were unfolding in India. It is likely that Irwin had much to learn about the nature of Indian politics. His thinking about Indian government was doubtless influenced by the post-First World War situation. Irwin had to find his feet in India, and it is clear that he drew on the experience and expertise that the governors in particular were able to offer. The provincial governors had had a long career in India and were the most senior, knowledgeable and experienced members of the ICS. This book is essentially an exploration of the extent of the governors' role in the government of British India and of their attitudes towards and influence on the aspirations of nationalist India. Given the prime role of the governors in developing and providing policy advice to Irwin at the Centre, it is to them we must look to determine the honest intentions and sincerity of the British regarding Indian independence.

One can identify two overarching policies which Irwin and the governors consistently used to govern India and maintain British rule. The first was to provide sound government and administration through various techniques which included the deliverance of constitutional reform.

The second was to deal directly with nationalism and emergency within the law of India. The British hoped that the delivery of sound government would help them in neutralising rising Indian nationalism, particularly amongst the rural classes. The details of the issues dealt with by Irwin and the governors in the period 1926–1931, and the approaches they adopted in ensuring good government and administration and lawfully dealing with Indian nationalism are explored.

Chapter 1 of this book defines the governors' status in British India and the nature of their relationship with the Centre. Chapter 2 examines the governors' working of the Montford Reforms. It establishes the governors' contribution to government and the nature of their professional relationship with the Centre under that particular heading. The chapter reflects their attitude towards the reforms and hence their approach to meeting these aspirations. It will be seen that the governors did not use the complexity of dyarchy to confuse nationalist aspirations but attempted to transparently deliver, including through collaboration, the policy outcomes required by these reforms.

A major theme during Irwin's viceroyalty was the work required to support the activities of the Simon Commission. It is difficult to identify any work which includes any detailed examination of the role and functions of the governors of British India in the important tasks relating to the Commission. The same can be said of the governors' contribution to Irwin's initiatives relating to his Dominion Status Declaration and the first Round Table Conference. The predominant focus, in the available literature, is on Lord Irwin and his decisions without identifying how far he was influenced by others. Chapters 3 and 4 closely examine the degree to which the governors influenced Irwin, the various secretaries of state for India and the British Government in making their important policy decisions in relation to the Commission, the Declaration and the first Round Table Conference.

From the time Lord Irwin landed in India, in 1926, until his departure five years later, a major challenge his viceroyalty faced was making terms with rising Indian nationalism, within the law of India and the politics of Britain. Chapters 5–8 address how the governors interacted with the Viceroy and the British Government, in dealing with the various manifestations of 'direct' nationalism. These included communal disturbances, revolt, civil disobedience and non-cooperation, the activities of trade unionism and communism, and of course the activities of Gandhi.

Given that the authority in matters relating to all-India civil defence and security was held by the Viceroy, it is identified how far he consulted with and was influenced by the counsel and policy advice of the governors in the overall response to the nationalist and security challenge. The degree to which the governors agreed with Irwin in his attitude and approach to dealing with nationalism is established. This is particularly interesting given Irwin's future role as British Foreign Minister, before the Second World War and modern history's view that he and Chamberlain significantly erred in their dealings with Hitler, in offering a policy of appeasement.[28]

The complexity of advice given by the governors, the differing policy approaches to the problems at hand and the decisions taken by Irwin are examined in detail in this volume to determine the degree to which the governors were, in effect, the well-springs of the wisdom used in the attempt to settle the Indian 'problem' which existed between 1926 and 1931. It is established that analysts of Indian history have given too much credit to Lord Irwin and the secretaries of state in their administration of India, and too little to the *Satraps*.[29] It is revealed that Irwin's consistent skill was his willingness to take advice from the governors and work with them within a governors' Raj. This fact also has interesting implications for the historical record of the performance of other Viceroys.

It must be acknowledged that there were governors, of the Irwin era, who held reactionary views regarding Indian independence but this was recognised by Irwin who aligned himself with his more liberal governors, consistently drawn from the ICS. Through this analysis it is established that the governors were not perfidious but provided advice which could only culminate in the outcome of Indian independence.

Endnotes

1. See the following publications for evidence of this: Bridge, *Holding India to the Empire*; Brown, *Modern India*; Baker, *The Politics of South India: 1920–1937*; Tomlinson, *The Indian National Congress and the Raj, 1929–1942*; Gallagher, 'Congress in Decline', pp. 155–211; Moore, *Endgames of Empire*; Rumbold, *Watershed in India*.
2. The Commission's conclusions were contained in the *Report of the Indian Statutory Commission* (hereafter *Report of the Simon Commission*). The Commission was chaired by Sir John Simon, an eminent lawyer and British Conservative MP.
3. M.K. (Mahatma) Gandhi (1869–1948), Indian patriot, social reformer and moral teacher. In the movement for Indian independence, he dominated the Congress, instituted civil disobedience and advocated non-violence.

4. Formed in December 1885 to unite various Indian political societies under one umbrella with the objective of achieving a vague goal, then, of home rule. See James, *Raj*, p. 352.
5. In Irwin's time the three presidencies were Bengal, Bombay and Madras. The six provinces were the United Provinces of Agra and Oudh, the Punjab, the Central Provinces and Berar, Bihar and Orissa, Assam and Burma.
6. P.G. Robb's book, *The Government of India and Reform,* identifies the ability of Lord Chelmsford, another Viceroy, to consult with his governors and to work for consensus, as will be seen in Chapter 2, pp. 38–41. This trait of consultation might be seen as a personal quality. Other viceroys, such as Lord Curzon could be autocratic.
7. This term is not intended to imply that the governors literally ruled India but rather to highlight and emphasise their importance in British India's administration.
8. See, p. 222 for biographies of the governors and secretaries of state who worked with Irwin. These biographies are largely drawn from *The India Office List* which was published yearly, until 1947, under the direction of the Secretary of State for India in Council. Note: Acting governors filled in for small periods and had little opportunity to influence policy. See also a map on p. *x* identifying the presidencies and provinces and their respective governors during Lord Irwin's viceroyalty.
9. E.F.L. Wood, First Earl of Halifax, (Lord Halifax *Fullness of Days*); Viscount Halifax, *The Indian Problem*; Lord Irwin, *Some Aspects of the Indian Problem*; Lord Irwin, *Speeches*; Viscount Halifax, 'The Political Future of India', pp. 420–430; Viscount Halifax, 'India: Two Hundred Years', pp. 104–115; Viscount Halifax, 'Indian Constitutional Reform', pp. 198–216; A. Campbell Johnson, *Viscount Halifax*; A. Roberts, *Holy Fox;* The Earl of Birkenhead, *Halifax;* S. Hodgson, *Lord Halifax*; S. Gopal, *The Viceroyalty of Lord Irwin.*
10. A. Misra, *The Administration of the United Provinces of Agra and Oudh under Sir Malcolm Hailey*; M. Hailey, 'India', pp. 844–855; M. Hailey, 'India—1983', pp. 620–632; M. Hailey, 'The Future of Colonial Peoples', pp. 277–278; M. Hailey, 'India in the Modern World', pp. 401–412; Lord Hailey, *The Future of Colonial Peoples.* Note: Hailey also wrote a number of publications when involved in later work on African colonial issues. J.W. Cell, *Hailey.*
11. The Earl of Lytton, *Pundits and Elephants.*
12. F. Sykes, *From Many Angles*; F. Sykes, 'The Indian States and the Reforms', pp. 48–68.
13. W. Marris, *India*; W.S. Marris, *Civil Government for Indian Students,* p. 298. (reference to Marris, Sir W.S. Translation of Homer's Odyssey, 1925, quoted in O'Malley, *The Indian Civil Service*, p. 298.)
14. G. de Montmorency, *The Indian States and Indian Federation*; *India Today and Tomorrow.*
15. H. Butler, *India Insistent*; W.S. Razi, 'Sir Harcourt Butler on the Indian educational and political situation in the early twentieth century', pp. 349–355;

D. Awasthi, 'Sir Spencer Harcourt Butler and his eastern Oxford', pp. 159–166; D. Awasthi, 'Sir Spencer Harcourt Butler and University Education in India', pp. 855–865; G. Minault and D. Lelyveld, 'The Campaign for a Muslim University', pp. 145–189; D. Awasthi, *Administrative History of Modern India*; W. Holdsworth, 'The Indian States', pp. 1–16. The *Report of the Indian States Committee* was published in London in 1929.

16. J.H. Kerr, *Settlement Reports of Saran and Darbanga*; J.H. Kerr, *Rampini's Bengal Tenancy Act 1913 and 1918*; Sir A. Muddiman, *Memoirs*; H. Wheeler, *A Chaukidari Manual*. (Note: a Chaukidari tax is one levied to defray the cost of a town or village).
17. Birkenhead, *Halifax*, p. 217. Note Birkenhead the author, was the son of Birkenhead, the Secretary of State for India.
18. Campbell Johnson, *Viscount Halifax*, p. 246.
19. *Ibid.*, p. 299.
20. Hodgson, *Lord Halifax*, p. 122.
21. Roberts, *Holy Fox*, p. 25.
22. Gopal, *Lord Irwin*, p. 135. See also R.G. Ayres, 'The Impact of Viceregal Attitudes towards Gandhi on Imperial Policy 1929–1934'. The supposed pervasive influence of Irwin has been captured by Ayres in the following quotation drawn from his research: 'all of the major policy decisions which were carried out during his term were initiated or greatly influenced by him [Lord Irwin], including the Simon Commission, the Dominion Status declaration, the Round Table Conference and the Delhi settlement with Gandhi', p. 10.
23. Darwin, *Britain, Egypt and the Middle East*, p. XIII.
24. Darwin, *Britain and Decolonisation*, p. VII. See also Darwin, *The End of the British Empire*; Darwin, *The Empire Project*; Darwin, *Unfinished Empire*, for accounts of the impact of the Second World War on Britain's transition from empire and imperialism.
25. Marlowe, *The Late Victorian Empire*, p. 166. Marlowe quotes Hirtzel in the India Office writing to a colleague in 1919 that the old type of imperial rule was 'dying in India ...'.
26. Darwin, *Britain and Decolonisation*, p. 32.
27. *Ibid.*, p. 82.
28. Gilbert and Gott, *The Appeasers*.
29. Holder of provincial governorship in ancient Persian Empire.

1

The Governors: Their Constitutional, Legal and Personal Standing

This chapter identifies important elements of the constitutional, legal and personal standing and status of the governors of British India, at the time of Lord Irwin's viceroyalty. These elements will be explored, in relation to the governors' position within their provinces and in the context of their relationship with the Viceroy and the Centre, in order to understand the formal and personal parameters within which they functioned in India. These understandings are a necessary background to an identification of the nature of the governors' involvement in government and administration.

The legal, formal authority and definition of the governors' functions can be found in the *Government of India Act* of 1919,[1] which was the constitutional rule book for India in the period 1926–1931, and until this Act was replaced by its successor in 1935. The 1919 Act was derived from an earlier constitutional progression contained in the Morley–Minto Reforms of 1909—the Indian Councils Act which increased Indian participation in government by drawing in the more liberal nationalist elements of the growing Indian political class. The 1919 Reforms, driven to a large extent by increasing political awareness amongst a growing educated population, and an expectation of reward for India's war service, were more substantial.

The reforms decentralised political and administrative power from the Government of India to the provinces in a form of political experiment called dyarchy,[2] which introduced a greater measure of provincial autonomy than had existed under the previous Morley–Minto Reforms. Dyarchy involved a dual system of government in which Indians were given a degree of representative control over certain less politically sensitive areas of government (the transferred) at the provincial level, whilst the colonial rulers remained in charge of those subjects (the reserved) they identified as of critical strategic, military, economic, political and security importance. The power to administer the reserved subjects was held by the central government but could be devolved to the governors and their executive councils for provincial purposes as appropriate.

The system was designed, ostensibly to provide Indians with the political/administrative experience necessary to take on more critical and politically important areas of government. The 1919 Act contained provisions for review of constitutional progress and was intended to be evolutionary. Interestingly, Harcourt Butler and other men to become governors had been involved in the formulation of the 1919 Reforms. Butler held firm views regarding the need to decentralise the powers of the 'ponderous plodding Government of India',[3] apart from any view regarding constitutional progress. The principal political characteristics of the pre-reform regime had been 'the concentration of authority at the centre; the control over legislative functions exercised by the Executive and the ultimate responsibility of Parliament for the whole of the Indian Government'.[4] The trend towards increasing the powers of provincial governments and governors had its origins in the recognition of more being gained in dealing with such important matters as ensuring sound administration and meeting the challenge of rising Indian nationalism at the provincial government levels, while assigning to the Centre, matters of Imperial concern.[5] The complexity of dyarchy, introduced by the 1919 Act, reflected an essential duality of purpose of increasing provincial governmental powers, and an objective of ensuring the political provincial India proper constitutional and parliamentary training to offset nationalism.

The 1919 Act had introduced a constitutional system which had profoundly altered the power relationship between the Centre and the provinces. Previously, local governments had been fundamentally agents of the Government of India. 'They were wholly responsible for all their acts to, and derived all their powers from, the central government'.[6] After 1919, the local provincial executive was divided in two, with accountability for transferred subjects, theoretically at least, back to the electorate and reserved subjects, technically, to the British Parliament through the Governor and Governor-General. Even in the case of the reserved subjects, the Governor and his executive had a level of political independence which was to increase as the constitution evolved and convention developed, and was to be only qualified by controversies which attracted viceregal intervention. While local governments continued to act as agents for the Centre in some respects, for example, for customs and for shipping, the legal and constitutional powers of the governors had been significantly increased, as set out in the 1919 *Government of India Act*, by intention.

By Irwin's time, the 1919 legislation had caused the local governments and Government of India to drift apart with a consequent swing of power to the provinces. This is reflected in a letter written by Sir Malcolm Hailey in June 1926, in response to a suggestion by Irwin that a conference of governors be regularly held. Hailey advised Irwin that

> in the pre-reform days, when financial or administrative sanction was needed for a great variety of matters which are now decided by Local Governments on their own authority, the contact was much closer...[now] the pendulum has swung rather too far the other way.[7]

The vast geographical size of India, and the reality of the difficulty of prompt and effective communications between the Centre and the provinces also tended to increase the trend towards magnifying provincial autonomy. Wise viceroys, such as Lord Irwin, acknowledged, where merited and appropriate, the importance of local expertise in good provincial administration. At the very least, under Irwin the tendency was for mutual consultation and consideration, of contentious matters, with the governors rather than for autocratic and peremptory viceregal direction. 'I am only writing to utter what I believe probably to be a wholly unnecessary word of caution'.[8]

Under the 1919 Constitution, the governors were the rulers of their provinces and were the ultimate source of power, albeit under sanction, but only in some instances, from a distant Viceroy and an even more distant Secretary of State. Given the intent, authority and outcome of the 1919 legislation and the practical reality of the requirement for good government in the provinces, tacitly acknowledged by the Centre, it is not unreasonable to claim that the governors were, in many important respects, the actual rulers of British India. It was through the medium of the governors and their panoply of administration that the Raj made its major, direct and real contact with the vast population of India and became conscious of their aspirations, political, economic and otherwise. Drawing on their long experience it was particularly the Civil Service governors who understood the diversity and needs of the people. It was to the governors that their Indian subjects looked for the evidence and practice of sound British administration. After 1919, the governors became constitutional tutors to an important layer of the Indian political and administrative class, which chose to cooperate.[9] The governors had significant influence over their ministers and executives. 'Nor could the enormous influence of the governor as an expert be ignored; it tended to weaken ministers' importance and initiative and reduce them to the advisers of a more or less independent governor.'[10] The governors also rewarded cooperation amongst other collaborationists such as the commercial and landed classes.

The 1919 Constitution further increased the real powers of the governors in a number of important respects: First, the central government was required under the new Act to abstain from legislating on provincial subjects 'except where those subjects are declared by the Rules of Classification of the Act [(Part V Sec 45 (A)].'[11] The Rules of Classification set out the principles by which the administrative subjects would be classified as either reserved or transferred. Dyarchy did not operate at the Centre. Second, was the fact of the transfer of some 46 major administrative and governmental areas to the provinces to their control.[12] Third, under the Act, administration of central subjects would be transferred to the provinces.[13] This provision also tended to increase the governors' powers. Fourth, the fact that the non-official membership of the Central Legislative Assembly were inexperienced, varied greatly in quality, did not always understand the effect of their own amendments and that their drafting was frequently at fault,[14] would tend to some degree to indicate the Assembly was poorly skilled and ineffective. This factor would reinforce the importance of the legislative councils in the provinces and the relative power of the governors in the all-India administrative hierarchy.

A Section of the 1919 Act, relating to local governments, provided:

> ...every Local Government shall obey the orders of the Governor-General in Council, and keep him constantly and diligently informed of its proceedings and of all matters which ought in its opinion, to be reported to him, or as to which he requires information, and is under his superintendence, direction and control in all matters relating to the government of its province.[15]

On a strict reading, this wording would appear again to reinforce a view that the Viceroy was in fact constitutionally the principal ruler of India. Analysis indicates, however, that the nature of the relationship between the central and provincial governments had changed as a result of the 1919 legislation. With the introduction of dyarchy, the central government lost influence over the transferred subjects and could only intervene generally

> ...(1) to safeguard the administration of all-India subjects, (2) to decide questions arising between two or more Provinces, failing agreement between the Provinces concerned, (3) to safeguard Imperial interests, (4) to determine the position of the Government of India in respect of questions arising between India and other parts of the empire and (5) to safeguard the exercise of powers and duties imposed upon the Secretary of State or the Secretary of State in Council regarding the [Indian] High Commissioner [in London], borrowing and the services.[16]

With regard to reserved departments, no rules were made under the 1919 Act to relax the control of the Governor-General or Secretary of State. Any loosening of control in this area was to be left to convention.[17] While on the face of it, Part V Section 45 of the 1919 Act seemed to reflect the absolute power of the Governor-General in Council, in fact there had been a reduction in the level of control of the central government, the Secretary of State and the British Parliament over transferred subjects. As practical experience of government under the reforms developed, it was intended that forming conventions would reflect a relaxation in central control over reserved subjects as well. Given the complexity of administering dyarchy, and the chaotic nature of the political framework within which it operated, it is not surprising that the development of these constitutional conventions would have been severely stunted. However, loosening of authority and control over provincial government and administration, by the Centre inevitably meant an increased provincial autonomy and hence increased power of the governors.

Under the 1919 Act, the governors had obtained significant powers to exercise influence and patronage. The governors appointed ministers to administer the transferred subjects at the governors' pleasure and not for the life of the legislative councils. Ministers could be removed without the governor giving any reason.[18] The governor consulted was guided by his ministers' advice but if he disagreed, then he could take contrary action. The governor had significant power to override the will of the councils and ministers, particularly where he could certify that any Bill affected the 'safety or tranquility' of provinces. The governor had unilateral power, in the case of emergency to authorise expenditure. He had the power to pass any Bill relating to a reserved matter, subject to agreement by the Governor-General and Secretary of State.[19] Given the complexity of dyarchy and the overlapping nature of the various reserved and transferred portfolio subjects, the use of the word 'relating' in the legislation gave the governor wide powers over areas outside the reserved. In many respects, the Governor was equivalent in function to the modern Australian Prime Minister but was more powerful, particularly as there was no real cabinet or parliamentary checks and balances. The Governor was only accountable in a political sense to the Viceroy, the Secretary of State and the British Parliament, and in a moral sense to his king and himself. The 1919 Act required that the three presidency governors be appointed by the king, while the provincial governors be appointed by the king after consultation with the Governor-General.[20]

The position and status of the governors were not the same.[21] Even though they were commonly designated as governors, the presidency and provincial governors were paid at different levels and their varying status was reflected by their mode of appointment. While 'there is nothing in law which prevents a civil servant being appointed to a Presidency Governorship',[22] this category was routinely appointed from the ranks of distinguished men, including politicians and the aristocratic class, where the king had an unfettered choice. These men were the most senior in rank of the governors, their three presidencies of Bengal, Bombay and Madras, being the oldest, richest and most politically important of the British Indian territories. Acting viceroys were conventionally drawn from Bengal, the senior presidency, but an exception was Lord Goschen of Madras. Even so, in seeking out a replacement in 1929 in the House of Lords for Lord Goschen, the Secretary of State, Lord Peel was to observe 'the difficulty is that they are apt to regard one of the Presidency Governorships if they are at all ambitious, as something of a shelf...they are apt to consider that nothing short of the Viceroyalty is worthy of their talents'.[23]

The six provincial governors had their origins in the ICS with the senior Governor in this class coming from the United Provinces of Agra and Oudh, the largest and most populous of the provinces. The fact that the provincial governors were appointed by the king, as recommended by the Secretary of State, after consultation with the Governor-General was intended to facilitate the appointment of the best men from the ICS. The appointment of Lord Sinha[24] in 1920, who was not an ICS officer, as Governor of Bihar and Orissa indicates that exceptions to this general rule were possible. His qualifications would also, presumably, have made him an exemplary presidency governor.

An authority for the formal superintendence and control over the governors, exercised by the Governor-General, Secretary of State and the British Parliament through the Monarch, was set out in the governors' Royal Warrant of Appointment.[25] The Warrant of Appointment was intended to encapsulate, for the governors, the formal line of authority which existed between the king, Parliament, Governor-General and themselves. The governors were required also to undertake an Oath of Allegiance to their sovereign.[26] However, in reality this power structure had evolved, following principally upon the 1919 *Government of India Act*, to allow an analysis of British India during Lord Irwin's time as being a governors' Raj.

While the several governors differed formally in power and status, they wielded almost identical powers, and were to be guided by an Instrument of Instructions,[27] issued on appointment by the Secretary of State in Council. The Instrument of Instructions set out for the Governor included not only specific directions relating to action in particular circumstances of government, but also importantly defined for him the British Parliament's behavioural requirements in the context of the Governor's moral and ethical duty towards India and its people, consequent upon the 1919 *Government of India Act.* In other words, the Instructions defined the Parliament's expectation of how the governors were to acquit the intentions of the Montford Reforms. These were their corporate governance rules.

The Instructions also attempted to define those gubernatorial practices which, for an infant legislature, might usefully become parliamentary conventions over time. They contained reference to the British objective of providing an opportunity for the development of governmental experience and expertise by Indians.[28] The Instrument set out the governor's responsibilities across a wide range of matters under some twelve headings. These included the safety and tranquility of his province; the proper administration of both the transferred and reserved subjects; that inappropriate commercial monopolies were to be avoided; the interests of the European and Anglo-Indian communities were to be safeguarded; the public services were to be protected in the legitimate exercise of their functions; the educational need of the Muslim community was to be provided for as well as the advancement of the depressed classes.

However, of particular interest to the underlying theme of this book is that the Instrument also provided, in relation to constitutional advance, that the Governor was 'to further all changes tending to make India fitted for self-government [and to]...restrict the exercise of the power to act in opposition to his ministers' advice, which is vested in him under the 1919 Act'.[29] Clearly, the underlying spirit of the 1919 Reforms was to achieve a legislative environment where government was achieved by a minimum of interference and direction by the governor of his Indian ministers. On the face of it, the governors were not intended to be autocrats, certainly not by constitutional authority.

The Instrument of Instructions set out the governor's responsibilities, and the various provisions of the *Government of India Act* provided the legal authority for their governmental powers. The Simon Report,[30] identified the real importance of the Governor in any discussion of the provincial executive.

> He is...appointed by His Majesty by warrant under the Royal Sign Manual, and the head of the province in all matters of dignity and precedence; he is not only the chief patron of innumerable institutions and endeavours, and the dispenser of unending official and personal hospitality; he is also the actual and working head of the Executive, presiding over its full meetings, and providing by his influence, advice and sometimes even direction, the cohesion between the two sides of government, which would otherwise be wholly lacking.[31]

The Governor, in the Executive Council, took part in all discussions, had the casting vote and had the power to overrule the majority in certain circumstances.

He thus 'shares to the full and in every detail his colleagues' responsibility to the British Parliament for the proper administration of the reserved departments'.[32] In case of the Legislative Council, the Instrument of Instructions and provisions of the 1919 Act required that he be guided by the advice of his ministers, that he should attempt to place the responsibility for Council decisions on them and only in exceptional circumstances overrule them.[33]

The Simon Report identified that the Governor, in his work with his executive and legislative councils, must 'exercise great tact and discretion and a constant watchfulness'.[34] This was so particularly when the Governor presided over joint meetings of the two councils held to consider matters which were not clearly defined as the responsibility of one council or the other and joint decisions, or at least understandings, appeared necessary. The Governor was therefore a vital part of the 'day-to-day administration' and also 'the authority in reserve'. The Governor clearly had a most important role in ensuring the probity and proper governance of the administration of his presidency or province. The Simon Report also pointed out that 'there is no statutory provision defining the qualifications for a Governor or the period for which he shall hold office. The customary period is five years'.[35] A 'job description' is available in the form of the Instrument of Instructions and the 1919 Act, but can a set of 'selection criteria' for the various governorships be found?

It has already been identified that the two categories of governors, the presidency and the provincial, were drawn from different backgrounds of achievement and standing. The presidency governors most often had their origin in British politics, with an aristocratic background being a useful advantage. The provincial governors were drawn from the ICS, with all the concomitant benefits of Indian experience. It can be observed that a high level of personal qualities would have been required of the governors to deliver the difficult elements of their 'job description'.

Professionally, the governors were men of high achievement. With the possible exception of Lord Lytton[36] who may have relied to some degree (given his later record in India) on the name of his father, who had been a largely successful Viceroy in the nineteenth century, the presidency governors had established their own reputations and had proved themselves, by most standards, as men of distinction in Britain. Lord Peel felt that 'for these Governorships a man with Parliamentary experience is…I won't say… essential…but anyhow desirable'.[37]

The biographical data,[38] on the provincial governors of the period under study, contained in *The India Office List*, reveals a cadre drawn predominantly from men with long experience of Indian administration and politics. This was an elite group, recruited to the elite ICS, with the highest educational qualifications predominantly from either Oxford or Cambridge. 'Between 1892 and 1914 Oxford obtained 48.2 per cent of the places [in the ICS], Cambridge 29.5 per cent'.[39] In 1938 'all but one of the eight provincial governors in India…were Oxonians',[40] reflecting this historical pattern. During Irwin's period, of the seventeen presidency and provincial governors, six were drawn from Cambridge and seven from Oxford. It can be asked whether the classical university education of these governors was a foundation for a philosophically liberal approach towards democracy and government, which they took to India (a classical university education, at that time was often an extension of a classical school education, as was the case for Hailey at the Merchant Taylor's School). However, two of the more conservative presidency governors, Lytton and Jackson, were educated at Cambridge qualifying this assumption, as will be seen. Presidency Governor Lord Goschen, educated at Oxford, seems to have been more aligned with his ICS colleagues in his approach to the Indian future. The ICS governors were men who had spent their lives in India and had risen through the ranks to reach the top level of their service as provincial governors.

> Seniority rather than selection by merit normally determined promotion [in the ICS], except in the realm of prize postings at the highest levels, for example, Secretary, Chief Secretary, Governor. Only the meritorious were appointed to these posts, which carried extraordinary responsibilities and amazing pay, pomp and circumstance.[41]

Over a long career of service in India, in the provinces and sometimes at headquarters in Delhi, they had risen to be governors, the high point of their careers. The criticality of these ICS men, in ruling India, is pointed to by Ferguson when making the point, 'Perhaps more than anything else, the British Empire was an empire based on local collaboration; how else could fewer than a thousand ICS men have governed a population of 400 million Indians?'.[42] The precise numbers of the ICS in 1930 are provided by O'Malley. 'It is a small body consisting of only 1,014 men on 1 January, 1930; its effective strength at any one time, after deducting the number of men on leave, may be taken as from 800 to 900.'[43]

Both Seal and Yang argue that British rule in India had a 'soft centre'[44] or could be described as a 'limited Raj'.[45] Their argument supports a view that while the British could not be pushed into the sea, essentially because the Indian population continued to be too divided against itself (as the events of 1857 had shown), British rule was, in fact, not all pervasive or powerful and relied heavily on extraneous support. The British relied not only on collaboration, at almost every level, but also on other measures such as the influence of awe and splendour when the rulers chose to flaunt themselves, on control by manipulation, on policies of divide and rule (though seen later in the text) between races and religion and on princely support. Seal also points to the huge prestige or *izzat* of the administration (ICS) and the consequent gulf between ruler and ruled, which factor could only tend to reinforce the apparent power of the British in the eyes of the native population.[46] It can also be noted that this prestige (of the ICS) was also identified by those fellow Europeans who did not understand the 'organisation and procedures of the bureaucracy'.[47]

Yang identifies 'The lack of penetrating state institutions',[48] and that thus, in effect, real British physical power ended at the level of the local market police station. In the context just outlined it was the ICS and most importantly the governors at the apex of the system who kept the vast Indian population in thrall and awe of British rule. Even so the British did need to manifest themselves. Further, even though real British power may have ended at the level of the markets the ICS did contain a cadre which had experience and understanding of India down to that level if not further. Lord Hailey's career which included a period as a Settlement Officer in the Punjab, bringing him into extensive contact with the Indian population exemplifies this point. The ICS and its heads had an expertise (including in Indian languages) and experience indispensable to the British rule of India.

Regarding the selection of the governors and the rulers of the presidencies, it appears that they were selected primarily on the basis of personal reputation and connection in Britain. Lord Lytton was asked to go to India by Edwin Montagu, then the Secretary of State for India, in 1921.[49] Sir Frederick Sykes recounts he was offered the Governorship of Bombay in 1928 by Lord Birkenhead.[50] While one can assume a certain personal connection between the secretaries of state and the prospective governors in these cases, and thus knowledge of personal qualities, qualifications relating to their actual prospective performance may have not been the overriding requirement. It may not be coincidental that both Lytton and Sykes, and to some degree other presidency governors under Irwin, were of a different personal quality to the provincial governors, and tended to adopt a different demeanour towards the Viceroy.[51] Sykes, for example, was most critical of Irwin's policy of 'steady pressure' towards the nationalists and Gandhi.[52] The presidential governors certainly lacked the long Indian experience held by the provincial governors and had not developed a consequent ability to understand and be understood by the Indians they ruled.

While there was no precedent for a man from the ICS to be appointed as a permanent presidency governor, it was acceptable for one to be appointed in an acting capacity. Sir Stanley Jackson, Governor of Bengal, had requested leave for a period of three months from June 1930, for health reasons, and Lord Irwin asked Sir Hugh Stephenson, Governor of Bihar and Orissa, who had served in Bengal, to act. In considering this request, which he did reluctantly, Stephenson took into account a number of considerations. In a frank response to the Viceroy, he indicated that the difficult security situation in Bengal would not make it easy for him.

> In a three months' acting capacity I should be in a much weaker position to deal with things than in my permanent appointment; an acting man can't do much more than carry on while on the other hand he may have a crisis sprung upon him at any moment, especially in Bengal.[53]

Stephenson referred to a difficulty he would have with an old colleague, Moberly,[54] who was the senior executive officer in Bengal and who would normally have been expected to act as Governor. He also pointed out that he would also lose financially, as the expenses in Bengal were much greater and Jackson had set a high standard. He was also looking forward to 'getting into a new house at Ranchi'. The possibility of three months in Bengal would complicate matters.

> Purely from my point of view there seem to be no attractions in favour of changing temporarily a Province where I am well in the saddle for a much more difficult one where the surroundings will be to a large extent strange and to some extent hostile.[55]

Stephenson concluded his letter by indicating to Irwin that he was, despite all considerations, 'prepared to carry out your instructions; but you have given me an opportunity of saying how I feel about it, so I have frankly'.

In the event Stephenson was indeed directed. 'I am afraid that I am forced to return to the proposal that you should go to Bengal for the three months'.[56] Stephenson consequently took charge of Bengal on 5 June 1930 in Calcutta, in accordance with 'the normal rule, which the Secretary of State has in the past emphasised and to maintenance of which the Government of India attach importance, that charge of office of Governor should be made over at headquarters [in this case Calcutta]'.[57]

Some of the personal qualities which provincial governors were expected to hold can be identified in correspondence between Lord Irwin and Lord Birkenhead in their consideration of appointments within the ICS, including to the office of Governor. The first example was in January 1927, when Irwin wrote to Birkenhead discussing a replacement for Sir Charles Innes, who was to be appointed as Governor of Burma later in the year, as the member for railways and commerce on the Viceroy's Council.[58] In recommending Sir Geoffrey de Montmorency as Innes' replacement, Irwin succinctly set out his personal qualities for Birkenhead. Apart from knowing and being on excellent terms with all the leading commercial men throughout India

> ...he combines exceptionally detailed knowledge of all sides of Indian life with good judgement and a wide grasp of general political conditions and would be a very valuable recruit to my Council. He has confidence, to a very conspicuous degree, of Indians of every class and in every province of the country. He would be excellent in debate and in Assembly, and I can recommend him from every point of view.

In the event, de Montmorency declined the position on the grounds of ill health at the time but his qualities had clearly marked him as a future Governor, which he became, of the Punjab in 1928.

In correspondence with Birkenhead in February 1927, concerning a replacement for Sir John Kerr, the Governor of Assam, Irwin indicated that he would have preferred 'an Assam man' as successor and that he had written to Kerr for suggestions.[59] Kerr replied suggesting as the only possible candidate, Botham,[60] his Finance Member, but adding that he had little experience outside Assam which might be a drawback. Irwin then checked with Sir William Marris, who had been the Governor of Assam from 1921 to 1922 and who knew Botham. Marris advised that he did not think Botham was 'cut out for a Governor as he is not keenly interested in administrative questions and lacks decision'.[61] Irwin went on to rule out another Assam man, Bentinck,[62] who had been a very good district officer but lacked wider experience and could not be appointed over Botham. Irwin also ruled out Donald,[63] a member of Lord Lytton's Executive Council who had been recommended by Lytton, on the basis of 'what I saw of him in Calcutta' and his reputation for laziness. After full consideration, Irwin was to recommend Laurie Hammond as the Governor 'of this somewhat backward province'. Hammond was a Member of the Governor's Executive Council in Bihar and Orissa and had been spoken of very highly by the Governor, Sir Henry Wheeler. Hammond

> ...has had thorough administrative training and has been both Financial and Chief Secretary. He is tactful both with Europeans and Indians, is hospitable and a sportsman and would do the social side well. He is described as having an active mind and would I think have the breadth of view necessary to a Governor.[64]

In the event, Birkenhead and the king were to accept Irwin's recommendation and Sir Egbert Laurie Lucas Hammond was to serve successfully as the Governor of Assam from 28 June 1927 until 10 May 1932, when he retired from India.

In March 1927, Irwin was considering replacements for the governors of the United Provinces and Burma. Irwin first made enquiries regarding the qualifications of many officers in those provinces which may have suited them to the position of Governor. Sir William Marris put forward the name of his Private Secretary O'Donnell[65] as the man to succeed him. In discussing O'Donnell with Birkenhead, Irwin advised he had

> ...met O'Donnell at Allahabad in December and have made some independent enquiries about him. My conclusion is that though he is undoubtedly capable, and intellectually above average he is somewhat lacking in the necessary driving power and personality. I have also been given to understand that if faced by a really critical situation he is apt to be jumpy and might not stand the strain.[66]

Turning to Burma, Irwin was to advise Birkenhead that the Governor of Burma, Sir Harcourt Butler, had put forward two names, Sir James McKenna and Sir William Keith,[67] which only needed to be considered. With respect to McKenna, Butler advised 'he is played out and deficient in initiative or decision. Keith is very unpopular and has bad judgement. He is also a fanatic for the separation of Burma from India'.[68] In looking outside the provinces for men to fill the two governorships, Irwin advised Birkenhead that the obvious candidates seemed to be Muddiman, Innes, Montagu Butler, de Montmorency and possibly Bray and Thompson. Irwin also indicated that the option of appointing a distinguished Indian or somebody from England, possibly Sir Frederick Whyte[69] had been suggested. Irwin informed Birkenhead:

> I do not know of any Indian whom I should wish to recommend at the present juncture and I should not wish to propose you should choose somebody from home and pass over the Services. De Montmorency may I think be left out as it would be much better to consider him for succession to Hailey [in the Punjab] in due course.[70]

De Montmorency had long Punjab experience and had also worked closely with Hailey. Irwin's final choice fell on Muddiman and Innes.

> Both are men of outstanding ability and have deserved well of Government. Muddiman's extensive knowledge of constitutional questions, his experience as Home Member and his thorough grasp of administrative and judicial

> matters fit him well for the post of Governor. He is popular with Indians is cheery and hospitable. Innes has much impressed me by the thoroughness of his work. Both he and Lady Innes possess great natural courtesy and charm and he inspires confidence in all with whom he comes in contact. Harcourt Butler supports Innes for Burma on the basis of his commerce experience.[71]

Both men were accepted, to their high positions, by Birkenhead and the king.

At the beginning of 1928, Irwin was considering a suitable replacement for Hailey in the Punjab. As previously noted, Irwin had earlier reserved de Montmorency for consideration for this province and indicated to Birkenhead that the only other candidate was Montagu Butler, who was then Governor of the Central Provinces.

Irwin informed Birkenhead:

> Montagu Butler has had at first sight a more distinguished career than de Montmorency and has had very wide experience as District and Secretariat officer and as President of both the Provincial Legislature and Council of State. I formed a high opinion of his administrative and political sagacity when I visited the Central Provinces last year. At the same time I know many people who describe him as having a good many brains but not certainly the bigness of his brother Harcourt Butler, and doubt whether he would have had such a distinguished career if he had not been the younger brother of such a brilliant man. Montagu is not popular with officials and regarded as a political wire puller.[72]

Again Birkenhead and the king were to accept Irwin's recommendation for Sir Geoffrey Fitzhervey de Montmorency as the Governor of the Punjab.

Montagu Butler believed, in fact, there were strong elements of undue influence at work in the process of selection of governors and that it worked against him. 'He [Birdie][73] thinks Hailey has him [Irwin] in tow and says that he is running and will run de Montmorency for the Punjab. He has never heard any criticism of me or my work; in fact the contrary.'[74] 'He [Birdie] told me Muddiman was a great friend of Lady Stephenson and got Stephenson the job [in Bihar and Orissa]. Muddiman also got the Home Membership for Crerar.'[75]

Montagu Butler was disappointed and could not understand not being selected as Muddiman's replacement in the United Provinces or later Hailey's replacement in the Punjab and had written to Irwin saying so.[76] Following personal discussions on this sensitive matter in Delhi, Irwin advised Butler that he had informed the Secretary of State of Butler's preference for an extension of his appointment in the Central Provinces.[77] Irwin informed

Butler that Lord Peel had indicated he could not make any promises on the threshold of a British General Election, and that there were no precedents either for the extension of a governorship, for more than a few months, or for reappointment to the same province and that Irwin would have to 'show cause'. Given Irwin's view, and that of others, Montagu Butler may have been fortunate Irwin evidently did show cause, and that his governorship in the Central Provinces was extended until September 1933. In any case, it seems, the Central Provinces were not a hardship. 'The Monty Butlers are very happy at Nagpur, and it strikes me his billet must be one of the softest and pleasantest going!.'[78] Evidence that conditions did vary from province to province in both comfort and responsibility for the governors is contained in a Hailey letter written in 1928, after his transfer to the United Provinces. 'I naturally find conditions here very different to those of the Punjab, particularly as regards the position of the Governor himself'.[79] He describes the requirement of personal rule in the Punjab, and the need 'to interest himself in the innumerable details of the administration and to interview an astonishing number of people'. This was not so much the case in the much larger United Provinces.

In writing to Irwin, in May 1927 about a replacement for Muddiman as Home Member, Birkenhead was to make reference to 'the remarkable dearth of men of outstanding character and ability at the top of the Service in the various Provinces at the present time'.[80] Birkenhead was to ascribe this situation to the tendency of the previous Viceroy, Lord Reading, 'who hated changes of personalities around him', to limit the movement of district officers to headquarters and thus restrict the acquisition of important experience.

> On the face of it this is bad for the district officers, whose outlook and ambitions become limited to the districts; for Government, whose choice of men is restricted; and for the secretaries themselves, who get increasingly out of touch with the real life of the country.[81]

Birkenhead was clearly conscious of the importance of broad experience, gained not only at the provincial and district level but also at headquarters, to the capacities of good governorship. Birkenhead was also of the view that everything being equal promotion should be on the basis of merit and not seniority.[82]

The correspondence between Irwin and Birkenhead, quoted above, demonstrates the important role the Viceroy had in making personal assessments of candidates for provincial governorships. While there certainly was a requirement for high formal academic qualifications and for professional success to ensure upward movement through the ranks, more esoteric criteria were applied at the very senior levels of the ICS from which the provincial governors were drawn. The Viceroy and his confidants appear not to have had these personal selection criteria formally set out but to have drawn from an unwritten code.

As far as can be established from the Irwin/Birkenhead record, a 'good' Governor was expected to have had a wide knowledge and experience of India. This could combine, ideally, with particular expertise in a province drawn from personal service there and from work at headquarters. He might be a Punjab man like Hailey or de Montmorency. He was required to have a grasp and understanding of political conditions in his province and its implications across India. He was expected to have good judgement, be confident, show initiative and be regarded as a decision maker. Being a sound debater was regarded as an asset, as was the possession of both mental and physical energy, enthusiasm and a breadth of view. He was required to show interest and have training in administration and have other professional skills such as in constitution making. He was expected to show tact and understanding when dealing with both Indians and Europeans and to inspire confidence in the people he led. He must not hold any emphatic bias of any kind. He was to be a popular man of personality and presence, needing to be cool in an emergency. He should be a good entertainer and in this regard an attractive and supportive wife was an important asset. To achieve an appointment to a governorship, it also helped to have connections including family who could assist one's career, directly or indirectly, as was the case with Lord Lytton and Montagu Butler.

In discussing Harcourt Butler and Malcolm Hailey, Woodruff describes highly competent men of principle with strong commitment to service.[83] These men were friendly and had a well developed sense of humour and proportion. They liked the India in which they lived, the work they did, and the peoples they governed. A letter written to Harcourt Butler's son, after the Governor's death in 1938, by an Indian noble, gives some sense of his achievements and of the regard in which he was held amongst his Indian friends and associates.

> In him I have lost a noble friend, a sincere well-wisher and a great benefactor. He had been loved as no man had ever been loved in Oudh before; although he has left this world yet his high achievements will survive for times to come.[84]

Butler had, in fact been so successful in nurturing friends and collaborators during his time in India that the *Taluqdurs*[85] of Oudh were to make him a member of their association.[86] He was the first and perhaps the only European to have been given this honour.

It is interesting to note another element of a Governor's selection criteria was that he was expected to wholeheartedly accept the Reforms of 1919. '...the reforms were accepted by the heads of provincial governments and members of the governor-general's council...absurd for the British Government to entrust high office to men who were not genuinely in favour of the reform movement'.[87] Logically this factor would have produced, over time, a cadre which supported progressive reform and constitutional advancement in India.

These were the important elements of selection criteria, then applicable to the provincial governors of British India. It is noteworthy that Irwin was unable to recommend any Indian for appointment to permanent governorships, at least in 1927.[88] The fact that Irwin would not consider anybody from Britain for provincial governorships demonstrated the importance he placed on the loyalty of the ICS. In those times, as these positions were much more than ceremonial, men from outside the ICS, such as military officers were not deemed appropriate, as they are in the more modern era in territories still under the Crown.

Irwin and his governors were cognisant, nevertheless of the political sensitivity of passing over senior Indians for permanent governorships. They were happy to consider them in an acting capacity, which to them had the added advantage of offering guided training and experience in line with the intentions of the Montford Reforms. In 1928, Hailey put forward the Nawab of Chhitari, an Indian noble, who had acted in Muddiman's position after his death, as a candidate to act for him in the United Provinces.[89] *New India* was highly critical of the passing over of the Nawab in favour of Lambert who had been his junior on the Executive Council.[90] At the end of 1929 Irwin was discussing with Montagu Butler a replacement for him and selected an Indian, Shripad Balwast Tambe, senior member of the Central Province's Excecutive Council, to act for him.[91]

In May 1930, Sir Charles Innes was planning a leave in England and attendance at the first Round Table Conference. Innes found himself unable to recommend Sir Joseph Maung Gyi, as acting Governor in his absence, following consideration of the advantages and disadvantages which he set out in a note to Irwin.[92] Innes advised Irwin that factors for Sir Joseph's appointment included: 'he is senior Member of Council and Vice President. He is thoroughly loyal and has great political courage; if he is not appointed there will be a political outcry'. However, Innes listed the factors against appointment as including: 'he is a party politician and had used his patronage dishonestly; he was financially and morally corrupt; he could not be trusted to carry out Clause VII of the Instrument of Instructions to governors [relating to the public interest and unfair discrimination]'. In short Innes advised that Sir Joseph had a bad reputation and would be a bad appointment. Despite Innes' strong views on Sir Joseph's failings, Irwin was to give greater weight to the political dimension, including in India proper. 'I feel that the broad political argument has greater weight if you pass him over than a direct slur, and though it might not matter a great deal in Burma, it will certainly produce the worst possible effect in India at a critical moment'.[93] Irwin pointed out he would have 'two European Councillors looking over his shoulder', and that these matters are 'questions of degree and of argument'.

Very high standards of probity and competency were expected of British administrators without exception, but Irwin was to tolerate apparently lower standards in a Burman in the interests of political expediency. This attitude might also be interpreted as a reflection of an underlying imperialist British view that, in any case, an Indian or Burman could probably not be trained to British standards for innate reasons of race and culture.

When there was a requirement to fill the offices of Viceroy and Governor-General on an acting basis, the Governor of Bengal was normally selected, as was the case when Lord Lytton acted for Lord Reading in 1925. The Presidency of Bengal was regarded as the senior of the three presidencies as it was the major territory established by the British, was the site of the original capital until 1910 and original seat of the Viceroy. However, Sir Stanley Jackson was passed over in favour of Lord Goschen, the Governor of Madras, on the occasion of Lord Irwin's return to England in 1929. Irwin broke the news to Jackson by advising him that the Secretary of State recognised Goschen's five successful years as Governor and that if Irwin's leave had not coincided with the end of Goschen's term, 'you [Jackson] as senior Presidency Governor would have naturally been the person to act'.[94] Birkenhead preferred to reward merit and competency in presidency governors, as he did with the ICS including governors there derived, rather than seniority.

In distinguishing the respective approaches to selection of presidency and provincial governors (and acting governors) it would not be surprising to note a difference in attitude, displayed by these categories to the person of the Viceroy and his authority. The presidency governors, particularly the aristocrats could be understood to regard themselves as equal in personal status if not in standing or rank in India. They did not owe Irwin their appointments. The provincial governors had risen through ICS ranks consequent upon performance and their final promotion had been due to the favourable assessment of the Viceroy. They could be expected to be his loyal servants, but nevertheless carrying with them into their new role and association with the Viceroy all the elements of personal quality which had identified them in the first place, and which excluded obsequiousness and sycophancy. They could be expected to continue to give frank and fearless advice. Given the nature of these men and the long experience of India held by them, and the relative inexperience of Irwin in comparison, it is not surprising that he would place considerable reliance on their advice, not only on provincial but also on all-India matters. This would be particularly so with Hailey, de Montmorency, Harcourt Butler and Innes, as will be shown in later chapters. These men had significant influence and input into important all-India policy matters and decisions over and above that of the other governors. Later chapters will also show that it was primarily the presidency governors, particularly Lytton and Sykes who gave Irwin the most concern in the administration of their admittedly difficult jurisdictions.

The presidency governors enjoyed the personal privilege, an anomaly of historical tradition, of corresponding directly with the Secretary of State, which they did on a regular basis at least once a month, not always copying this correspondence to the Viceroy even for information.[95] The correspondence of these governors with Irwin does reveal, but only infrequently, copies of dispatches involving important material written to the Secretary of State. There does not appear to have been a strict convention of consulting with the Viceroy prior to writing or of copying all correspondence of this nature through his office. All the provincial governors met the requirement of writing only to the Viceroy, with him then involving the Secretary of State as appropriate. Given the possibilities of views and advice diverging from the Viceroy on important all-India matters being communicated from the presidency governors direct to the Secretary of State, and influencing his decision making, there was potentially a strong chance of confusion and inefficiency in administration. Effectively, the Secretary of State had an independent source of information and one which could reflect, not only diverging views but also tensions between the Government of India and the presidencies. For example, this special status 'Lord Lloyd,[96] as Governor of Bengal [*sic*, actually Governor of Bombay] did not hesitate to exploit to the full when he wished to take stronger action against Gandhi's first civil disobedience campaign than the Viceroy Lord Reading was at first prepared to approve'.[97]

An examination of the presidency governors' correspondence with Lord Birkenhead, reveals that he used this avenue to compare and balance other correspondence from India. In writing to Sir Leslie Wilson, the Governor of Bombay, in November 1924 Birkenhead indicated 'it will be of the greatest value to me, if you will express freely your own views, so that I do not have to rely merely on impersonal official correspondence',[98] as he established his relationship with his governors at the beginning of his period in office. It is noteworthy that the governors used their privilege of access not only to keep the Secretary of State apprised of their personal perspectives of matters within their jurisdiction but also to obtain personal favour, as Lord Lytton did on matters of personal leave. From the Birkenhead Papers it can be seen that the Secretary of State actively used his correspondence with the presidency governors to obtain information, but avoided issuing directions on policy matters, thus minimising any complications with the Government of India. The practice of secretaries of state differed in the matter of direct communications with the presidencies. A contrast to Birkenhead was provided by Lord Peel who annoyed Governor Lytton by barely acknowledging his correspondence. Peel advised Lytton's wife, 'tell him to write about anything he likes but India. I get enough about India in my official papers'.[99] This may also have reflected a personal view Peel held of Lytton and the value of his correspondence.

The Government of India had always been conscious of the possibility of difficulties arising from the opportunity given to the presidency governors to turn direct to the Secretary of State. In his book, *The India Office*, Sir Malcolm Seton, Deputy Under-Secretary of State for India, contends, 'The right had not always been viewed with benevolent eyes by the Government of India, but restrictive rules and the modern standardisation of Indian administration… prevent the danger of cross purposes in the official correspondence'.[100] Nevertheless, the option of being able to write directly to the Viceroy's chief, on any matter, must have been a tempting possibility, particularly in circumstances of real or imagined personal tensions with the Viceroy.

While the provincial governors did not have a direct line from India to the Secretary of State they had the potential, based on their knowledge and experience, to exercise more personal and immediate influence on him in London through appointment to the Council of India.[101] Two of the provincial governors who served with Irwin, Wheeler and Marris, were both appointed members of the Council in 1927 and 1928 respectively, and Wheeler served for two, five year terms. A Commissioner of the Bengal Police Service during Irwin's time, Sir C.A. Tegart, was also appointed in 1931.[102] The Council was a very powerful body, chaired by the Secretary of State, in the administration of India,[103] and would have offered ample opportunity for the two governors to influence and contribute to Indian affairs. Their provincial colleagues, therefore, also had on the face of it, an informal, indirect and personal line, available to them to influence the Secretary of State's decisions on India.[104]

It is not surprising that a matter of considerable personal importance to the governors was that of salary and allowances. These emoluments comprised salary, a sumptuary (or incidental personal) allowance, a contract grant (to cover the cost of running their establishment), a tour fund, a state conveyance and motor grant, a presents and charities grant, and maintenance and other minor allowances.

The economic and political importance of the presidencies was also reflected in the salaries their governors received. It was laid down in the second Schedule to the 1919 *Government of India Act*, that the Governors of Bengal, Madras and Bombay were entitled to receive a maximum of 128,000 rupees per annum. During Irwin's time, the Governors' annual salary was 120,000 rupees.[105] This was around 9,200 British pounds at the approximate rate of exchange of 13 rupees to the pound in 1931.[106] The Governor of the United Provinces, which had been recognised as senior amongst the provinces in 1833, was also entitled to a maximum of 128,000 rupees per annum, equivalent to the presidencies. In 1919, the Governors of the Punjab and Bihar and Orissa received 100,000 rupees and the governors of the Central Provinces and of Assam received 72,000 and 66,000 rupees per annum respectively.[107] These salaries compared to a British Cabinet Minister's who received in the vicinity of 5,153 British pounds, or 67,000 rupees, per annum in 1935.[108]

However, the governors bore some extra costs which affected their income. In August 1927 Irwin wrote to his brother-in-law, and British MP, Lane Fox, who was to become a member of the Simon Commission but also had under consideration the possibility of taking up a presidency governorship in Madras or Bombay. Irwin responded to his queries relating to the cost of holding a governor's office.

> I have no doubt that Bombay is more expensive than Madras, in as much as it is a general hotel; and I think Leslie Wilson told me last year that it had cost him something like four or five hundred a year out of his own pocket in addition to his screw [salary]. Goschen told me last week that, except for some complication due to the situation as it was when he took over—which he hoped to get put right—he was just square on his pay…Goschen, on the other hand, lost two or three thousand pounds in directorships.[109]

That the presidency governors were experiencing some real or imagined financial stress is evidenced in them seeking pay increases. In June 1927, Irwin had had the benefit of a letter from Wilson, copying a note to Lord Birkenhead from the three presidency governors, seeking the payment to them of an additional 8,000 rupees to the maximum annual salary of 128,000 rupees, allowed in the second Schedule of the *Government of India Act* of 1919. Their letter pointed out that the Viceroy and all the other governors received the maximum salaries allowed under the Act and that there had not been a pay increase since 1880, despite the imposition of taxes on these salaries since then.[110] In their letter the governors either chose not to spell out or did not know why this apparently highly anomalous situation existed, and simply based their claim on comparison and cost of office against the background of possible reductions in their contract grants. The matter, in the event was resolved by Irwin and Birkenhead not agreeing to an increase in the governors' salaries, but acceding to waive, during the term of office of all three current presidency governors, the reduction in the contract grants which had been proposed.[111]

Another important factor in relation to payment of salary and emoluments was the increase in responsibility each Governor had experienced since the 1919 Reforms. In the context of the Lee Royal Commission held into the Public Services in the early 1920s, and its refusal to increase pensions to governors and councillors, Governor Hailey was to advise Lord Lee.

> I have had a very considerable experience of the Governors and close personal acquaintance for very many years with Members of Council. I can say with confidence that the amount of work and responsibility now falling on both of them is out of proportion to that encountered by their predecessors...[112]

In an examination of the mechanics of the governors' capacity to influence policy development, with the Government of India and with other British Indian jurisdictions, it is useful to note Lord Irwin's early attempt to set up annual governors' conferences. The governors' attitude to this initiative and the considerations they saw as pertinent to his suggestion, reveal some of the matters pertaining to the policy as well as personal relationship between the Centre and the provinces and presidencies. In June 1926, shortly after his arrival in India, Irwin sought the governors' comment on his proposal that they arrange periodical meetings to coordinate policy development and discuss general administrative questions, with as few support staff as possible.[113] Lord Chelmsford, Viceroy from 1916 to 1921, had been in the practice of holding annual conferences, involving governors and Irwin may have been taking the lead from him.[114] The governors' replies indicate a range of considerations they had in mind affecting their attitude to the matter.

Governor Marris acknowledged to Irwin the value of a conference on general grounds in the context of the value of personal contact, but identified two main difficulties.

> The machinery of Provincial Governments is complex, and on many matters a Governor would hesitate to commit his Government without having previously prepared the way. And secondly, the conditions of the Provinces are so different from one another that the common ground is relatively small.[115]

This response, on the surface of it would seem odd on the grounds that the first difficulty would presumably be overcome by circulating an agenda, supported by briefing, in advance. The second ignores the raft of policy matters of the time which were common and of vital importance to all provinces and which are largely referenced here. Marris was writing, no doubt, with the rather jaundiced memory of Lord Chelmsford's conferences in mind which he described as 'most jejune',[116] but nevertheless went on to set out a list of matters that occurred to him as suitable for discussion. These included

> ...(1) communal ill-feeling, (2) corruption in the public service, (3) protection of minorities, especially Muslims and Anglo-Indians, (4) relations between Governors and their Ministers, (5) control of local bodies [municipal and district boards], (6) preparation of the case for the Parliamentary [Simon] Commission, (7) composition and procedure of the Parliamentary Commission and (8) the future position of the Indian States.[117]

Each of these topics of interest to Marris will find some degree of reference in this book, contradicting his view that there was little common ground between the provinces. In fact his list is hardly comprehensive. Marris did, however, provide pertinent insight into the relationship between presidency and provincial governors and their relative status with regard to policy advice.

> It is, I suppose, fair to say that Presidency Governors' opinions are formed on less direct contact with Indian life than those of *mufassil*[118] Governors, but that this lack of immediacy is compensated for by their wider experience of men and affairs in other fields.[119]

This comment tends to confirm the central importance of the ICS governors and their long Indian experience to the effective administration of India. It would also indicate that the two categories of governors brought complementary professional attributes to their consideration of matters of common concern, such as at a governors' conference.

An interesting insight into the views held by the ICS governors of their colleagues, the 'politician' governors, is provided in the record of a meeting of the India Committee of the Royal Empire Society, held in September 1930, to examine the Simon Report. The meeting was chaired by Sir John Kerr, a previous Governor of Assam who had left India.[120] The Committee agreed they should recommend a position of a deputy governor, drawn from the ICS, to support and assist presidency governors to overcome their inexperience in Indian affairs. One Committee member went so far as to 'suggest very strongly that no Governor should be a politician from home; let them find their governors in India from the ICS, or Indians, or Europeans in commerce'. The Chairman said they 'could mention that the functions of the governors were such that they could only be coped with by people conversant with the country'. The lack of relevant Indian experience held by appointees to presidencies was acknowledged directly, and somewhat naively by Sykes on arrival in Bombay in 1928. Responding to his welcome address he said:

> My previous experience has been gained in offices far different in character to that which I am about to assume, but during the last few months I have done my best to make myself acquainted with some of the many very complex and difficult problems with which it will now be my duty to deal.[121]

The *Indian National Herald* was extremely critical of the appointment of this inexperienced Governor stating the position demanded 'the most intimate knowledge of the traditions and temperament of the people and a thorough grasp of fundamentals of its complex problems'.[122]

Ignoring any benefit of complementarity, Marris suggested two conferences, one for the presidency and one for the provincial governors, and made the point that he believed the Viceroy 'would get a clearer view of what one may call the foreground and the background of Indian politics by viewing the two things separately',[123] but indicated he would be delighted to attend a joint conference as appropriate.

Sir John Kerr replied to Irwin with similar feelings that 'so far as Provincial subjects are concerned, I rather doubt whether there would be sufficient material for a yearly meeting'.[124] He believed any meeting should confine itself, mainly, if not entirely to reserved subjects so as not to offend ministers. Kerr placed value, like Marris, on personal contact between the governors and listed communal tension, the relations of governors with their Legislative Councils and their ministers and matters relating to the Montford Reforms (the Simon Commission) as possible matters for discussion. Governor Hailey, with his usual enthusiasm and perceptiveness, replied 'I should myself welcome an annual meeting, for there are many questions which it would be of great value to discuss'.[125] He identified, as a problem to be overcome, the tendency of local governments and the Government of India to drift apart since the 1919 Reforms.[126] Sir Leslie Wilson, who had been the Governor of Bombay since Lord Reading's time, felt

> ...that there has not been that close touch that there should be between the Viceroy and the Governors; and, with Reading, the difficulty was got over to a certain extent by my writing to him on the 1st of every month a personal letter, dealing with matters in the Presidency which he might not know of from purely official reports.[127]

However, Wilson was very skeptical about the value of nine governors sitting around a table and expressed a preference for each Governor to meet the Viceroy as a matter of course each year.

In the event Irwin, despite the attractions of a governors' conference, seems to have preferred Wilson's advice as it wasn't until July 1930, that the governors met with Irwin in Simla, together, for the first and last time. At that meeting, the two principal agenda items were the Civil Disobedience Movement and the Simon Commission report. The nature of the policy process followed at the Simla Governors' Conference will be discussed in Chapter 8.

Since 1864, the Government of India had moved its headquarters from Calcutta and then New Delhi to Simla for a period of around five months during the hot weather on the plains of India.[128] The Punjab Government came up from Lahore initially in 1871–1873, and then continuously from 1876.[129] The headquarter of the British Indian Army was found in Simla.[130] Even though Sir Walter Lawrence,[131] from personal experience at Simla, believed that the summer capital was 'too small for two "Lart [sic] Sahibs"[132] much less for three',[133] their concurrence did provide an ideal and lengthy period each year for the Viceroy and the Governor of the Punjab to consult in circumstances ranging from valuable personal and private discussions to formal written memoranda.

Sir Malcolm Hailey's energy and ability[134] and his extensive access to the Viceroy while Governor of the Punjab and later, underpinned his substantial, solicited and often unsolicited policy advice to the central decision-making authority of the Raj. Governor de Montmorency enjoyed the same privileged access to the Viceroy after he became Governor of the Punjab in 1928, and it will be seen he also exercised considerable influence with him.

Given this framework of colonial governance, the following chapters will define the degree to which the governors individually and as a cadre contributed to the governing of India and the extent to which India was a governors' Raj.

Endnotes

1. The Consolidated Government of India Act, 1919, London, 1919.
2. Dyarchy is a compound of two Greek words *di*-twice+*archia*-rule, and means government by two rulers. See A. Appadorai, *Dyarchy in Practice*, p. 3.
3. Danzig, 'The Many-layered Cake', pp. 57–74, 60. Danzig argues here that the 1919 Reforms not only stemmed from a need to meet Indian political

aspirations but also met a preference in the provinces for less central interference. This provided a trade-off to the conservative governors for their agreement to a measure of liberal political reform at their provincial level.

4. *Report of the Indian Statutory Commission*, Volume I, p. 111.
5. Keith, *A Constitutional History of India*. See generally pp. 247–265 for the increase in provincial powers consequent upon the *Government of India Act* 1919.
6. Mukherji, *The Indian Constitution*, p.189.
7. Halifax Papers, Hailey to Irwin, 26 June 1926.
8. *Ibid.*, Irwin to Lytton, 1 June and 22 November 1926, in which Irwin acknowledges the authority of the Governor over aspects of his approach towards nationalism, but asks Bengal to keep him informed prior to any change in policy.
9. H. Butler, *Collection of Speeches*, pp.146–162. See Sir Harcourt's speeches on the Montford Reforms in which he provides advice to the Burmese Legislative Council in 1923, and to young officers in 1926, on the constitutional principles involved.
10. Keith, *Constitutional History*, p. 279.
11. *Ibid.*, p. 275.
12. The major items were local government, medical administration, public health, education, public works and water supplies, land revenue administration, famine relief, agriculture, fisheries and forestry, ports, the administration of justice, industrial matters and police. The major areas reserved to the central administration were the defence of India, external relations, relations with Native States, communications, shipping, criminal and civil law, trade and sources of all-India revenue including taxation.
13. See Rule 46 of the Devolution Rules. This Rule provided for the Governor-General in Council to employ the agency of the Governor in Council for this purpose.
14. Reading Papers, Memorandum titled 'Opinions of Governors and ICS officials regarding constitutional advance, 1923–1924'. No day or month reference. Provided as briefing to the Muddiman Committee, which examined, in 1924, the progress of the Montford Reforms.
15. Part V Section 45 (1) *Government of India Act* 1919.
16. Mukherji, *The Indian Constitution*, p. 190. See also Appadorai, *Dyarchy*, p. 47.
17. Appadorai, *Dyarchy*, p. 49.
18. Mukherji, *The Indian Constitution*, p. 229.
19. *Government of India Act*, 1919 Sections 52 (1), 52 (3), 72D, 72E (1).
20. *Ibid.*, Section 46 (3).
21. Mukherji, *The Indian Constitution*. See pp. 214–220 for annotations and analysis relating to S. 46, *Government of India Act* 1919.
22. Parliamentary Debates in the House of Commons on the *Government of India Bill*, 1919, quoted in Mukherji, p. 215.
23. Halifax Papers, Peel to Irwin, 27 March 1929.

24. Satyendra Prasanna, Sinha. Baron of Raipur (1863–1928). First Indian to be appointed: Advocate General of Bengal; a member of the Governor-General of India's Executive Council; Parliamentary Under Secretary of State for India; a member of the House of Lords; a Governor of a British Province. Governor of Bihar and Orissa, 29 December 1920 to 29 November 1921. Retired due to ill health.
25. We do hereby authorise and empower you the said...to take upon you, hold and enjoy the said Office...subject nevertheless to the superintending, directing and controlling power vested in Our Governor-General of India in Council as by the Government of India Act or any other Act or Acts of Parliament now in force is provided or by any rules lawfully made there under. And also subject to such instructions and directions as you the said...shall as Governor or Governor in Council of Our said Province of...from time to time receive under Our Royal Sign Manual or under the hand of one of Our Principal Secretaries of State. (NAI, Home/ Establishments, File 475/31)
26. Sykes Papers, Oath of Allegiance.
27. See Appendix 1 for full text of Instrument of Instructions drawn from Mukherji, *The Indian Constitution*, pp. 216–218. The Viceroy was also issued with similar Instructions.
28. *Ibid.*
29. *Ibid.*, p. 216.
30. *Report of the Simon Commission*, Volume I, pp. 154–157.
31. *Ibid.*, p. 154.
32. *Ibid.*
33. *Government of India Act*, 1919, Section 52, (3).
34. *Report of the Indian Statutory Commission*, Volume I, p. 155.
35. *Ibid.*
36. For example, demonstrating a certain defect in character, Lord Lytton while Governor had threatened to resign, rather petulantly, a number of times over personal leave matters. See Birkenhead Papers, Lytton to Birkenhead, 24 December 1924.
37. Halifax Papers, Peel to Irwin, 27 March 1929.
38. See p. 222.
39. Symonds, *Oxford and Empire*, Oxford, 1986, p. 191.
40. Ferguson, *Colossus*, p. 207.
41. Potter, *India's Political Administrators*, p. 32.
42. Ferguson, *Collosus*, p. 215.
43. O'Malley, *The Indian Civil Service*, p. 2.
44. Seal, *The Emergence of Indian Nationalism*, p. 343.
45. Yang, *The Limited Raj*, p. 225.
46. Seal, *Indian Nationalism*, p. 137.

47. *Ibid.*, p. 137.
48. A.A. Yang, *The Limited Raj*, p. 6
49. Lytton, Pundits and Elephants, p. 8.
50. Sykes, *From Many Angles*, p. 331.
51. Gopal, *Lord Irwin*, pp. 135–136.
52. Sykes, *From Many Angles*, pp. 382–386.
53. Halifax Papers, Stephenson to Irwin, 8 January 1930.
54. Sir A.N. Moberly. Member of the Bengal Executive Council from 1926.
55. Halifax Papers, Stephenson to Irwin, 8 January 1930.
56. *Ibid.*, Irwin to Stephenson, 25 February 1930.
57. *Ibid.*, Irwin to Jackson, 31 May 1930.
58. Birkenhead Papers, Irwin to Birkenhead, 9 January 1927.
59. *Ibid.*, Irwin to Birkenhead, 15 February 1927.
60. A.W. Botham. C.S.I., C.I.E., ICS, 1897. Member of the Assam Governor's Executive Council.
61. Birkenhead Papers, Irwin to Birkenhead, 15 February 1927.
62. A.H.W. Bentinck. C.I.E. ICS, 1897. Member of the Assam Legislative Council.
63. Sir J. Donald. ICS, 1895. Member of the Bengal Governor's Executive Council. Note Donald was knighted in June 1927 despite Irwin's views of him.
64. Birkenhead Papers, Irwin to Birkenhead, 15 February 1927.
65. Sir S.P. O'Donnell. ICS, 1896. Member of the United Provinces' Governor's Executive Council. Secretary to the Government of India's Reform Office in 1920. Acting Governor of the United Provinces in 1926.
66. Birkenhead Papers, Irwin to Birkenhead, 21 March 1927.
67. Sir J. McKenna. ICS, 1894. Various positions including with the Government of India; Sir W.J. Keith. ICS, 1895. Various positions including acting Governor of Burma in 1925.
68. Halifax Papers, Irwin to Birkenhead, 21 March 1927.
69. Note, Whyte was not an ICS man but an academic and politician (M.P. for Perth City 1910–1918). Previously the President of the Legislative Assembly in New Delhi, 1920–1925.
70. Birkenhead Papers, Irwin to Birkenhead, 21 March 1927.
71. *Ibid.*
72. *Ibid.*, Irwin to Birkenhead, 19 March 1928.
73. Birdwood, Field Marshal Lord. Commander-in-Chief in India, 1925 to 1930.
74. Montagu Butler Papers, Butler to his wife Hannah, 4 August 1927.
75. *Ibid.*, Butler to his wife, 11 July 1929. Sir J. Crerar. ICS, 1900. Member of the Governor-General's Executive Council, 1927–1932.
76. Halifax Papers, Montagu Butler to Irwin, 1 August 1928.
77. *Ibid.*, Irwin to Montagu Butler, 7 March 1929.
78. Hailey Papers, Birdwood to Hailey, 17 January 1926.
79. *Ibid.*, Hailey to Brown (*Times of India* journalist and secretary of the East India Association), 23 August 1928.
80. Birkenhead Papers, Birkenhead to Irwin, 26 May 1927.

81. *Ibid.*
82. *Ibid.*, Birkenhead to Irwin, 9 August 1927.
83. P. Woodruff, *The Men Who Ruled India: The Guardians*, Volume II, London, 1963, p. 290.
84. Harcourt Butler Papers, Bahadur Shah to Victor Butler, 4 March 1938. Harcourt Butler died on 2 March and it is interesting to note his friend Bahadur Shah's letter had been written from 'Butler Gunj', an address in Lucknow.
85. Great land owners.
86. Harcourt Butler, *Speeches*, p. 119.
87. Keith, *Constitutional History*, p. 299.
88. Birkenhead Papers, Irwin to Birkenhead, 21 March 1927.
89. Halifax Papers, Hailey to Irwin, 8 September 1928.
90. *New India*, 1 December 1928.
91. Halifax Papers, Irwin to Montagu Butler, 9 November 1929.
92. *Ibid.*, Innes to Irwin, 15 May 1930.
93. *Ibid.*, Irwin to Innes, 27 May 1930.
94. Halifax Papers, Irwin to Jackson, 6 October 1928.
95. B.B. Misra, *The Administrative History of India*, p. 250. See also Seton, *The India Office*, p. 48.
96. G.A. Lloyd. Baron of Dolobran. Governor of Bombay, 1918–1923.
97. Campbell Johnson, *Viscount Halifax*, p. 246.
98. Birkenhead Papers, Birkenhead to Wilson, 27 November 1924.
99. Lytton, *Pundits and Elephants*, p. 30.
100. Seton, *The India Office*, p. 49.
101. *Ibid.*, p. 3.
102. *The India Office List*, p. 168. Sir C.A. Tegart. Indian Police Service 1901. Commissioner, Bengal Police Service, 1925–1931, with responsibility for anti-terrorism.
103. Seton, *The India Office*, pp. 28–38.
104. Note: it has not been possible to establish whether Wheeler and Marris were contacted by the provincial governors in order to influence the Secretary of State, but it is not unreasonable to suspect this channel was used, particularly upon return to England after their Indian posting, 'over dinner'. Hailey communicated with at least one Member of the Council of India providing Indian intelligence. See Chapter 5, p. 106.
105. Halifax Papers, Wilson to Irwin, 16 June 1927.
106. Tinker, *Viceroy*, p. 117.
107. Mukherji, *The Indian Constitution*, p. 215. See also p. 291 of *The India Office List* (1936) which indicates these salaries had not increased, at least, in the period 1919 to 1936.
108. Potter, *India's Political Administrators*, p. 33.
109. Halifax Papers, Irwin to Lane Fox, 11 August 1927.
110. *Ibid.*, Wilson to Irwin, 16 June 1927.
111. *Ibid.*, Irwin to Birkenhead, 14 October 1927.

112. Hailey Papers, Hailey to Lord Lee, 4 March 1926.
113. *Ibid.*, Irwin to various governors, 18 June 1926.
114. *Ibid.*, Marris to Irwin, 4 November 1927.
115. *Ibid.*, Marris to Irwin, 25 June 1926.
116. Naive, simplistic and superficial.
117. Hailey Papers, Marris to Irwin, 25 June 1926.
118. The word *mufassil* describes a territory of India outside the boundaries of the original British settlements at Bengal, Bombay and Madras. Hence a *mufassil* Governor is a provincial governor.
119. Halifax Papers, Marris to Irwin, 25 June 1926.
120. Royal Empire Society Papers, minutes of meetings of the India Committee held to consider The *Report of the Indian Statutory Commission*. Meeting of 19 September 1930.
121. *Times of India*, 8 December 1928.
122. *Indian National Herald*, 8 December 1928.
123. Halifax Papers, Marris to Irwin, 25 June 1926.
124. *Ibid.*, Kerr to Irwin, 26 June 1926.
125. *Ibid.*, Hailey to Irwin, 26 June 1926.
126. *Ibid.*
127. *Ibid.*, Wilson to Irwin, 21 June 1926.
128. P. Kanwar, *Imperial Simla*, p. 37.
129. *Ibid.*, p. 41.
130. *Ibid.*, p. 40.
131. Sir W. Lawrence. Lord Curzon's private secretary from December 1898 to 1903. Curzon was Viceroy from 1898 to 1905.
132. The Indian pronunciation for Lord but correctly spelt Lat. See Lawrence, *The India We Served*, p. 81.
133. The third Lat Sahib was the Army Commander-in-Chief.
134. Cell, Hailey.

2

The Montford Reforms and Dyarchy

This chapter deals primarily with the Governors' interaction and relationship with the constitutional system known as 'dyarchy'. It sets out to identify the nature of their connection with this system. Consistent with the underlying theme of this book, emphasis is placed on exploring the governors' contribution to the introduction and operation of dyarchy at the presidential and provincial level, and their relationship with the Government of India at the Centre on this constitutional arrangement. It is not intended to provide here a detailed description of the machinations of the governors working dyarchy in their provinces. Rather this chapter identifies the governors' attitudes and intentions towards constitutional change in India. It will establish whether the governors genuinely entered into the spirit of the Montagu Declaration and subsequent reforms and whether and how their attitudes influenced rising nationalism. It is important to establish whether the governors, as a group, were inhibitors of nationalist aspirations or fundamentally supporters and encouragers. The chapter explores the phases of development and implementation of the Montford Reforms and dyarchy which were significant policy areas to which the governors, to varying degrees, were involved and contributed.

Dyarchy was introduced in India, consequent upon the 1919 *Government of India Act*, in 1921 with the active personal involvement of Edwin Montagu, Secretary of State for India, the Viceroy, Lord Chelmsford and the imperial bureaucracy both in England and India. Given that a number of the governors of the period of Irwin's Viceroyalty were then rising through the ICS ranks, it will not be surprising to find that some of these men had a significant and personal influence on the form that dyarchy was to take. We know, in particular, Sir Harcourt Butler as a Governor and Sir William Marris,

Sir Alexander Muddiman and Sir Geoffrey de Montmorency, in their ICS capacities, were personally involved in policy development and preparations for the introduction of dyarchy. An interesting element will be to establish how far these men were able, diligently, to apply dyarchy in their provinces in the form and with the intent the system was finally agreed by the British Parliament.

It can be argued that the British had embarked upon a pathway of constitutional reform, which would lead, perhaps not with direct intention, to Indian independence, at the time of the dissolution of the East India Company and Queen Victoria's proclamation of 1 November 1858. Britain then had the choice of accepting 'Indians as what they had now become, subjects of the Queen, "fellow citizens" who could be tutored in the art of government in preparation for ruling themselves'.[1] Indian government was now beholden to the British Parliament and electorate through the Secretary of State for India and the Governor-General and Viceroy. Considerable political change in Britain at the end of the nineteenth century had extended the vote to the working classes and 'produced a breed of radical Liberal and, later, Socialist politicians keen to expose what they took to be injustices in the daily administration of India and to reprimand those responsible'.[2]

From this impetus and beginning, with its origins in the Mutiny or Rebellion of 1857 a passage to Indian independence had become discernible and, with the benefit of hindsight, was to turn out to be traversable. A real issue of continuing concern for Indian nationalism was to be how long it would take to negotiate the path. History shows a British reluctance to concede constitutional advance without pressure being applied to the Raj. Increasing Indian education along Western lines, carrying with it ideas of democracy and equality, a free vernacular press and the formation of the Indian National Congress in 1885 provided the initial and continuing catalysts to Indian nationalism. Political pressure, which was initially moderate but ultimately radical, and included extremism, led to the Morley–Minto Reforms of 1908, which introduced Indian representation in central and provincial councils, and thus the beginnings of representative democracy in India. The First World War and its social and educational impact, as well as India's significant contributions of manpower, material and money further increased political pressure on Britain to reward India for its support in the form of more democratic advancement.[3] This came in the form of the Montagu Declaration of 1917 and the Montford Reforms encapsulated in the *Government of India Act* of 1919, which some historians see as a political concession for India's contribution to the war effort.

The Montagu Declaration of 1917 was repeated in the opening paragraphs of the Preamble to the 1919 Act. The Preamble set out the British formula for constitutional advancement with key elements relating to

> ...the increasing association of Indians in every branch of Indian administration; the progressive realisation of responsible government; British India as an integral part of the Empire; progress by successive stages; with the time and manner of each advance to be determined only by Parliament; and Parliament to be guided by the degree of cooperation received from Indians to whom new opportunities would be conferred.[4]

The intent of the British Parliament reflected in the Preamble to the 1919 Act and in particular the respective interpretations of the Indian nationalists and the British, of these words quoted above were to form an important basis of the tensions and significant differences between them into the future. It can be asked justifiably whether delayed or accelerated constitutional advance was the real motivation underlying the Declaration. The general historical approach is to view constitutional reform in terms of the result of the application of various forms of indigenous pressure against the British, rather than the outcome of planning for the distant future. The British had set a pathway, and tests in the Preamble would be the governors' and the wider British benchmark the Indians would have to meet to merit further constitutional advance. But how far and in what way did the governors respond to indigenous pressure?

It is also interesting to note the intention, contained in the final paragraph of the Preamble, to give the provinces and consequently the governors 'the largest measure of independence of the Government of India' possible. It was the provinces that were to administer dyarchy and not the Government of India.[5] It was the governors who were required to implement and administer this complex constitutional system, in what was to be an increasingly hostile political environment.

Historians have chosen to interpret the British intention contained in the Montford Reforms in different ways. In his article 'The Montagu–Chelmsford Reforms (1919): A Re-assessment',[6] Philip Woods identifies a number of approaches to this issue. Woods indicates

> ...there has been a general tendency to lump the [Montford] Reforms together with the 1909 and 1935 reforms as examples of the British attempt to hold on to their essential powers by the means of using constitutional concessions to divide their opponents and to distract them from the key elements of power which the British skillfully retained for themselves.

He indicates that research revealed the British had no real timetable for transfer of power and concessions in that direction were most often wrested from them by consistent nationalist pressure.

Further that 'reforms which started with any liberal intent were soon made safe by the conservatism of the Government of India, local governments and the bureaucracy'.[7] Even so, Woods believes the reforms were 'much more liberal and educative in intent than has been acknowledged',[8] and that 'in 1917, there was a remarkable change of view among key policy makers',[9] towards a more liberal outlook. This book explores the governors' role in this change.

The system of dyarchy which was introduced into the Indian presidencies and provinces was an experiment. It was innovative in form, complex and to a significant degree capable of differing interpretation as to application. At its broadest level it can be seen fairly as an intended opportunity for the Indian political classes to obtain the necessary parliamentary, governmental and administrative experience, in due course, to run their country. By the early 1920s, dyarchy was to increase the political power and influence held by Indians at the local and provincial levels. 'Most seriously, at the local level, important changes had taken place which were to shift the balance of local control decisively against the colonial government...and deposited crucial power into Indian hands'.[10]

In the context of this new system, and in the prevailing environment of nationalist hostility and pressure, did the Governors work dyarchy towards the liberal outcomes which Montagu intended or did they, by manipulating the ample opportunity offered by the complexity of the reforms, use them cynically as a brake on constitutional evolution? Was there pressure between the Centre and the presidencies and provinces in achieving outcomes and if so, how were these resolved?

Appadorai's, *Dyarchy in Practice*, published in India in 1937, is a valuable contemporary analysis of the introduction and working of dyarchy from its inception in 1921 until 1936, when a new Government of India Act came into operation. The book's conclusions point to a range of considerations useful to an understanding of the governmental environment within which the Governors of British India operated.

The introduction of this bifurcated system had not been universally welcomed, or during its operation universally applauded even by those with the best of intentions, whether British or Indian, politically moderate or extreme. The system's defects were manifest. First amongst these was the fact that the dyarchical system reflected a fundamental distrust of Indian capacity to govern, which was politically to far outweigh the available benefits for gaining constitutional training and experience. The system was an open provocation to the nationalists, who responded accordingly by initially boycotting the Legislative Council elections, then obstructing the operation of the councils and generally taking any opportunity to harass and criticise, both from within and without the legislatures. The fact that the British maintained control of the strategically important subjects of government, including control of money and finances, defence and law and order, reinforced the cynicism felt in nationalist quarters towards British intent.

The mechanics of the system itself were inherently flawed as the subject matters of the two sides of government inevitably overlapped. For example, every Bill on the transferred side which contained a penal clause required the involvement of the law and order, reserved side of government to enforce the provision. This fact compromised the ability of ministers on the transferred side to develop and implement their own discrete policies or indeed to understand where their ministerial responsibilities began or ended. Where the Governor was required to exercise his powers to decide on points of conflict between the two halves it was easy to accuse him of bias against those elected to the Legislative Council. He could not function as a truly impartial judge in these matters as his political allegiances were seen to lie elsewhere. Appadorai identifies that arrangements were made in some provinces to overcome this problem. 'The substance of these arrangements is to leave to joint deliberation the point at issue, and to trust to mutual goodwill for preventing friction, and finally leaving it to the Governor to decide'.[11] However, these approaches were merely patchwork remedies in a fundamentally dissatisfied and hostile political environment.

It has also been pointed out that dyarchy being a divided government could only be a weak government. Factually, the government, comprising the Governor and ministers responsible for transferred subjects and their counterpart executive councillors responsible for the reserved subjects, was divided in its loyalty to the respective authority of the provincial legislature and effectively the British Parliament. This fact did not lend itself to cohesion and common effort particularly in relation to difficult issues which would be delayed or postponed.

> On account of the interdependence of functions, the want of organised parties and of a separate purse, it [the transferred half] is compelled to seek the support of the reserved half [and vice versa], and in so doing, to compromise. Too much compromise is inimical to strong and efficient government.[12]

This situation was further complicated by the shortage of experienced ministers, a factor inherent in the reformed system introduced in 1921 and after each respective Council election.

The provisional nature of the 1919 *Government of India Act* was reflected in the intention set out in the Act to review its provisions and included the possibility, not only of extending, modifying but also of *restricting* responsible government. This was another serious impediment to the development of sound government within the provincial councils. In the eyes of politically aware Indians, this review encapsulated a patronising approach which severely aggravated the more nationalist politicians, who were unwilling to tolerate the concept of India having to prove itself a good constitutional pupil in order to advance to a further level of responsible government. The reference to any possibility of going backwards to a restriction of what already existed was pure anathema. The fact that dyarchy was a transitional arrangement only hastened the calls for its early end and compromised intentions to make the system work through, for example, the development of governmental convention, a feature of constitutions which are allowed to develop and are not constructed.[13]

An ostensible objective of dyarchy was to introduce the electorate and their representatives in the legislative councils to the concept of ministerial responsibility back to the electorate through Council members. An important element of this principle was that if the electorate and Council found that the Council members or ministers had been irresponsible and had thus lost the confidence of the Council, then ministers would be required to resign. Analysis by Appadorai indicates that over the period 1921 to 1928 there were a total of 49 government defeats, if support from the official bloc was omitted and 21 defeats if otherwise, without ministerial resignation.[14] Apart from not observing the principle of ministerial responsibility, ministers had not developed strong links with a political party and therefore could not command parliamentary support. Dyarchy was still fundamentally undemocratic despite its intentions.

Generally in the United Provinces, Madras, Bihar and Orissa and in Bengal, ministers were only able to continue in office with the support of the official bloc, severely eroding the development of the principle of ministerial responsibility.

> The absence of stable parties, the existence of the official and nominated bloc; the attempts at working dyarchy in a unitary way; the joint purse; the overriding powers vested in the Governor; the rights of the civil services; the right of the Secretaries of direct access to the Governor and the interdependence of functions of government all combined to obscure and delay the growth of responsibility.[15]

In a real sense, given the powers of the Governor to override or personally to endorse legislation, ministers were, in fact, ultimately responsible to the Governor and not the electorate, which indeed was often unable to understand the difference between reserved and transferred subjects, adding a further layer of complexity to the relationship between the electorate and legislative councils.

It can be seen from this analysis that the work of the governors at the provincial level, with respect to dyarchy, was complicated, highly politically charged and had all-India implications. Dyarchy was generally viewed as having failed partly because of its inherent administrative flaws but also because of the timing of its introduction with the hard line nationalists or Swarajists from 1922 refusing to operate any system out of their complete control, let alone a hybrid. The governors were faced over the period from 1922 to 1925 with continuous obstruction in the councils, and in Bengal and the Central Provinces the governors had assumed responsibility for all departments. At the end of 1925 a split occurred in the nationalist approach to destroying the councils from within, and new approaches to achieving nationalist aims were developed.

The Reforms Inquiry Committee or Muddiman Committee set up in 1924 to consider whether adjustments to the 1919 constitutional arrangements were necessary, declared that, 'while it was too soon to pronounce that dyarchy had succeeded, it was premature to say that it had failed'.[16] This view had been at least partially derived from the advice of several governors, who had responded to Viceroy Reading's request for briefing, on how the reforms were working in their provinces, for Muddiman's Committee.[17] They believed that while there were problems with dyarchy, benefits of constitutional advance were being achieved.

In the time from the introduction of the Montford Reforms in 1919 to Lord Irwin's departure in 1931, there had been four general elections under the 1919 Act. These were in 1920, 1923, 1926 and 1929–1930. Thus, there had been a period of around eleven years and the experience of four elections, in which practical knowledge of how to achieve the goals set by the Montford Reforms was built, to the end of Lord Irwin's Viceroyalty. This experience was to be analysed by committees[18] appointed by the provincial legislative councils in order to report to the Simon Commission.[19] Without exception each of the provincial committees, regardless of their stated attitude to dyarchy, sought significant changes to their governmental framework. The underlying thrust of their reports indicated that genuine and consistent attempts had been made to work dyarchy, but they were largely complicated not only by the system's own inherent complexity but also by the external influences of nationalism and communalism. The provinces generally believed that they had learnt constitutional ways by experience, acknowledging the constructive involvement of the governors and advising that they were ready for further constitutional advancement. A characteristic Committee comment made reference to dyarchy as having by and large worked in their province because of the 'spirit of harmony and cooperation'[20] which existed despite the system's complexities. Even though seeking change, the committee reports were essentially politically benign and remarkable for the conservatism of the constitutional goals they identified, in contrast to what the nationalists sought. This might be seen as some indication that the authors had indeed developed a level of parliamentary responsibility, and the political maturity the governors had been seeking to nurture.

In Bengal, the impact of the Swarajists from 1924 and communalism from 1926 had made dyarchy unworkable, but elsewhere, and even to a degree in the Central Provinces, dyarchy had been made to work. The governors had successfully achieved a level of cooperation, with the moderate and cooperating Indian political class, which was essential to the ongoing British rule.[21] Bridge's hypothesis that British constitutional reforms were not really intended to hand over power in any immediate sense can be seen as consistent with the reality of dyarchy in practice.[22]

Appadorai set out the flaws and failures of dyarchy in operation. Were the governors sufficiently astute and prescient to identify these weaknesses, and hence the inherent ineffectiveness of the Montford Reforms in their capacity to deliver truly liberal constitutional reform as was intended, before their implementation?

In the context of establishing the attitude of the governors to the legislation introduced at the end of 1919, it is of particular interest to note their views of the impending system expressed at the Annual Meeting of governors, held in January 1919, with the Viceroy. As has been noted some of the governors of the Irwin era had been intimately involved in the formative stage of dyarchy. The meeting with Chelmsford was, effectively, the last significant opportunity the governors had to provide their input into the shape of the impending constitutional reforms. During the period from 1916 to the end of 1918, the British Government, the Government of India and the governments of the provinces had been engaged in a process of consultation and development of the concepts leading to the construction of the *Government of India Act*.[23] However, this process of consultation had, evidently, not fully taken into account the views of the provinces to their satisfaction.

At the January 1919 meeting, the heads of provinces were asked to consider the report on the reforms jointly prepared and agreed in India by Montagu and Chelmsford at the beginning of 1918.[24] This document had been largely written by William Marris, who was to become Governor of Assam in 1921, and of the United Provinces during part of Lord Irwin's Viceroyalty.[25] Lord Chelmsford, Chair of the Governors' meeting, had set out three principles against which he wished his joint report to be considered, namely: the goal of progressive realisation of responsible government; that substantial steps towards this goal be taken at once and that this policy be carried out by stages. Chelmsford asked the governors to consider how to achieve these goals. 'If we can arrive at an agreement as to the method of carrying out the fundamental principle, viz, the transfer of responsibility we shall at all events have cleared the ground and we can then examine the machinery which will be necessary'.[26]

As Lieutenant-Governor of the United Provinces, Sir Harcourt Butler had had considerable input into 'formulating a scheme alternative to that of the joint report and to develop it in some detail'.[27] This alternative scheme, prepared and agreed by Butler, other Lieutenant-Governors (Sir M. O'Dwyer and Sir R. Craddock),[28] and Chief Commissioners (Sir B. Robertson and Mr N. Beatson-Bell)[29] was put forward as their input into Chelmsford's discussion of his joint paper. These dissenting senior officers indicated that they supported the principles of the joint report but also that they took full account of the depth of the existing criticism of dyarchy. They summarised their position as follows:

> Bengal and Bihar and Orissa treat the main question, [the transfer of responsibility] as closed to discussion, but the former is dubious and the latter guarded in its opinion. Madras is in favour of instituting sub-provinces but otherwise would fall in with the majority opinion. All other Governments have declared against a dualised executive and wish to maintain the unity of administration.[30]

While the Governor of Bengal and the Lieutenant-Governor of Bihar and Orissa[31] believed the adoption of dyarchy was a forgone conclusion, the other governors went on to identify what they regarded as the significant defects of what was being proposed. They believed that dyarchy would cause legislative, administrative and financial friction at the governmental and executive levels, dividing the government against itself, at a time when there was a dire need for cooperation and association. Their alternative scheme 'would do away with the distinction between reserved and transferred subjects and it should be open to the Governor to give any portfolio to any member of his [Legislative] Council whether he should be official or non-official'.[32] The dissenting parties believed that this would secure an effective unitary government. Further, they indicated that they wished to see a substantial elected majority and to give the Legislative Council very real powers in the matter of legislation and supply.

> We urge that this constitution will provide an executive which, though responsible to the Secretary of State will be largely accountable in practice to the Legislative Council. This will be a more *liberal* scheme than that proposed during the period of transition, in that, in the words of the announcement [of 1917] it will associate Indians with every branch of the administration.[33]

It can be argued the note signed off by Butler and his four colleagues, on the face of it, reflected an attempt to formulate a more practical and democratic constitutional model than that in the event adopted. It predicted quite accurately the difficulties, as set out earlier in this chapter, that would be experienced in the provinces under dyarchy. It is remarkable that these senior provincial officials, who could be expected to have reflected a more reactionary attitude to reform, identified and sought what they agreed was a more progressive approach as desirable. They referred to their scheme as being more liberal than dyarchy. This is particularly so in the case of Lieutenant-Governors O'Dwyer and Craddock, who both later gained reputations as reactionaries in England for fulminating, in the press, against any concession towards constitutional reform in the face of nationalist pressure.[34] In his autobiography, O'Dwyer describes their alternative scheme as liberal and makes reference to 'a liberal component for the association of Indians in a unitary government' which the dyarchical model lacked.[35]

The dissenting governors' scheme was not adopted, therefore one can only theorise over any comparison of the possible effect of its implementation with that of dyarchy and any view that the alternative scheme may have been more liberal. However, the point to be made is that the dissenting governors, even including O'Dwyer and Craddock, put forward an alternative scheme which, at least in principle, contained strong reference to a desire to offer even more liberal reform than ultimately contained in the 1919 *Government of India Act*. How far did Harcourt Butler and his gubernatorial colleagues, and later their successors apply the liberal principles of the 1917 Montagu Declaration to the administration of dyarchy, a system to which Butler at least was fundamentally opposed? To what extent did the governors of the Irwin period nurture the development of a constitutional system which had been identified by so many observers as flawed in its concept and operation, in order to advance the constitutional evolution of India? Despite the flaws identified in the dyarchical system, did the governors' implementation and operation of dyarchy reflect a main intention of introducing liberal reform?

At the level of the British reactionary, dyarchy was seen as a capitulation to the Indian *literati* which provided the very small, politically active, and as the reactionaries perceived it, the fundamentally self-interested political class of India at that time. Britain had forfeited the interests of the politically illiterate masses of India to the unrepresentative and educated elite.[36] Again, how far can the governors of British India, in the period between 1926 and 1931, be seen as reflecting these reactionary views? Is it possible that this class resisted political progress in India and can this be detected in their correspondence with Lord Irwin? Alternatively, is it possible to establish that, following the implementation of the Reforms of 1919, the governors were inclined to display a degree of moral intention to work the Reforms in the spirit they were intended and with sympathy for nationalist aspirations? If Irwin was a liberal in conservative disguise how many of the governors by their practice can also be seen in this way, or were they consistently conservative or even diehards in the O'Dwyer model? How far did the governors try to work dyarchy?

It is with this background of the development and implementation of dyarchy, and of the difficulties of its general administration, that a specific consideration of how the governors approached and managed the scheme follows. Is it possible to identify any cynicism or underlying theme of gubernatorial 'subversion' in their constitutional keystone association with dyarchy? How constructive were they? This section will show the range of attitudes held by the governors in relation to the operation of dyarchy and to the implications held within the scheme of constitutional evolution, which they had to operate. It will reveal a spectrum of opinion varying from those governors who warmed to the task to those who were perplexed by it, and preferred the 'old' system. The range of views and approaches shows how far sighted some were and how others held to more myopic perspectives. As we shall see this division was primarily between the ICS Governors and those appointed to the presidencies.

Of the governors of Lord Irwin's time nine had administered dyarchy before his arrival as Governor, namely: Sir John Kerr in Assam; Lord Lytton in Bengal; Sir Henry Wheeler in Bihar and Orissa; Sir Leslie Wilson in Bombay; Sir Harcourt Butler in Burma; Sir Montagu Butler in the Central Provinces; Viscount Goschen in Madras; Sir Malcolm Hailey in the Punjab; and Sir William Marris in the United Provinces. Some of them, as has been seen, had been involved in the system's development. Other men to become governors under Irwin, with the exception of the future presidency governors, worked as senior officers in the ICS. These men were Sir Geoffrey de Montmorency, Sir Laurie Hammond, Sir Hugh Stephenson, Sir Alexander Muddiman and Sir Charles Innes. All these men would have been very familiar with the concept of dyarchy and its complexities. Given the ICS pedigree of the provincial governors it will be interesting to differentiate between them and the governors of the presidencies in relation to dyarchy.

As previously noted Sir Harcourt Butler as the Lieutenant-Governor of the United Provinces had revealed his negative attitude towards dyarchy to Lord Chelmsford at the beginning of 1919, before the reforms were introduced. Despite his reservations and practical experience of dyarchy, his wish to impart constitutional expertise is reflected in a speech he gave at the opening of the Legislative Council in Lucknow in 1921, when dyarchy had been in place for well over a year.[37] In his speech Butler advised the councillors that he had concerns with the number of motions from the Council addressed to the Government of India on matters that were the central government's concern. Butler informed them there was a need to become a practical legislative body and to concentrate on matters within their powers.

> I attach the more importance to this because I am a confirmed believer in the devolution of powers to local governments; and I do not see how we can expect the Government of India to leave us alone in matters that concern us if we do not leave them alone in matters which concern them.[38]

Further:

> I perceive a tendency among some of you, when out-voted to appeal at once to the Government of India. It is anomalous under a constitutional system of government such as we now have. May I remind you that no progress in constitutional government is possible until the minority accept the will of the majority. That is the very root and essence of representative Government.[39]

While the councillors did not yet understand the bounds of their constitution and authority, the tendency to appeal to the Government of India was bound to be inevitable in an undemocratic system. It also might be cynically seen as compromising any wish Butler, himself, had to run his province unfettered by interference from the central government, thus complicating provincial independence.

In a document, dated May 1923, Butler set out some impressions of the working of the reforms while he was Governor of the United Provinces during 1921 and 1922.[40] Butler indicated that he believed the reforms would not truly work until the non-cooperators had entered the legislative councils. But, that his attempt to work the Government on a unitary basis by supporting the ministers had worked well and the main problems were between 'Mussalman and Hindu'. However, he identified the main difficulties as: 'the divorce of the Governor from real touch with the Legislative Council; the impossibility of securing anything like secrecy under the reformed constitution and the feeling of insecurity and dissatisfaction in the [civil] services'.[41]

Butler's objective of achieving political education was complicated by non-cooperation and communalism. The fact that the Governor had little direct regular contact with the Legislative Council limited his ability to provide immediate guidance to its membership which, at least in the early 1920s, was a constitutionally naive group and one which did not understand the fundamental principle that democracy provides for the will of the majority. The Governor's role was further complicated by ministers having not learnt the importance of confidentiality, and by a conservative, mainly European, Civil Service which was not yet happy to accept the transfer of political power to Indians. But fundamentally Butler had revealed that the Raj could not operate without cooperation, even within the constitutional system which had been provided.

Harcourt Butler was transferred to Burma as Governor at the beginning of 1923 and on 3 March addressed the first meeting of Burma's Legislative Council.[42] He noted that only 10 per cent of the qualified electorate had bothered to vote, and therefore there was a clear need to educate the public to take advantage of their democratic opportunity. He also advised that the cardinal condition of healthy reform must be that it is real and not have too many safeguards.[43] He referred to his preferred alternative scheme (that had been known as the scheme of the five *Satraps*) rejected by the British Parliament and said 'I deferred to their [the Parliament's] ability and experience, and did my best in the United Provinces to make their scheme a success...what matters most is not the letter of the constitution, but the spirit in which it is worked by all concerned'.[44] In his book *India Insistent*, Butler reinforced this view: 'The craziest constitution will work if supported by experience and a sense of compromise: the wisest will not work without them'.[45] Butler further advised the Burmese Council at its inaugural meeting that 'it is a real and honest scheme, that the ministers do have large powers, that the vote of the Council does dictate policy in the transferred subjects and that the Legislative Council is now the centre of political gravity'.[46] The fact that dyarchy did work to an extent, even though it could be classified as 'crazy' as a constitutional system, reinforced the importance of the elements of experience and compromise which Butler had identified and of cooperation. The Report of the United Provinces Provincial Committee, to the Simon Commission, had attributed any smooth operation of dyarchy to individual goodwill. The Burmese Committee had said that the reforms in Burma had worked more successfully than anywhere else. These views may have owed something to Governor Butler's skills in nurturing collaboration and constitutional reform in both jurisdictions.

In an official memorandum of 26 July 1924, written over a year after becoming Burma's Governor, Butler indicated that he believed the various governments of India were trying honestly to work dyarchy but were not being met halfway.[47] He revealed that

> ...this is a disappointment but not altogether a surprise to many who, like myself, have been in favour of political concessions to Indians from a period long antecedent to the Reforms. I am not a pessimist as to the future, but I am very much afraid of a catastrophe if we go too fast.[48]

Here is direct reference to a British official view of the difficulty of setting any definite timetable for constitutional reform. History knows that India was given Independence in a sense 'ready or not', but Butler, an imperial bureaucrat, believed at that time, that there was a continuing need for considerable development including of political education and of safeguards to protect the interests of the masses and minorities.

Butler's period as a Governor concluded when he departed from Burma at the end of 1927, and was appointed Chairman of the Indian States Committee, in which capacity he was to examine the future of the relationship between the Indian princes and British India.[49]

Butler had exercised a clear role in building constitutional tradition in both the United Provinces and in Burma including dealing with the manifestations of political inexperience and naivety. The record indicates that, despite his personal scepticism of the constitutional system he was required to work and indeed his active opposition during its formative stages, he worked dyarchy constructively and to the best of his ability. The United Provinces and Burma had presented him with the special challenge of assisting to build political systems from their foundations. Despite the complications of the non-cooperation movement and communalism, Butler established a record of constructive contribution to the constitutional development of his two provinces, and contributed to the advancement of the progressive objectives of the Montford Reforms.

The *Rangoon Times* was generous enough to recognise this. 'Our present Governor has had the unique experience of seeing the Reforms launched in two provinces, and in both cases the new constitution has endured without the shaking attacks on it such as have been made elsewhere...largely due to Harcourt Butler's tact and amiability'.[50] It is not entirely clear, from the record, how Butler saw the evolution of these constitutional developments concluding, in relation to the British place in India and India's place in the empire, although he must have suspected what the outcome of the measures which had been put in train would be. Examination of other governors' records will establish whether Sir Harcourt Butler's attitude to the introduction of dyarchy was typical of the overall gubernatorial approach.

Turning to Hailey, Governor of the Punjab and the United Provinces respectively and regarded generally as the most competent Governor of his time, it is interesting to note that his biographer, Cell has only three references to Hailey and dyarchy in his book, one of them being in relation to Hailey and Africa.[51] Cell indicates that while Hailey could be a tough protagonist, in opposition to Indian nationalism, he did with prescience recognise the need for Britain to respond to nationalist aspirations. When required to be tough by British Government policy he was, but 'when their policy [towards nationalism] shifted in 1917, permitting more latitude, his did too'.[52] Cell quotes from Hailey's response to a circular request from the Viceroy Lord Hardinge,[53] written during the First World War, for input into the policy necessary to deal with rising nationalism. The revolt of Asia was already a fundamental force of the twentieth century, and Hailey wrote, 'it appears to be sound statesmanship to take every reasonable opportunity to meet this growing feeling of responsibility and independence'.[54] While Cell does see Hailey's attitude to nationalism as ambivalent, given his conservative ICS background, he acknowledges that by the early 1930s Hailey 'fully recognised [that] Indian politicians possessed a degree of influence over their countrymen no alien government could hope to match',[55] and the British needed to take this into account.

Drawing from the implications of a note written by Lord Hailey on Lionel Curtis[56] in 1958, Cell answers the question, 'Given that he [Hailey] had to carry out the policies of his superiors, what were his own principles?', by indicating, 'His sympathies lay with the [Indian] Liberals, men like the Allahabad lawyer Sir Tej Bahadur Sapru'.[57] This might not be surprising as the more extreme nationalists saw the Indian Liberals as collaborators. Cell has thus described Hailey as a person who, while conditioned as a 'Guardian'[58] by his early work in rural India, could bend flexibly with the trend of an age. Hailey believed that 'although by definition any transitional system must possess severe defects, at the provincial level dyarchy had actually worked well'.[59] The Indian historian Misra, in his not entirely sympathetic work on Hailey, acknowledges the Governor had tried hard to make dyarchy a success.[60]

In a letter written in October 1930 to Irwin,[61] Hailey described the technique, which the Swarajists had adopted, of putting forward 'untouchables' as candidates, thus ensuring the withdrawal of higher castes who were then to see the political contest as being beneath their dignity. In making reference to the democratic principle, Hailey commented:

> ...eventually it will be recognised that administration lies in the hands of the Councils and their Ministers, and, if they are so composed as to lose largely in popular estimation, then it will be difficult for them [Council and Ministers] to gain that general 'consciousness of consent' which is necessary if administration is to be successful.

Hailey had outlined personal concern for the development of democracy within the training ground of dyarchy, and revealed his underlying philosophy further, in the same letter, by indicating a preference for a majority Swarajist Ministry working dyarchy than for a government to not to work at all.

A practical example of Hailey's intention to employ one of the important British objectives for dyarchy, to train Indians in constitutional process, is contained in a letter he wrote to his Minister for Agriculture, the Honourable Sardar Jagundra Singh, in 1927.[62] Hailey offered constructive criticism of one of the minister's speeches to the Legislative Council, advising he should avoid 'exhortations'.

> I think you need to pay rather more attention to the concrete work before the Legislative Council, the answers to questions, the criticisms in debates etc. It will not do to rely on generalities with it. Your power for doing good work depends, in the long run, on the terms on which you stand to Council...You must not mind my saying this.[63]

Hailey, nevertheless, felt a degree of frustration at the difficulties inherent in implementing dyarchy and the responsibilities placed on governors for over-sighting and supervising the system. He advised Hirtzel,[64] at the India Office, that any advance in reforms 'will throw more on our shoulders' further increasing the contrast with the 'old days of the Lieutenant Governors... (whose work) was delightfully easy'.[65] Hailey found it difficult to work with

> Ministers whose least and most venal defect is lack of administrative knowledge, and with heads of departments whose work is constantly being thwarted...by a Legislative Council...one's officers are amateurs, the crew half-politicians and the passengers nearly all Bolshevists.[66]

Hailey's views and experience of operating dyarchy were common to most of the ICS governors, as was his intent to participate fully and constructively in the process of constitutional evolution set by the Reforms of 1919. The Governor's underlying philosophy was contained in his view that it was impossible to continue 'autocracy' and 'those of us who were of a more liberal frame of mind, honestly believed that a step such as the Reforms Scheme was a proper advance in the direction of self government'.[67] However, in common with most of the governors nothing on the record can be found which indicates Hailey had identified a real time frame or end point for British rule and the adoption of Indian self-government. In fact his article 'India—1983'[68] written in 1933, while referencing political reform, barely hints at the prospect of the British leaving India. The title speaks for itself.

Sir Geoffrey de Montmorency, who had long experience in India and had worked closely, and in sympathy, with Hailey, succeeding him in the Punjab, identified the significant increase in provincial autonomy as the outstanding achievement of the Montford Reforms. While acknowledging that at the time it was felt that dyarchy worked 'creakingly' in the provinces, 'a new kind of political life and freedom of initiative in Provincial affairs sprang into existence',[69] which led directly to the provincial autonomy of the 1935 *Government of India Act*. There is no tone of disappointment or bitterness in the references, in his booklet on India written in 1944, to constitutional reform stemming from the 1919 Act. In his publication, the Governor described his time in charge of the Punjab positively, reflecting an overall personal viewpoint that his experience of dyarchy was essentially constructive.

Sir William Marris, as an Indian civil servant, had had the opportunity for considerable input into the policy development and drafting of the reforms producing dyarchy. The reforming Montford joint report had in fact been written 'with distinction and earnestness largely by William Marris'.[70] As a civil servant, his skills as a scribe would have been called upon, but there is little doubt he would have had the opportunity to contribute to the policy discussions surrounding the formulation of the joint report which gave birth to dyarchy. Some indication of Marris' early view of the constitutional future of India, and his political philosophy was recorded by Lord Hailey in 1958, in a note on Lionel Curtis, describing Curtis' role in the development of a democratic approach to India. Cell drawing from the note indicates that 'in 1909, it seemed, during a trip to Canada, Sir William Marris [then a civil servant] had persuaded Curtis that, however distant, self-government was the only intelligible objective of British policy in India'.[71]

Appadorai writes that Marris, in the face of his difficulties with his ministers not supporting the policy of the reserved side of government, completely abandoned the experiment of dyarchy. He refused, categorically, a Reforms Enquiry Committee recommendation that he should implement joint deliberation of the reserved and transferred sides of government, at least on important matters.[72]

Sir William succinctly set out for Irwin, four of what he saw as the major complexities of dyarchy.

> ...(1) that each side of the Government is affected, indeed frequently disturbed by the operations of the other side; (2) that there is no human possibility of agreement either on the 'administrative record' or on 'policy'; (3) that conceptions of 'policy' are humanly bound to colour presentation of the 'administrative record' and (4) that any attempt at boiling down the whole material into a composite picture or into agreed on conclusions is doomed to failure.[73]

Clearly Marris, through practical experience, had not found dyarchy an easy pathway of constitutional development, but his intent and underlying attitude to making the Indian people fit for self-government is reflected in his words to Irwin at the start of his viceroyalty. 'Whenever I write on these matters I feel that I lay myself open to criticism of not accepting, or believing in the policy [contained in the Montford Reforms]. I do really believe in it but I think we went about it in the wrong way'.[74] Marris felt that politically, for reasons of religion and community, India was too immature to embrace the democratic principles contained in the dyarchic experiment. Marris believed in the spirit of the Montford Reforms but that the timing of their implementation was far too early.[75] In his reply to Marris, Irwin acknowledged the Governor's diagnosis of the state of the administration and its likely further decline but supposed 'that this was part of the price that we ought to have foreseen—and perhaps did foresee—that we should have to pay for the constitutional effort we thought it wise to make'.[76]

Sir Alexander Muddiman, who succeeded Marris as Governor of the United Provinces, was like his predecessor closely involved in assisting with the drafting of the 1919 *Government of India Act*. He had been sent to London to ensure that the views of Lord Chelmsford and the Indian Legislative Department were fully represented during the final drafting of the Bill.[77] Again, as with Marris one can assume that to fulfil this role Muddiman would have had not only a high degree of technical expertise related to the legislation, but also a philosophical commitment to the liberalising intent of Lords Montagu and Chelmsford. Given that Muddiman died prematurely in June 1928, there is little material on the record which can be used to establish his definitive intention for democratic reform in India.

Sir Charles Innes succeeded Harcourt Butler as Governor of Burma at the end of 1927. In an October 1928 memorandum prepared for the purposes of the Simon Commission, Innes set out his underlying approach to constitutional advance in India.[78] Innes advised Irwin of his frank view that, while the reformed constitution had worked with comparative smoothness in Burma, frailties in the democratic framework, including lack of political education in the electorate and the weakness of the working of responsible government, meant that Burma was not ready for constitutional advance. Nevertheless, Innes believed political pragmatism required that Burma be given the same degree of advance as would be given to other provinces. Innes wrote that despite any view that dyarchy may have failed, he felt entitled to assume that there would be, as an outcome of the Simon Commission review, no change in the goal of establishing responsible government in India. 'In our view it is neither possible nor desirable to go back on the announcement of August 1917 that it is the object of His Majesty's Government ultimately to establish completely responsible Government in India'.[79]

Innes set out his democratic philosophy for India by stating:

> ...in our view it would be wiser to get as far away as possible from dyarchy and from the implications in the preamble to the Government of India Act 1919 which are so much resented. The idea that the people of India are definitely on trial as to their future for self-government should be abandoned. For once an advance towards self-government has been made it is impossible to go back, and it is almost equally difficult to remain stationary. Successful constitutions grow; they are not constructed in stages.[80]

In using the term 'self government' and indicating its inevitability, Innes was in effect acknowledging, and in no sense denying or resisting, India's inexorable move towards independence, even though he was still unsure of its timing and of the future nature of the British connection. Governor Innes had transparently set out for Irwin and the Simon Commission a liberal attitude towards the constitutional future of India.

Sir Hugh Stephenson, the Governor of Bihar and Orissa, writing to Irwin on matters relating to preparations for the Simon Commission, suggested that British policy makers, in deciding on Indian fitness for constitutional advance, were tending not to look beyond the workings of the Legislative Councils.[81] Stephenson believed

> ...the real question is how far have the Reforms affected the every-day life of the country which is going on below the surface? Are the constituent bodies in the State, especially the middle classes, small landholders, traders and above all the peasants being trained in any degree for the future? Is all this surface turmoil leaving them entirely untouched, or has the long process of training them to be a *self-governing nation*[82] begun? Are they being led towards democracy? We can no longer be satisfied that the welfare of the masses simply consists in good administration on the lines that we think we know are best for them.[83]

Once again a British Governor uses the term, in what can be seen as a rhetorical question, 'self-governing nation' and coupling this with the word 'democracy', leaving little doubt of his view of the future of India.

Sir Montagu Butler, Governor of the Central Provinces since 1925, (and Sir Harcourt's brother) set out his views of dyarchy in a July 1927 letter to Irwin.[84] Butler advised that no worthwhile answer could be given about the success or failure of dyarchy, because the Province 'was rushed by the Government of India Act from the benevolent autocracy of a Chief Commissionership straight into the unfamiliar machinery of Council Government'.[85] He believed the British had moved too quickly and this inexperience in Council processes was followed by the instability caused by Swarajist disruption resulting in abeyance of the constitution, in the Central Provinces, from 1924 to 1927. For two years of this period, Governor Butler had administered both the transferred and reserved subjects. Despite the frustration surrounding the failure of dyarchy in the Central Provinces, reflected in his letter, Butler still reported with satisfaction that he was able to identify a further increasing association of Indians in the administrative work of the Province. That the Governor was actively involved in imparting parliamentary training is contained in a speech to his Legislative Council, where he advised that 2000 questions on notice in 1927 were counterproductive and could not be dealt with.[86] One of the objectives, of the Montford Reforms, designed to achieve democracy by increasing Indian competency in the art of government, was being imparted, at least.

Sir Laurie Hammond, the Governor of Assam, expressed similar frustration to Montagu Butler in his report to Irwin of the operation of dyarchy in his Province.

> Less than four per cent of the total population have a vote; of these probably seventy five per cent are illiterate and do not understand what it means or appreciate its value. Their 'representatives' in Council are afraid to risk their seats by agreeing to finance necessary schemes of development and still find the best or only electoral cry is to oppose the Government. The Province has, in fact, already been given a constitution about fifty years too soon...[87]

Hammond had identified the complication of an elite democracy which the British wished to avoid. It was not the educated who were, and would be, the problem, vis-à-vis democracy, but the uneducated. Hammond had contradicted the views of the Assam Provincial Committee Report to the Simon Commission and of his predecessor, Sir John Kerr,[88] that the reforms had worked entirely smoothly in Assam. However, he had not expressed any open resistance to the objective, of moving towards greater democracy, set by the Montford Reforms. He had indicated his dissatisfaction at the framework provided for doing so, thus aligning with the views of Marris.

What were the views and attitudes of the presidency governors, without the background of their ICS colleagues in the reform process, towards implementing the resultant innovative measures and developing democracy in India? Sir Leslie Wilson, an ex-politician and the Governor of Bombay, in a letter to Irwin of December 1926, described the complexities of appointing ministers following the 1926 elections.[89] Wilson, while regarding Swaraj[90] as a 'futile policy', in wrestling with the difficulties of constructing a ministry which would support a functioning government, pragmatically recognised the importance of dealing with the Swarajists. He believed in 'meeting those, more than half way, who were showing signs of a greater desire towards constitutional government'.[91] His approach to the 1926 election outcome, and the need to appoint ministers to ensure stable government, may be seen as an exercise of his skills as a politician in identifying the need for compromise and for keeping key Indians on side.

Wilson admitted that the construction of his ministry was an experiment

> ...but one I think I am justified in making, as it is to my mind, of the greatest importance to get as many as possible who show any inclination to get away from that ridiculous policy of obstruction in the Council, and opposition for the mere sake of opposition, and without acceptance of responsibility that opposition ought to mean.[92]

But Wilson further noted that his opponents could expect nothing from Swaraj and that he would not hesitate for a moment to use his full powers of certification (of overruling) to ensure proper government. The Governor's attitude towards opposition and obstruction did not seem to take into account the reality of the political environment in which he was functioning, as had his ICS colleagues in similar circumstances. But Wilson's political skills may indeed have been demonstrated by his never having had to use his powers of certification in the difficult political circumstances then existing in Bombay.[93] However, his references to the hopelessness of the goals of Swaraj and his willingness to use extreme measures against it, as necessary, can be seen as manifestations of an undemocratic inclination.

The Governor's conservative approach to the prospect of real constitutional advance in India is later reflected in exchanges, in the context of the Simon Commission, with Irwin on the form that the future Indian constitution might take. He advised Irwin that if the Simon Commission advocated any advance in self-government at all, they could do it in one of two ways. 'One, to give more freedom to the Provincial Governments, and hold on to control in the Central Government, or vice versa'.[94] Not surprisingly, Wilson expressed a preference for strengthening the powers of the provincial governors. He also expressed a wish to alter the franchise to strengthen rural voting power, particularly in the Viceroy's Assembly, against urban interests, openly admitting his advocation of 'a policy of *divide et impera*'.

Wilson further reinforces a view that he was not really interested in constitutional advance in India and that he was uncomfortable with its implications when he questioned the likely attitude of Indian ministers, in a unitary government as suggested by Irwin, towards European staff: 'Are they to be left to the tender mercies of an Indian minister in charge of the department in which they work?'.[95] And '...are great questions such as irrigation—large works like the Bhatgar Dam and the Sukkur Barrage—to be left to a decision of an elected Assembly?'. [96] In Wilson's proposal for constitutional reform 'a strong check on Indian Ministers was essential'.[97] Wilson did not seem to be aware that history was moving. Given Irwin's perceptions of the Indian constitutional future, as expressed in his 1929 Declaration, in which he reinforced the view that the Montagu Declaration of 1917 implicitly contemplated Dominion Status, Irwin clearly had more in common with the governors of the ICS cadre than with Wilson who must have perplexed him.

Evidently Sir Frederick Sykes, Wilson's successor, and again a politician, had more in common with his predecessor than with Irwin and the provincial governors. Sykes succinctly sets out his view of constitutional evolution in India in his biography, *From Many Angles*.[98] Here he records a statement he made to the Bombay Legislative Council in February 1930, in which he directly challenged the appropriateness of the Irwin Declaration by stating that 'a Constitution cannot be given to a sub-continent by a mere political phrase'. Sykes' address was an extraordinary challenge to the Viceroy and towards the policy of constitutional advance which Irwin was in the process of implementing. A real factor with which constitutional advance in India had to contend was the attitude of men like Sykes, Wilson, Lytton and Willingdon as governors and later as viceroys. However these men were prevented from governing in the autocratic way that they would have wished by the liberal pressures contained in the reform process itself, and the more progressive political opinion of the age. However, even Sykes had to acknowledge the inexorable advance towards self government put in train in 1919. '... whatever the ultimate constitution of this country may be, we must expect it to represent a great advance towards responsible self government'.[99]

Lord Goschen in an address to the East India Association,[100] whilst on leave in England at the beginning of 1929, referred specifically to the working of the reforms in his Presidency, Madras.[101] He advised his audience that dyarchy had largely worked in Madras for four fundamental reasons. First, because of the adoption of a 'First Minister' system involving his selection by the Governor, and that minister selecting his two colleagues. Second, since the reforms it had been customary to hold cabinets involving both the reserved and transferred sides. These two innovations generated loyalty and cohesion leading to joint cabinet responsibility. Third, the ministers genuinely attempted to work the reforms. Fourth, because 'the Legislative Council was divided into two parties and not into numerous factions'. Goschen gave credit to his predecessor, Willingdon, for successfully establishing dyarchy in Madras (see below) but there can be little doubt Goschen himself can also be complimented for the presidency's relative constitutional stability. The address also contained reference to Goschen's view of a constitutional future for British India. 'The immediate need is to develop responsible self-government in the Provinces, by handing over all branches of the local administration to the Provincial Legislative Councils under certain safeguards'.[102] While being more critical of dyarchy, Goschen was to repeat these views to the association exactly a year later, after his departure from India, as reported by *The Hindu*.[103]

Goschen, a politician and an aristocrat, was more sympathetic, than Sykes or Wilson, to Indian nationalism when he wrote to Lord Irwin in February 1929. Advising Irwin that he was depressed about the attitude of the Simon Commission which had then arrived in Madras he went on to say:

> ...what I object to is being regarded, as I shrewdly suspect some of us are, as a visionary, a guileless person under the influence of Indians, one who thinks that all will be well in the best of [Indian] worlds if we grant them sufficient advances in Government. Personally, I do not think so, but as I have said before what I think the diehards will not realise is our present position and the hopes, if not promises, that have been held out to India.[104]

In his letter Lord Goschen placed himself in the liberal camp by indicating British policy needed to take the reforms forward by advancing self-government and that the advance needed to be immediate. Irwin would have been comfortable with Goschen's attitude and approach to Indian democratic aspirations during the period he acted as Viceroy later in 1929.

Goschen describes the role of his predecessor, Willingdon, another politician, in instituting dyarchy in Madras, in a note to Lord Peel, Secretary of State, which he had copied to Irwin.[105] He advised that Willingdon had attempted to create parliamentary government on Western lines, and by using caste and religious divides, a party system. While Goschen felt that the excessive strength of communal feeling had inhibited his predecessor's objective, his policy had achieved 'a greater success than could have been obtained by any other system'.

Willingdon had spelt out directly his vision to Peel, during his first term as Secretary of State, for a future India when he advised that the 'one difficulty in all this is the retention of the British element which is absolutely essential, which every thinking Indian knows is essential, and which, if we gave the Indian full responsibility, he would think more essential than ever'.[106] Willingdon's future India required a British presence confusing any concept of full responsibility. While Willingdon experienced difficulties working dyarchy under the reforms, he was generally regarded as successful in Madras.[107] However, in a letter to his close friend Harcourt Butler, he expressed his contempt for dyarchy. 'I hated dyarchy always as you know and am glad to think that will go'.[108] Given his views of the impracticality of the severing of the British connection and his record as Viceroy of inaction and of marking time,[109] it is not surprising to read his words again to Butler in April 1930, prior to becoming Viceroy at the beginning of 1931, that despite the Government of India's commitment to Dominion Status for India, it is a status that 'India can't possibly have'.[110]

And Willingdon was obviously unhappy with Irwin's policy approach to constitutional advance in India.

> He (Irwin) first of all issues a, to my mind, totally unnecessary proclamation, assuring Indians of Dominion status which is impossible in India, and we are told his reason for this is to reassure Indians of our sincerity in working towards their looking after their own affairs.[111]

Willingdon, as Governor of Bombay, Madras and Viceroy, can only be classed as a reactionary, certainly in contrast to the ICS Governors of Irwin's time. Willingdon's use of the words 'our sincerity' contained in the quote above seems to hint that he may have been willing to have been less than sincere when it came to India's constitutional aspirations.

Lord Lytton in Bengal revealed his commonality with Willingdon in what seems a contradictory approach to constitutional advance in India. On the one hand, in discussions with Indian politicians and businessmen in Calcutta on his arrival in 1922, he was able to define Swaraj as 'the ultimate constitutional independence of India, that is to say, the people who live in India should govern themselves instead of being governed from London'.[112] However, Swaraj did not mean racial independence to Lytton. 'If Swaraj meant sharing with the British, then I was for it all the time, but if it meant getting rid of the British, then I was against it from the beginning and would fight it at every stage'.[113] It is not surprising given Lytton's attitude that his period as Governor was difficult and that his policies towards Indian nationalism diverged from the Government of India and the Secretary of State. For example, in 1924, in dealing with Swarajist obstruction within the Legislative Council, in relation to the rejection of a demand for the salaries of school inspectors, Lytton sought to sheet home the issue of constitutional responsibility to the Swarajists, by serving notice on the inspectors. Lord Reading was unhappy with this action as it was at variance with the consistent policy of conciliation that had been followed by the Government of India, at this time, in the face of Swarajist provocation.[114]

Lytton, in fact achieved very little during his term as Governor beyond developing a strong feeling of personal impotence in the face of the realities of Indian politics. His attitude was succinctly spelt out in his opening of the first session of the third reformed Bengal Legislative Assembly as reported in *The Statesman*, Calcutta, in January 1927. After five years experience he was able to say:

> Of the defects of the present Constitution I have been provided with plenty of evidence. Of the lines on which it can be improved opinion is for the less unanimous, and of the success of the experiment already made evidence is more difficult to produce.[115]

Lytton was the one Governor of Irwin's time who, because of his own personal limitations, demonstrated no real inclination for intellectual involvement in, or positive contribution to, the contemporary political debate. However, it is interesting to note, as Wood points out, that it was in fact Montagu, himself who persuaded a reluctant Lytton to accept his Bengal posting in the first place. 'Montagu had perceived how difficult it was to find men as governors who would faithfully carry out the intentions of the reforms enthusiastically. Lytton, however, perfectly reflected Montagu's belief that what was needed now was a touch of political imagination combined with racial goodwill'. [116] Lytton, as a Presidential Governor, had apparently started his term as Governor, initially as a liberal and ended as a reactionary, jaundiced by his experience.

The governors, principally those trained within the ICS and most often with a personal attachment to India and the Indian people, understood the democratic forces abroad and saw the fundamental contradiction between the continuance of British rule and the legitimate aspirations Indians held for their future. Despite the difficulties of administration and politics presented by the system of dyarchy the governors did persevere with its implementation. They used the Montford Reforms to impart political experience and training to Indian politicians in the practice of constitutional government. The governors also identified the importance of educating the public in the principles of democracy. They set out to achieve these outcomes and to a significant degree they were successful in this. In wrestling with the complexities of the dual governmental system imposed upon them, which some of them had resisted, they did not resile from the underlying intent of the Montagu Declaration, reiterated by Irwin.

Generally, the Civil Service governors were in advance, in terms of their progressive attitude to the constitutional future of the subcontinent, of other British participants in political India, including most of their presidency gubernatorial colleagues. British commercial interests, the largely reactionary army, whose careers and purpose were threatened and British 'diehards' continued to resist constitutional progress and its conclusion. While the various governors had their own, sometimes differing personal views about the efficacy of dyarchy, they had implemented government policy in good faith. They were aware of and supported the overall thrust of the Montford Reforms but some had reservations about the mechanism used to achieve the Reforms' ends. The liberal intent of the Reforms was acquitted mainly by the Civil Service governors with Irwin.

The next chapter focuses on the governors' contribution to key policy issues surrounding the appointment and implementation of the Simon Commission. It explores the governors' considerable involvement in this all-India matter, including their failure to anticipate Indian sensitivities to British policy.

Endnotes

1. James, *Raj*, p. 297.
2. *Ibid.*, p. 312.
3. See generally Rumbold, *Watershed in India*. Also Robb, *The Government of India and Reform*.
4. Preamble to *The Consolidated Government of India Act, 1915–1919*. See Appendix 2 for full Preamble.
5. Seton, *The India Office*, pp. 58, 60.
6. Philip Woods, 'The Montagu–Chelmsford Reforms (1919): A Re-assessment', pp. 25–42. See Woods, *Roots of Parliamentary Democracy in India*, for a full exposition of 'the making and early working of the Montagu–Chelmsford Reforms' and of the British intent behind them.
7. *Ibid.*, p. 26.
8. *Ibid.*

9. *Ibid.*, p. 28.
10. C.A. Bayly, *The Local Roots of Indian Politics*, p. 244.
11. *Ibid.*, p. 357.
12. *Ibid.*, p. 359.
13. *Ibid.*, p. 363.
14. *Ibid.*, p. 368.
15. *Ibid.*, p. 369.
16. *Report of the Reforms Enquiry Committee* (Muddiman Report), p. 37.
17. Reading Papers, Reading to various Governors, 21 April 1923. Willingdon (Madras), Lloyd (Bombay), Lytton (Bengal), Marris (United Provinces), Maclagan (Punjab), Wheeler (Bihar and Orissa), Sly (Central Provinces), Kerr (Assam).
18. All these committees, each five to seven in number, included one European, with the exception of Bihar and Orissa which did not have a European member. The Central Provinces did not form a committee as the result of the Swarajist agitation.
19. See *Report of the Indian Statutory Commission,* Volume III, presented in May 1930 for details of the Committees' Reports.
20. *Ibid.*, Volume, III, p. 35, provides a typical reference.
21. For example, in Madras Justice Party non-Brahmin legislators and in the Punjab the loyalist landlord-dominated Unionist Party were willing to do business with the government.
22. Bridge, *Holding India to the Empire.*
23. Rumbold, *Watershed in India*, pp. 54–126.
24. *Ibid.*, p. 155.
25. *Ibid.*, p. 108.
26. Harcourt Butler Papers, MSS EUR F116/75.
27. *Ibid.*
28. Sir M.F. O'Dwyer. ICS, 1882. Lieutenant-Governor of the Punjab, 1913–1919. Sir R.H. Craddock. ICS, 1882. Lieutenant-Governor of Burma, 1918–1922.
29. Sir B. Robertson. ICS, 1883. Chief Commissioner of the Central Provinces, 1912–1920. Sir N.D. Beatson-Bell. Chief Commissioner of Assam, 1918–1921.
30. Harcourt Butler Papers, MSS, EUR, F116/75.
31. Earl of Ronaldshay, (by succession Marquess of Zetland). Governor of Bengal, 1917–1922. Secretary of State for India, 1935. Sir E.A. Gait. ICS, 1882. Lieutenant-Governor of Bihar and Orissa, 1915–1920.
32. Harcourt Butler Papers, MSS.EUR, F116/75.
33. *Ibid.*, My italics.
34. Harcourt Butler Papers, Willingdon to Harcourt Butler, 22 February 1933.
35. M.F. O'Dwyer, *India as I Knew It*, p. 387.
36. M.F. O'Dwyer, 'Three Years of Reform in India', pp. 353–369. O'Dwyer, *India as I Knew It*, p. 244.
37. Harcourt Butler Papers, MSS EUR F116/91, Speech to the Legislative Council at Lucknow, 24 October 1921.

38. *Ibid.*
39. *Ibid.*
40. Harcourt Butler Papers, MSS EUR, F116/91.
41. *Ibid.*
42. H. Butler, *Collection of Speeches*, p. 146.
43. *Ibid.*, p. 147.
44. *Ibid.*, p. 148.
45. Butler, *India Insistent*, p. 77.
46. Butler, *Collection of Speeches*, p. 150.
47. Harcourt Butler Papers, MSS EUR F116/91.
48. *Ibid.*
49. I. Copland, *The Princes of India in the Endgame of Empire*, provides a definitive account of British policy towards the Princely States in the context of the devolution of British power in India. This includes an account of Harcourt Butler's contribution to this policy.
50. *Rangoon Times*, 6 March 1926.
51. Cell, *Hailey*. See Cell's index.
52. *Ibid.* p. 54.
53. C. Hardinge. Baron Hardinge of Penshurst. Viceroy from 1910 to 1916.
54. Cell, *Hailey*. Hailey response to Hardinge circular, 30 August 1915, quoted in Cell, p. 55.
55. *Ibid.*
56. L. Curtis, (1872–1955). Liberal thinker and author who was one of the first proponents of dyarchy. See O'Dwyer, *India as I Knew It*, p. 374.
57. Cell, *Hailey*, p. 57. Sir T.B. Sapru (1875–1949). Lawyer and leader of the Indian Liberal Party, who, like M.R. Jayakar, favoured discussions and dialogue with the British. Sapru and Jayakar were involved in mediation leading to the meeting of Irwin and Gandhi at the end of 1929.
58. Woodruff, *The Men Who Ruled India*, Volume II, p. 289 (Woodruff also includes Harcourt Butler in this category).
59. Cell, *Hailey*, p. 56.
60. A.K. Misra, *The Administration of the United Provinces of Agra and Oudh under Sir Malcolm Hailey*, p. 189.
61. *Ibid.*, Hailey to Irwin, 7 October 1930.
62. Hailey Papers, Hailey to S.J. Singh, 1927. Note, no day or month reference.
63. *Ibid.*
64. Sir F.A. Hirtzel. India Office. Permanent Under-Secretary for India. Retired July 1930.
65. *Ibid.*, Hailey to Hirtzel, 18 July 1929.
66. *Ibid.*
67. Lytton Papers, Hailey to Lytton (acting Viceroy), 22 June 1925.
68. Hailey, 'India—1983'.
69. de Montmorency, *India Today and Tomorrow*, p. 2.
70. Rumbold, *Watershed in India*, p. 108.

71. Cell, *Hailey*, p. 55.
72. Appadorai, *Dyarchy*, p. 138.
73. Halifax Papers, Marris to Irwin, 4 November 1927.
74. *Ibid.*, Marris to Irwin, 1 June 1926.
75. Marris, *India*, p. 26.
76. Halifax Papers, Irwin to Marris, 17 June 1926.
77. *Ibid.*, Irwin to Wedgwood Benn, 11 September 1930.
78. *Ibid.*, Innes to Irwin, 6 October 1928.
79. *Ibid.*
80. *Ibid.*, Innes to Irwin, 6 October 1928.
81. *Ibid.*, Stephenson to Irwin, 16 August 1927.
82. My italics.
83. *Ibid.*
84. *Ibid.*, Montagu Butler to Irwin, 13 July 1927.
85. *Ibid.*
86. Montagu Butler Papers, *Speeches of His Excellency Sir M. Butler*, Volume I, p. 46.
87. Halifax Papers, Hammond to Irwin, 24 July 1928.
88. *Ibid.*, Hammond to Irwin, 28 July 1927.
89. *Ibid.*, Wilson to Irwin, 28 December 1926.
90. Defined here as the complete constitutional independence of India. Self-government. See F. Moraes, *Jawaharlal Nehru*, p. 67.
91. Halifax Papers, Wilson to Irwin, 28 December 1926.
92. *Ibid.*
93. *Ibid.*, Wilson to Irwin, 14 March 1928.
94. *Ibid.*, Wilson to Irwin, 31 May 1928.
95. *Ibid.*
96. *Ibid.*
97. *Ibid.*
98. Sykes, *From Many Angles*, p. 381.
99. Sykes Papers, Speech at a luncheon of the Bombay Branch of the European Association, Bombay, 10 March 1930.
100. The East India Association was founded by Dadabhai Naoroji (British MP and Indian nationalist) in 1866, in collaboration with Indians and retired British officials in London. It was a platform for discussing matters and ideas about India.
101. Goschen Papers, Address to the East India Association, Caxton Hall, Westminster, London, 20 January 1929, titled, 'The working of the reforms in Madras'.
102. *Ibid.*
103. *Hindu*, 20 January 1930.
104. Halifax Papers, Goschen to Irwin, 26 February 1929.
105. *Ibid.*, Goschen to Irwin, 4 January 1929.
106. Willingdon Papers, Willingdon to Peel, 25 September 1922.

107. Tinker, *Viceroy*, p. 126.
108. Harcourt Butler Papers, Willingdon to Butler, 5 May 1929.
109. Tinker, *Viceroy*, p. 140. Also see Macnamara, unpublished Masters' thesis, 'Lords Willingdon and Lytton', generally for Willingdon's record as Governor of Madras and constitutional advance.
110. Harcourt Butler Papers, Willingdon to Butler, 5 April 1930.
111. *Ibid.*, Willingdon to Butler, 18 July 1930.
112. Lytton, *Pundits and Elephants*, p. 22.
113. *Ibid.*
114. Reading Papers, Reading to Lytton, 10 April 1924. Also see Macnamara's unpublished thesis for Lytton's record generally as Governor in Bengal and constitutional advance.
115. Report of the Native Newspapers of Bengal, the *Statesman*, 13 January 1927.
116. Woods, *Roots of Parliamentary Democracy*, p. 259.

3

The Governors' Contribution to the Simon Commission

In 1926, after Lord Irwin's arrival in India, the issue of the Statutory Commission required by the 1919 *Government of India Act* was coming under initial consideration. Section 84A of the Act required that at the expiration of ten years after the passing of the Act, the Secretary of State would appoint a Commission with the objective of inquiring

> ...into the working of the system of government, the growth of education, and the development of representative institutions, in British India, and matters connected therewith, and the Commission shall report as to whether and to what extent it is desirable to establish the principle of responsible government, or to extend, modify, or restrict the degree of responsible government then existing.[1]

The appointment of the Statutory Commission was of considerable political importance to the British both in India and in Britain. From the Indian nationalist viewpoint there was particular sensitivity surrounding the ostensible purpose of the Commission. This was essentially to determine whether or not, in British eyes, India had sufficient political maturity to take the next step towards responsible government, however defined. The British would make a judgement as to the appropriateness of the next step in India's constitutional evolution. The British did not see the need, necessarily, to make concessions to the nationalists to embark on this process, particularly as the movement was in abeyance, and preferred to engage the Indian political moderates. For the British, a successful commission process and outcome would have demonstrated to all interested parties the sincerity of their intent for India, even if this was not agreed by the nationalists. Therefore, for Irwin and the governors it was an issue of considerable importance that the preparations and arrangements, both political and administrative, for the

Statutory Commission be managed efficiently and successfully. In England there was sensitivity, within the ruling Conservative Party, to ensure that the choice of the Commission membership did not fall to the Labour Party as a General Election was due coincidental on the tenth anniversary of the 1919 Act.[2]

Thus, in 1926 such matters as the nature and composition of the Commission, the scheduling of its travel to India,[3] the timing of its announcement and the Commission's objectives were prime issues for consideration by Lord Irwin and the governors. The extent and nature of the policy advice given by the governors on these matters will be examined in this chapter. It should also reveal Britain's true intentions towards Indian independence and whether Section 84(A) of the *Government of India Act* was deliberately drafted to permit the playing of a double game.

As early as August 1926 Irwin was receiving advice from Hailey in relation to the Statutory Commission regarding whether it be a Royal or a Parliamentary Commission.[4] The important distinction here related to the racial composition of the Commission. A Royal Commission could include Indians while a Parliamentary Commission confined to members of the British Parliament was unlikely to do so.[5] Hailey was aware that Lord Birkenhead had said in a speech, on 8 July 1926, that 'if he were the Secretary of State in 1929, it would be his duty to seek out for the *Royal* Commission the ablest body [of men] whom we could collect from the British Empire'.[6] Even so, the Governor was to advise Irwin that 'many of us feel that the most satisfactory Commission would be one composed entirely of Members of the two Houses'.[7] Hailey argued, in support of his view, that this arrangement would ensure an impartial view of India through British Parliamentary eyes. If the Commission was to include Indian politicians and be representative of all communities then Hailey believed no clear impartial view would be possible, concluding that 'Indians themselves, divided as they are at present on communal lines, would prefer a Commission composed as I suggest'.[8]

Hailey's suggestion had some impact as Irwin had sufficiently influenced the Secretary of State to change his mind on the nature of the Commission for Birkenhead to advise the Viceroy in September 1926.

> ...as to the personnel of the Statutory Commission you have persuaded me of the wisdom of your view. I too now think that the advantages of having Indians on the Commission are outweighed by the disadvantages.[9]

In the same September letter, Birkenhead was to inform Irwin that he had had discussions with the Prime Minister on the issue of the Commission, in which he (the PM) had indicated that 'his disposition was to leave the whole matter to you and me but there mustn't be the slightest risk of delay in selection of the Commission so much that an election might complicate the matter'.

In early 1927, the matter of the composition of the impending Commission was again at the forefront of Lord Irwin's mind when he sought advice from his confidants, Governors Hailey, Marris and also Muddiman, as yet a senior Indian civil servant, on the views of Birkenhead.[10] Irwin advised them that they would have an opportunity to discuss Birkenhead's views at Simla and the Secretary of State had set out a range of alternatives for consideration.

> ...(a) that the Commission should be parliamentary, but should not contain ex-Viceroys; (b) as above, but not excluding Governors; (c) that it should be mixed, i.e., Members of both Houses and others, excluding natives; (d) as in (c) but not excluding natives.[11]

It is highly relevant that Birkenhead in this same memorandum indicated he was still sensitive to the implications of not including Indians in the Commission's membership.

> I am well aware of the arguments in favour of the exclusion of natives, and my mind is absolutely open upon this, and indeed upon every other point: but you must remember that the arguments against the exclusion are *a priori* very strong.[12]

Birkenhead made it very clear there was real risk that without 'the least appearance' of an Indian, the Commission would be seen as having no authority. Given the existence of Indians of considerable distinction, their exclusion would 'make evident to all the world the "inferiority complex" with which we choose to brand the peoples of India'. But in a most revealing question Birkenhead may have signaled an underlying and duplicitous motive for his concern at the possibility of excluding Indians from the Commission.

> Are you quite certain that the presence on the Commission, both of Hindu and Moslem representatives, that the controversy which would follow, that the probability of divergent Hindu and Moslem reports, might not be of great assistance to you and us if the Commission took the view that a very considerable advance was not to be recommended at the moment when they report?[13]

What were the governors' views? In a comprehensive reply[14] to Irwin, Hailey reiterated his advocacy of a purely Parliamentary Commission on the basis of two essential factors. The first was that the Parliament needed to receive an accurate account of the working of the reforms. Hailey believed that a 'mixed' Commission would greatly complicate the information it would be bound to receive and that Parliament was most likely to only trust the views of members of its own body. Second, Parliament would need the views of open minded men unsullied by the politics of communal difference. Hailey was sure there were no Indians of such calibre to be obtained, even amongst people who were not politicians. They all owed an allegiance to their various factions and matters were further complicated by the existence of a wide range of sectional interests, the components of which would all claim a right to membership. Hailey acknowledged Birkenhead's position that a purely Parliamentary Commission would signal India's inferiority, but he believed a Commission which did not have an Indian majority would have the same effect. Again, Hailey took the opportunity to reinforce his view that the political consequences in India of the appointment of a Parliamentary Commission would not be great, and that the various factions would secretly welcome their opposition not being represented. Hailey was to reject Birkenhead's view that a 'mixed' Commission, which was likely to be a manifest failure due to internecine squabbling, would provide the British with an opportunity to postpone political advance, on the grounds that this argument was dialectical and not substantive.[15] However, Hailey was to acknowledge that if it was decided not to appoint a purely Parliamentary Commission then the non-inclusion of Indians would be indefensible.

Sir William Marris provided Irwin with the main arguments for a Parliamentary Commission as

> ...(1) that this arrangement emphasises Parliament's intention to keep the decision in its own hands, (2) that a Commission so composed may be expected to produce a report which Parliament will be disposed to adopt, and (3) that it avoids, in a way that gives no ground for reasonable objection, the admitted difficulties of a mixed Commission of Europeans and Indians.[16]

Making reference to personal discussions with the Viceroy in Allahabad, Marris advised that he nevertheless felt no certainty 'that we are on the right lines yet'. He felt there remained the need to find a formula for the establishment of the Commission which would be self-evidently the best outcome for all concerned and to make 'some bold departure which is not within the sight of any of us at present'. Accordingly, Marris affirmed that he was not 'enthusiastic about a Parliamentary Commission, unless it was a very small one and composed of men picked for their peculiar personal fitness and only incidentally as legislators'.[17] If in the event the forthcoming British General Election was to complicate the selection of a purely Parliamentary

Commission, as Irwin had suggested was possible in his letter of 18 April, then Marris advised he would not be unduly perturbed but on balance and at this juncture he hoped 'India may have the verdict of the Five Just Men'.[18] But Marris also agreed with Hailey that it would be difficult to find suitable Indians to effectively participate in any future 'mixed' Commission.

Irwin copied the Hailey and Marris correspondence to Birkenhead and drawing from the governors' views informed him that 'I am accordingly in favour of a Parliamentary Commission...*provided you can get a good enough team'*.[19] If this was not possible then Irwin felt the best alternative would be a Commission composed of four or five Englishmen, one Hindu, one Muhammadan, (of reasonable kind), one non-official European and one British Indian civil servant. He advised Birkenhead that both Hailey and Muddiman agreed with this view while he, Irwin, felt that Marris in suggesting five wise Englishmen 'underrated the political difficulties attaching to this plan'.

Hailey and Marris had put forward their views to Irwin on the issue of the composition of the future Commission in lengthy, strong and well argued letters. It is likely Muddiman would have provided his advice direct to Irwin through the Civil Service framework, perhaps verbally.[20] In advising Birkenhead, Irwin had followed Hailey's line, including on the likely lack of reaction amongst Indians against a purely British Parliamentary Commission. Irwin later confirmed his view in advice to Harcourt Butler, in June 1927, that 'a general boycott [of a purely Parliamentary Commission] is highly improbable'.[21] Both Irwin and Birkenhead were to turn out to be mistaken in ignoring Marris' reference to the whole question of the composition of the Commission needing further consideration. Marris had wished a more intensive analysis of the options on the basis of sensitivity to a most important consideration, namely the need to take into account likely Indian reaction to their non-inclusion in a body set up to determine their political future. The consequences of the snub were to occupy more of Irwin's time and energy over the next years than any further consideration of other options for the Commission's composition might have done. Even had he wished to do so, Irwin would have been constrained also by British Conservative politics and the archly conservative Birkenhead in considering, as a valid option, negotiation with the various nationalist factions on the make-up of the Commission.

Sir Hugh Stephenson,[22] Lord Goschen [23] and Sir Harcourt Butler,[24] agreeing with Hailey and Muddiman, were also to opt, in their advice to Irwin, for a purely British Parliamentary Commission, whilst Sir Leslie Wilson, after discussions with the Viceroy, wrote to him expressing a more prescient viewpoint.[25] Wilson advised Irwin that since returning from their discussions to his presidency he had been holding talks, on the personnel of the Commission, with key members of the Indian and European communities, and both groups had advised strongly against a purely Parliamentary Commission. Consequently, Wilson suggested a non-Parliamentary British and Indian Commission, consisting of some four or five prominent Englishmen, with representatives of the Hindus, the Muhammadans, the non-official Europeans, and the ICS. Wilson's position accorded with Irwin's second preference expressed to Birkenhead. This advice, however was qualified in forcefulness by the sentence in his letter, 'If I had not found opinion so strong about the exclusion of Indians, I should have still been in favour of a purely Parliamentary Commission'.

The high degree of policy influence exercised by these key administrators, particularly Hailey, Marris and Muddiman, on the Viceroy and thus indirectly with the Secretary of State and the British Government, on the vital question of the composition of the Parliamentary Commission, has been highlighted by the above references. The fact that the Commission was not to include Indian representation, was to reignite the energy and passion of the non-cooperation movement, to incite boycott and to isolate the British from proper dialogue with the nationalists, who in reality controlled India's future. If Irwin hoped an all-European Commission would be supported by the Muslims and Hindus, as it balanced the interests of both, he was mistaken.[26] The decision not to include Indians on the Commission was to be described by the Indian historian Gopal as Irwin's 'first and greatest mistake'.[27] By inference one might ascribe the same degree of error to the governors given their advice to Irwin and through him to Birkenhead. Indeed Gopal's view that the decision on the composition of the Statutory Commission was a major mistake is only entirely accurate if the allegation was intended to include the Viceroy's principal advisors, his governors. Collectively they had got it wrong. Given the intimate knowledge which all the governors must have had of Indian politics in their provinces and at an all-India level, drawn from the extensive avenues of intelligence available to them, it now appears extraordinary that they failed collectively to predict and identify to Irwin the scale of domestic opposition to not including Indians on the Commission. The governors, including the perceptive Hailey, had not discounted an adverse reaction, boycott and opposition on the basis that in any case the degree of it would not matter and the British were strong enough to resist extreme non-cooperation anyway. They had done this on a basis that boycott was unlikely and even if it occurred it would quickly die away. One can excuse Irwin for agreeing with his governors on such a fundamental matter, only on the basis of acknowledging the degree of influence they held over him, particularly at the beginning of his viceroyalty. One can excuse Birkenhead on the basis of it being understandable that he would tend to accept the advice of the experts in the field. One cannot interpret the governors' advice in terms of incompetence, for they were indeed experts on the complexities of political India, but perhaps on the basis of a degree of complacency and insensitivity to Indian aspirations.

The governors' majority position suggests they did not see the British as equal partners with political India in addressing constitutional problems, but as superiors in political tutelage and decision making. 'No single step could have been better calculated to drive deep the rift between Government and the ruled'.[28] Almost immediate evidence of this was contained in Congress calling, in December 1927 for a complete boycott of the Commission, and agreement to Jawaharlal Nehru's resolution demanding complete independence. The Indian Liberals and a splinter group of the Moslem League under Jinnah[29] joined in the call for boycott. The issue served to revive the flagging fortunes of the nationalist movement, and to catalyse trade unionism in the cities as well as youth leagues and student organisations. The British, far from being duplicitous, had bungled. Interestingly, Hailey's predominant role in this adverse decision was known to the Indian press as revealed in *New India* reporting, on 11 December 1928 that Birkenhead had decided on an all-British Commission on Hailey's advice. No mention was made of the Viceroy's role.

That the British at least understood the need to involve Indians at some level of the process of the Commission, is indicated by their consideration of options regarding establishing liaison between the Commission and Indian public men. Hailey was to forward de Montmorency's [30] ideas, vetted by him, on the matter in two notes to Irwin.[31] De Montmorency had suggested what he believed were the three available options for the selection of Indian co-adjudicators, whose function would be to sift evidence and judge the practical nature of suggestions put forward in evidence to the Commission. These were: (1) by nomination by government; (2) by nomination by parties or interests; (3) by selection by the legislatures. He discounted option (1) by saying the government would always be accused of having chosen the wrong men, and option (2) because he did not believe parties in India were sufficiently definite and representative, which left option (3). De Montmorency recommended that each of the legislatures 'elect a small body who, in the case of the Central Legislature, would assist throughout the enquiry where needed, and in the case of the Provinces, would assist the enquiry relating to each Province separately'. He saw eleven men (the number judged as related to effective representation of all-India) from the Centre advising on and criticising evidence and suggestions and providing advice on the relationship between the Centre and the provinces. Seven men (the number equating to the number of Parliamentary [Simon] Commissioners) from each of the provinces 'would be present during the enquiry and help the Commission in taking evidence and to criticise it'. De Montmorency identified that an advantage of this approach would be that any shortcomings in advice received by the Commission would be the responsibility of the legislatures and not that of the various Indian governments.

After considerable political upheaval within the Indian legislatures and threats of non-cooperation, following the announcement of the Commission in November 1927, eight of the nine provincial legislatures agreed, in a positive development for the British, to identify the level of political 'maturity' attained in their territories, and to cooperate with the Commission. Joint select committees appointed by the legislatures of the cooperating provinces were to prepare their own separate reports to the Commission, identifying recommendations for constitutional advance in India. The reports of these committees, were compiled in Volume III of the *Report of the Simon Commission*, published in May 1930. The Central Legislative Assembly and the Central Provinces chose not to participate in this process. Montagu Butler, given his province would not cooperate, suggested to Irwin the Commission should not visit the Central Provinces at all.[32] Irwin responded to this astounding policy advice by advising Butler that his approach would be a victory for non-cooperation. 'I should also have thought that minority opinion in the Province would strongly resent being deprived of an opportunity of expressing itself directly and on the spot'.[33] Butler was then to advise Simon that the 'main points' for his province were the raising of its status in order to be given a High Court and its financial position.[34] Non-cooperation by the Assembly was overcome to some degree by the Viceroy appointing an Indian Central Committee, consisting of four members of the Council of State and five members of the Legislative Assembly.[35]

In June 1927, Irwin referred a letter from Lord Birkenhead to Hailey for comment, in which the Secretary of State had, in discussing means of involving Indian opinion in the Commission process, criticised the option of a Select Committee of the Central Legislature, and suggested a Convention or Round Table as options. Another example of Hailey's standing and influence is provided by the fact of Irwin forwarding Hailey's advice to him direct to Birkenhead. The Secretary of State was to accept Hailey's advice against a Convention or Round Table and that a 'means should be found for focusing Indian opinion (other than newspaper opinion) on the proposals of the Commission, and this method [a Select Committee] would certainly have this result'.[36] In fact Hailey and de Montmorency had worked closely together on this policy advice to the Viceroy and Secretary of State.[37]

In November 1926 Irwin was to advise the governors,[38] in considering the matter of the announcement of the Commission, that it was probable the Secretary of State would decide to bring forward the Commission to 1928. If this was to happen Irwin identified some political advantage if the appointment in 1928 was announced in early 1927. Irwin saw the opening of the new Assembly in January 1927 as a good opportunity for any announcement in India, as it would provide the legislature with a feeling of 'confidence'. Irwin sought the governors' opinion on the tactical political advantage of his identified option.

Sir Leslie Wilson, Governor of Bombay, agreed completely with Irwin's suggestion.[39] Sir Samuel O'Donnell, the Acting Governor of the United Provinces, was also to agree on the basis of Irwin's reasoning,[40] as was Sir John Kerr, the Governor of Assam,[41] Sir Henry Wheeler from Bihar and Orissa,[42] Sir Montagu Butler from the Central Provinces[43] and Lord Goschen of Madras.[44] Each of these governors felt that as a matter of policy and tactics an early announcement of the intention to advance the appointment of the Commission to 1928 would be useful, because it would show good intent and effectively shorten the probationary period assigned to Indian constitutional development. Only Wheeler sounded a warning, indicating he hoped that no announcement of personnel for the Commission would be made. 'That would be fatal, as whatever it is, it would at once be bitterly attacked, and a movement set on foot to change it, add to it, or even boycott the Commission',[45] and give the nationalists a full year to prepare their opposition. Wheeler was prescient in identifying the risk of boycott unlike some of his peers. Sir Harcourt Butler from Burma and Lord Lytton from Bengal were the dissenters. Butler advised Irwin that he was against accelerating the announcement of the date of the Commission, as effectively there was little or no Indian demand for this and it would be foolish to provide a period for the nationalists to 'queer the pitch'.[46] Lord Lytton also advised against Irwin's suggestion as he believed any early announcement would be seen in Bengal by the obstructionists in his Council as a concession to their activity.[47] Both Butler and Lytton referred, in their letters, to forthcoming opportunities for personal discussion on these matters with the Viceroy. Irwin was able to advise Harcourt Butler, during their personal meeting in Calcutta in January 1927, that Birkenhead had decided against the Viceroy's suggestion of an early announcement, feeling that the acceleration of the Commission was 'our one card left, and that it was a pity to play it until we were certain it would take a trick'.[48]

These early exchanges on Simon Commission matters reflect the general pattern and process of policy making at this level, between the governors, Viceroy and Secretary of State, on the Simon Commission and across important Indian policy headings. They reveal the degree and nature of the governors' input and influence on the Viceroy and Secretary of State. These communications also indicate that the governors experienced a working environment where the Viceroy preferred to consult, actively sought input, provided opportunity for contributions from the governors on all-India matters, and was not autocratic in his approach. It was, of course wise for him to obtain provincial perspectives, but Irwin's style gave his governors the option of thinking beyond the boundaries of their territories too.

Hailey undoubtedly, of all the governors, had special influence with Irwin, stemming, principally, from his experience and abilities and facilitated by his special access, when in Simla, as Governor of the Punjab. This influence was again reflected in Irwin's reporting from the summer capital to Birkenhead in August 1927 'I had a long discussion with Crerar, Hailey and Blackett [49] last night with regard to the Statutory Commission'.[50] Irwin's note openly indicates the degree to which he relied on Hailey.[51] Irwin told Birkenhead that

> Hailey particularly was emphatic on two points: (1) the necessity of finding effective ways and means of having Provincial problems adequately considered by the Commission; and (2) the extreme danger of adhering to the distribution of time in the Commission's work between England and India that you at present contemplate. I agree with him on both points.

Drawing on the benefit of his talks with Hailey and his senior officials Irwin went on to warn the Secretary of State of the dangers of leaving a long gap between the announcement of the Commission and its visit to India. Irwin advised Birkenhead:

> I therefore feel very strongly that if it can in any way be managed, you ought to try and secure that the Commission should come out here for six weeks or two months next spring, to have a general look round and to, as it were, get going before Indian eyes.[52]

That the Viceroy's recommendation, influenced by his key adviser, was accepted is evidenced by the arrival of the Commission for its first visit from the beginning of February to the end of March 1928, and for its second from mid-October 1928 until mid-April 1929.

In the lead up to the announcement of the Commission in the British Parliament on 8 November 1927, Irwin wrote to his governors advising them of this date, the Commission's composition,[53] the timing of its visits to India, and to request them to prepare the way by meeting with principal political leaders in their provinces. Irwin specifically requested the governors to 'be careful to avoid giving the impression that we feel our case is a weak one',[54] and suggested they might 'do something with the Press'. The reference to the British 'case' being a weak one would seem to underline the possibility in Irwin's mind that it was indeed weak, that the British had made a mistake in the composition of the Commission and thus would need to defend it. Some governors were fully alive to the risk of appearing to acknowledge a weak British 'case' by defending it, and to the difficulty of defending it with political leaders and the press in any case. Marris' immediately telegrammed reply expressed deep concern at Irwin's approach to the issue.

> I am...convinced that action on the lines suggested in these Provinces [United Provinces] at least would do no good. We infer that expected announcement will not be acceptable to Indian views and that the object of discussion is to dissipate suspicion and disarm hostility.[55]

Marris advised Irwin that representations by him to the press and others would be of little avail in reducing the degree of any Indian irritation and suggested it would be better to wait upon events. Governor Wilson wrote in a similar vein,[56] as did Stephenson.[57] Marris, following up with a letter, emphasised his concern that any representations would merely provoke a view 'that Government have only taken this unusual step of persuasion and appeasement in advance, because they have a bad conscience in the matter or because they are nervous about the consequences'.[58] Marris believed that, in his Province, while there could be a reaction to the announcement of the Commission, it would not be very serious and Irwin's tactic would simply provoke a greater outcry. 'If there are attempts to boycott the Commission, I believe that they will fail under the pressure of events'. Other governors, Goschen of Madras,[59] the Governor of Burma,[60] the Governor of Assam [61] and Jackson of Bengal [62] all agreed to follow Irwin's request and Irwin was to excuse the dissenting governors from the actions he had suggested.[63] Hailey, in a late note indicated he had followed the Irwin strategy, and continued to advise his view that boycott could be discounted and even if that was wrong, the boycotters could achieve little anyhow.[64]

Irwin persevered with his plan of preparation for the announcement of the Commission, meeting with Gandhi and other important leaders to advise them of the British intention. Mohamed Ali Jinnah, who immediately recognised the flaw in the British plan, wrote to Irwin urging the inclusion of at least two Indians on the Commission, noting his regard for the Viceroy and indicating he did not wish 'any big move to be marred by a mistake during

Your Excellency's regime, and with which your name may be associated'.[65] By the time Jinnah was to provide Irwin with the correct advice it was too late for Irwin to rescind, and the result was disastrous.

The level of Indian opposition to the composition of the Simon Commission did indeed take the British by surprise and this is encapsulated in a short comment by Irwin to Lord Goschen, at the end of November 1927, agreeing with the Governor's view that 'the storm has been rather more violent than we expected'.[66] This represents a rather understated acknowledgement by Irwin and the Governor that they had collectively made a serious mistake. But Irwin may have learnt from his 'mistake', in dealing with the sensitivities of political India over the membership of the Commission. This was perhaps shown by the more sensitive and conciliatory approach he adopted towards Indian nationalism in later years, evidenced by his Dominion Status Declaration, the Round Table Conference in London, and his later Settlement with Gandhi.

The pattern of the Viceroy requesting policy input from the governors, reflected in the Simon Commission process and their various responses drawn from experience and the requirements of their own provincial circumstances, highlighted another difficulty of Indian administration. Namely, the complexity which faced the Viceroy in assimilating the governors' views and identifying a formula which would satisfy them individually, as far as possible, but would meet all-India requirements. Irwin's approach of seeking the views of the governors on all-India policy matters had the advantages of involving them in the decision making process, of obtaining their perspectives and the best range of views possible. However, a disadvantage was inevitably not always being able to satisfy the viewpoint of each province. The importance of Governor Hailey, and his summer location in Simla as Governor of the Punjab, established a distinct pattern of Hailey being consulted first, on Simon Commission matters, even though the detail of his advice may not have been always accepted.

The importance of Hailey and a select group of governors to Irwin is further shown by him confining his next request for policy advice,[67] on the important all-India question of reforms in the central government in the context of the Simon Commission, to only four governors: Hailey, de Montmorency, Innes and Montagu Butler, indicating the regard held by the Viceroy, certainly for the first three and their influence. It is notable that Irwin signed his covering letter 'Yours sincerely' to Montagu Butler and 'Yours ever' to the other three governors, perhaps denoting a differentiation of professional and personal familiarity between the Viceroy and those men. Irwin advised his interlocutors that the note he had prepared for their comment, was an attempt to examine some of the questions affecting the future constitution of the Government of India in relation to His Majesty's Government in Great Britain, and to the Central Indian Legislature. In a detailed twelve page analysis, Irwin identified the principal problem at the Centre to be the fact that

> ...we have created a predominantly popular legislature, subject to all the temptations of democratic bodies, and set it to work with an executive not drawn from the ranks of its elected members, which it has very partial power to control, and no power to remove. The legislature drifts naturally to irresponsible courses; while the executive, equally inevitably, is tempted to disregard a legislature, which it can always in the last resort override.[68]

Irwin advised the result was that the central machinery worked very clumsily and the 'constant abuse and defeat of Government in the legislature does no good to the general status of Government throughout India'. Irwin held a view that there was a need for a strong central government, and to establish a system which ensured greater harmony of function between the executive and legislature. He believed the way to establish harmony of function was to make the executive responsible to the legislature, and observed that achieving this responsibility without considerable restrictions and limitations 'is evidently impossible in India at the present time'.[69] Irwin identified the overriding factors creating the need for the restrictions and limitations as: (1) the Indian States; (2) the Defence of India and (3) Indian Foreign policy. In the Viceroy's estimation India was not yet mature enough to assume charge of these responsibilities.

Irwin's conclusion was:

> ...therefore if it is desired to introduce into the central Government a degree of ministerial responsibility to the legislature, it follows from the necessary restrictions outlined above that this can only be done through some division of subjects and control, such as dyarchy.[70]

He identified, as a possibility, a new form of dyarchy in which certain subjects would be transferred to ministers drawn from and depending upon the Assembly, while other subjects (foreign and political affairs and defence) would be administered by persons, appointed by the Crown, directly responsible to the Secretary of State for India. The legislature would have no control over the 'reserved' subjects, and would not be entitled to discuss them, but would vote their funding under a 'fundamental' law. Irwin went on to acknowledge and analyse the fact that even with those subjects which might be appropriate to transfer, such as finance, commerce, education and industries, the complicating factor was their relationship with the Secretary of State, the British Parliament and the provincial governments.

Irwin set out the extensive drawbacks to the introduction of any form of dyarchy at the Centre and indicated, 'The real question is whether it is desirable to break up the unity of the Central Government at all'.[71] He identified that the unitary nature of the government might be preserved

> ...while bringing the executive and legislature somewhat closer together than is the case at present, [if] a proportion of the Governor-General's Council should be appointed by the Crown from the ranks of the legislature.[72]

The Viceroy concluded his note by indicating the core issue was how to guarantee any government a majority in the legislature. Innes, de Montmorency and Montagu Butler,[73] responded to Irwin in lengthy, comprehensive and well argued submissions. Hailey does not appear to have provided a written reply, but would have taken the opportunity of his meeting with Irwin, later in 1928, to present his views. Hailey's influence with Irwin had continued after his transfer to the United Provinces in August 1928, and he had not been entirely supplanted by the new Punjab Governor, de Montmorency, as Irwin's policy intimate. This is reflected in Irwin's first letter to him as Governor of the United Provinces when, together with his congratulations, Irwin invited Hailey to New Delhi in November or Calcutta in December 1928, to discuss the problem of reform of the central government.[74] Consequently, given the opportunity of personal contact, Hailey's influence on this matter would have been substantial.

The three governors, in their written replies, pointed out the difficulties of operating dyarchy at the Centre. They acknowledged the tensions inherent in the need to reserve to British hands the core functions of foreign affairs, defence and the complications of the Indian States, while at the same time trying to introduce the principle of ministerial responsibility into an immature Indian political environment, further complicated by active nationalist opposition.

Innes identified the British dilemma succinctly.

> On the one hand, it [the British Government] cannot give immediate self-government without betraying its trust. On the other hand, if it does not give immediate self-government or something very close to it, it is going to make things very difficult in India and is in danger ultimately of driving India out of the Empire.[75]

Concluding, however that the British Government would not agree to the full reforms which would satisfy Indian leaders, Innes was to recommend that a review of the composition of the Central Legislature was the way forward.

Innes stated, 'We ought to devise some system whereby the Government can make its policy effective in the Legislature...It is of course a very difficult question'. He acknowledged his solution would involve a return to autocracy but he believed there was no perfect solution to this British dilemma.

Governor de Montmorency also saw the problem faced by the British and concluded some form of dyarchy, however called, was a real option.[76] His consideration of the problem started from a viewpoint that it was inevitable, in due course, that Indians would take over charge of all their affairs. In that circumstance, he believed, Indian politicians should be given the opportunity to gain experience as fully as possible across all portfolio matters, including foreign affairs and defence. The mechanism by which he envisaged this happening involved a bicameral legislature, in which deliberations on the hitherto reserved subjects, of foreign affairs and defence would be confined to an upper house. The lower house would be fully responsible for all other subjects but, through a system of Standing Committees or Boards, would be able to provide input into upper house deliberations. The Governor acknowledged a difficulty was 'that the popular side might say "I won't play" and as a political gesture refuse to serve on the Standing Boards',[77] but he believed his system would be defensible.

Montagu Butler commenced his advice from a less creative point of view advising Irwin, 'I am not sure I quite agree with the premises on which it [Irwin's note] is based. The central machinery does not seem to me to be working so very clumsily'.[78] While indicating he was not prepared to admit the need for any drastic change in the central government, he did acknowledge Irwin's position that changes of substance were, in fact, necessary by putting forward a rather obtuse solution. Butler's view was that over the years there had been a 'shifting of controlling power, in the provincial field from the Government of India, to the Governor corresponding privately with the Governor-General, and taking his lead from him'.[79] He advised Irwin that this trend must continue as a 'condition precedent to popularising the Central Government'. Butler was in effect putting forward a proposal for provincial autonomy with the necessary coordinating link maintained between the Centre and the provinces through contact between the governors and the Governor-General. Admitting 'that it was not a fully worked out scheme', Butler foresaw some elements of the Simon Commission conclusions for the future of India with his final sentence.

> The solution which seems so hard to find now will come of itself when the executive can be subordinated to the Legislature, and a truly federal form of Government can be set up with the spheres of the Central and Provincial Governments clearly and properly defined.[80]

Irwin had really set his governors a gordian knot,[81] a problem, in this case, impossible to solve, unless of course the British made a decision to withdraw from India. The British were unwilling, for whatever motive, to give up power over what they judged to be critical elements of government such as; foreign affairs and defence and relations with the Princely States. While they maintained this position it would be impossible to formulate a constitutional framework for India which would provide, by the Westminster definition, true responsible government. Irwin and the governors recognised this. In responding to Irwin on the matter, his trusted cadre attempted to identify a workable formula which even the Simon Commission was to find beyond it. In the framework within which the various governments of India and the Commission had to work, it was to prove impossible to assuage both British and Indian interests. To Irwin's credit he was to continue to attempt this task with the governors during the rest of 1928, and beyond when he recognised that the Simon Commission was not going to deliver a solution but to pour an accelerant on Indian discontent. The Dominion Status and Round Table initiatives represent the next major policy developments in the search for acceptable constitutional outcomes for the British and the Indian independence movements. Chapter 4 will explore the degree to which the governors contributed to these initiatives.

In the lead up to the Simon Commission's second visit in October 1928, the governors continued to respond to requests for background material and policy advice from Irwin importantly in relation to ideas for constitutional advance in the provinces. Innes, picking up on advice from Irwin that the Commission 'may mean to call on each local government to present a complete scheme for the future constitution of the Province',[82] was to advise him of his concern that this appeared to imply that the Commission 'has already arrived at the preliminary conclusion that we cannot go back or stay where we are'. Innes was alarmed that if this was the case then he should be advised thus avoiding unnecessary work. His advice implied that regression or standstill were still realistic options for Burma. Innes advised Burma's intention to put forward necessary background information for the Commission. This would include such subjects as the working of the government under the existing constitution, the working of the legislature, the electorate, the growth of parties, and the impact of the reforms on the different departments, as well as constructive policy proposals. All the material would be summarised in a general memorandum. This material would be supplemented in the case of Burma with memoranda on separation[83] (Burma from India) and on the Meston Settlement.[84] Innes advised his view that, while members of the Burma Legislative Council and ministers would canvass and endorse a range of options including for full provincial autonomy

> I have no doubt myself that this examination will warrant only one conclusion, namely, that provincial autonomy cannot be justified on any reasoned ground of political theory, and that as a choice between two evils it would be wiser to persevere with dyarchy for some time longer.[85]

At the beginning of October Innes, in providing Irwin with a nine page copy of the general memorandum, which he had drafted, confirmed his view, and that of his ministers, that Burma was not ready for advance in the context of Section 84A of the *Government of India Act.* As this position would be bitterly resented in Burma, Innes believed it would be very important, to avoid political turmoil not to put this in a form which would inevitably be seen by the Indian and Burma committees.[86] Innes acknowledged that practically, even given his and his government's views, it would be extremely difficult not to give Burma the same measure of advance as may occur in other provinces.

De Montmorency, now Governor of the Punjab, advised Irwin that his province's submission to the Commission fell into two parts, background and constructive policy as regards the local government in the future. He indicated that the policy submission had been 'prepared by Sir Malcolm Hailey and myself after prolonged discussions with the non-official Member and Ministers'.[87] As it had not been possible to obtain complete agreement with ministers and members, the second part of the main note consisted of Hailey's ideas, with the differing positions contained in separate memoranda. The Governor went on, in his letter to Irwin, to advise of his views on the actual presentation of evidence by provinces to the Commission, including by officials being restricted to advice on the current functioning of government. Sir Geoffrey felt it would be inappropriate for governors, council members and ministers to be examined on the second part of their submission, with the press present, especially given the differences of opinion.

Simon was later to inform Irwin that the memorandum submitted by Hailey and de Montmorency

> ...is a most remarkable document—far the most searching analysis and much the most practical Memorandum on the Provincial side which we have yet had before us. All the same, the difficulties stick out like quills out of a porcupine's back.[88]

In the last sentence Simon had identified the essential conundrum faced by the British, in being unable to extend fully responsible government to India, under a formula of wishing to reserve to themselves sensitive governmental functions. Hailey, complementing the de Montmorency memorandum, had also directly provided a paper to Simon discussing the complexities, with reference to India, of the meaning of responsible government. Simon responded, 'Thank you very much for your letter of October 29 enclosing the valuable and interesting note on the implications of this elusive phrase "responsible government". I am reading it with much profit'.[89] The Hailey/de Montmorency memorandum had put forward a scheme for the Punjab involving a Second Chamber, and the retention of dyarchy but with further subjects transferred and the abolition of the official bloc in the First Chamber. In the scheme, the reserved side, as a measure of compensation, would be allowed to carry to the Second Chamber demands on the reserved side refused in the First Chamber.[90] The degree of influence which Hailey and de Montmorency had on the final shape of the Simon Report itself is contained in Hailey's words. 'De Montmorency and I tried very hard in the Punjab and as a result finally proposed to the Commission a constitutional scheme which on the whole is very much like that which they have adopted'.[91]

Jackson put forward a view that, while the Bengal Government was considering four proposals for constitutional change, it would be inappropriate for Bengal to put forward any definite or preferred scheme for constitutional advance to the Commission.[92] Jackson noted he had seen the Punjab proposals prepared by Hailey and de Montmorency, whilst in Shillong, 'but it appeared to me that our experience would not permit of our agreeing to their suitability to Bengal'.[93] Apparently Stephenson had similar views to Jackson on contributions to the question of constitutional advance. At the beginning of November 1928, Stephenson, following discussions with Irwin in Simla in which the Viceroy had requested a contribution from him, had copied Irwin a memorandum to the Commission, from the reserved side of government, in which they had set out a formula relating to possible options for consideration in Bihar and Orissa. Referring to the Viceroy's wishes and pressure from Simon for some contribution, Stephenson advised:

> We have adhered more or less to our previous attitude that it is not for local Governments to suggest new constitutions. The line we have taken therefore is that if the Commission decide to do this or that, these are the safeguards that in our opinion are required.[94]

Stephenson's paper had evidently been submitted reluctantly. Governor de Montmorency, writing to Irwin from his residence 'Barnes Court' in Simla, had earlier provided him with a full page of reasons why Bihar and Orissa should submit a paper on their future constitution, despite any difficulties in agreement on a way forward they might have.[95] The importance of being at the Viceroy's right hand and Sir Geoffrey's special influence is reflected in the fact of Stephenson's rather belated submission.

Lord Goschen, in Madras, was to inform Irwin he believed it would not be possible to go backwards, or to stand still on constitutional reform. He and his ministers believed dyarchy must go and a form of unitary government be introduced.[96] All his ministers were against any extension of the franchise 'but we are in favour of dividing the constituencies up so as to make them smaller and the members therefore more responsible to their constituents'. By January 1929 Goschen's proposal had been refined to opt for provincial autonomy.[97]

Governor Hammond's submission to Irwin on constitutional advance in Assam involved giving 'all the power we can to the Legislative Council' but reserving appropriate powers to permanent officials to support the Governor 'when the inevitable breakdown occurs'.[98] This view was predicated 'on the assumption that there will be a strong Central Government', involving the Governor-General in Council being independent from the Legislative Assembly. Hammond copied this advice to Simon.[99] He had earlier advised Simon the frontier tribes 'should be left entirely outside the purview of the Legislative Council and should be administered by the Governor as Agent to the Governor-General'.[100]

The matter of the Simon Commission and its consequences were major policy issues for the British during Lord Irwin's Viceroyalty. This chapter has revealed the high degree to which the Viceroy sought out and depended on the advice of the governors of British India. This related not only to the context of seeking input on strictly provincial matters, relating to the Commission, but also on all-India policy in relation to constitutional advance and other matters. As with other policy circumstances this pattern was particularly so at the beginning of Lord Irwin's term. The governors also provided their personal advice direct to the Commission, most often through the Chairman, on matters concerning it. The Secretary of State and the British Home Government were also influenced by the governors, mainly through Irwin, on Simon Commission issues. In addition the governors influenced the Government of India through their own ICS Departments. The comprehensive advice the pro-consuls gave on the Simon Commission ranged across a predominance of significant aspects, from the mainly administrative arrangements to views on important policy. These matters included not only the composition of the Commission, but those relating to its announcement, procedure and advice on constitutional reform in the central and provincial governments. The Viceroy came to depend more on a small cadre led by

Hailey. That the governors' advice was fallible is revealed by the very serious error of providing a policy view that Indians need not be included as members of the Simon Commission. The governors had completely misread the situation regarding the composition of the Commission and hence altered history. This grave mistake was uncharacteristic of the governors and probably reflected a further misreading and overconfidence, amongst them, in relation to the determination and capacity of the nationalist leaders to challenge British rule. While appropriate representative Indian membership of the Commission would have been difficult to achieve, the mistake reawakened the nationalist movement which was to lead later to significant concessions being given to it by Irwin in the form of his Declaration and the Round Table initiatives. The extent of the strategic error was further exemplified by the necessity, for the British of Irwin's later pact with Gandhi, which to some extent temporarily rescued the situation for the Raj. If the governors had provided firm advice to Irwin and Birkenhead that it was vital there be some form of Indian membership of the Commission, then it would have been most likely accepted. In this case the British may not have been placed under the same degree of pressure by the nationalists during Irwin's viceroyalty. This chapter has clearly revealed the important influence the governors of British India had over vital affairs of state but does not identify any cynical or perfidious intent. The next will further reinforce the role of the governors in influencing critical British Indian policy.

Endnotes

1. 1919 *Government of India Act*, Section 84A (2).
2. Gopal, *Irwin*, Chapter 2, generally for further background.
3. The Simon Commission visited India from February to March 1928, and from October to April 1929.
4. Halifax Papers, Hailey to Cunningham, 21 August 1926.
5. There were two Indian members of the British Parliament at this time, one a Communist. See Gopal, Irwin, p. 19.
6. Halifax Papers, Hailey to Cunningham, 21 August 1926. My italics.
7. *Ibid.*
8. *Ibid.*
9. *Ibid.*, Birkenhead to Irwin, 23 September 1926.
10. *Ibid.*, Irwin to Hailey, Marris and Muddiman, 18 April 1927. Note Marris, as Governor of the United Provinces, was the senior of the provincial governors.
11. *Ibid.*, Birkenhead to Irwin, 23 March 1927.
12. *Ibid.*

13. *Ibid.*
14. *Ibid.*, Hailey to Irwin, 23 April 1927.
15. *Ibid.*
16. *Ibid.*, Marris to Irwin, 25 April 1927.
17. *Ibid.*
18. Five wise Englishmen.
19. Halifax Papers, Irwin to Birkenhead, 11 and 19 May 1927. Irwin italics.
20. No Muddiman reference in the Halifax Papers can be found on this matter.
21. Halifax Papers, Irwin to Harcourt Butler, 15 June 1927.
22. *Ibid.*, Stephenson to Irwin, 6 June 1927.
23. *Ibid.*, Goschen to Irwin, 6 June 1927.
24. *Ibid.*, Irwin to Harcourt Butler, 15 June 1927.
25. *Ibid.*, Wilson to Irwin, 2 July 1927.
26. Tomlinson, *The Indian National Congress and the Raj*, p. 15.
27. Gopal, *Irwin*, p. 21.
28. *Ibid.*
29. M.A. Jinnah (1876–1948). Member of the Legislative Assembly. Muslim Nationalist leader. President of the Muslim League. First Governor-General of Pakistan.
30. de Montmorency, who was a close colleague and friend of Hailey's, was at that time a member of the Punjab Executive Council and was to become Governor of the Punjab in 1928.
31. Halifax Papers, Hailey to Irwin, 22 and 24 May 1927.
32. Simon Papers, Montagu Butler to Irwin, 28 September 1928.
33. *Ibid.*, Irwin to Montagu Butler, 7 October 1928.
34. *Ibid.*, Montagu Butler to Simon, 13 December 1928.
35. See Halifax Papers, Irwin to various governors, 27 February 1928; Innes to Irwin, 28 February 1928; Muddiman to Irwin, 29 February 1928; Muddiman to Irwin, 2 March 1928; Wilson to Irwin, 5 March 1928; Stephenson to Irwin, 6 March 1928; Hammond to Irwin, 7 March 1928; Montagu Butler to Irwin, 9 March 1928; Hailey to Irwin, 12 March 1928; Hailey to Irwin, 23 March 1928 Jackson to Irwin, 13 March 1928; Hailey to Irwin, 28 May 1928. See also governors' replies to message from Irwin to various governors, 1 June 1928. These papers provide evidence of the extensive advice provided by the governors on this issue. Irwin also sought their advice on Commission procedure and on the taking of evidence. Halifax Papers, Hailey to Irwin, 23 March 1928; Irwin to Hailey, 25/26 March 1928; Simon Papers, 25 February 1928; Halifax Papers, Stephenson to Irwin, 12 October 1928; Telegram, Governor of Bengal to Viceroy, 13 October 1928; Wilson to Irwin, 4 February 1928.
36. *Ibid.*, Hailey to Irwin, 30 June 1927.
37. Hailey Papers. This reference reveals not only the significant communication between Hailey and de Montmorency on policy matters but also the extent to which they shared their experience and expertise. They also used this communication to forewarn and assist each other on important developments.

See de Montmorency to Hailey, 11 November 1928, in which Hailey is advised of the administrative arrangements de Montmorency had put in place for the Simon Commission in the Punjab.

38. Halifax Papers, Irwin to various governors, 17 November 1926. Irwin's letter was sent to eight governors excluding Hailey. It can be asked whether this fact indicated that Irwin had already discussed personally the matters canvassed with Hailey, demonstrating ease of access to each other, level of trust and hence the degree of Hailey's influence. Hailey may have been behind Irwin's tentative suggestion as to the timing of the announcement of the Commission?
39. *Ibid.*, Wilson to Irwin, 20 November 1926.
40. *Ibid.*, O'Donnell to Irwin, 21 November 1926.
41. *Ibid.*, Kerr to Irwin, 23 November 1926.
42. *Ibid.*, Wheeler to Irwin, 25 November 1926.
43. *Ibid.*, Montagu Butler to Irwin, 26 November 1926.
44. *Ibid.*, Goschen to Irwin, 16 December 1926.
45. *Ibid.*, Wheeler to Irwin, 25 November 1926.
46. *Ibid.*, Harcourt Butler to Irwin, 26 November 1926.
47. *Ibid.*, Lytton to Irwin, 25 November 1926.
48. *Ibid.*, Irwin to Harcourt Butler, 26 January 1927.
49. Sir B.P. Blackett. Finance Member, Governor-General's Executive Council.
50. Halifax Papers, Irwin to Birkenhead, 18 August 1927.
51. Hailey Papers. This reference is replete with requests from Irwin for Hailey's advice. Irwin to Hailey, 22 August 1927, provides yet another example of a viceregal appeal for help and guidance on Simon Commission matters.
52. Halifax Papers, Irwin to Birkenhead, 18 August 1927.
53. Hailey Papers, Irwin to Hailey, 20 October 1927. This letter advised Hailey the Commission itself would be parliamentary and that membership had been agreed by all political parties. Thus the governors had little or no role in the selection of the Commission's actual membership. See also file MSS EUR 77/63: Simon Papers on the 'Appointment of the Indian Statutory Commission'. Hailey Papers, Reed to Hailey, 8 January 1928 indicates a view of the generally low calibre of the commissioners apart from Simon and Viscount Burnham. The other members appointed to the Commission were Baron Strathcona, Edward Cadogan, Stephen Walsh, George Lane-Fox and Clement Attlee.
54. Halifax Papers, Irwin to various Governors, 10 October 1927. Irwin to Hailey and Hammond, 20 October 1927.
55. *Ibid.*, Telegram, Governor of the United Provinces to Viceroy, 11 October 1927.
56. *Ibid.*, Wilson to Irwin, 12 October 1927.
57. *Ibid.*, Irwin to Stephenson, 20 October 1927.
58. *Ibid.*, Marris to Irwin, 11 October 1927.
59. *Ibid.*, Goschen to Irwin, 11 October 1927.
60. *Ibid.*, Harcourt Butler to Irwin, 11 October 1927.
61. *Ibid.*, Hammond to Irwin, 11 October 1927.

62. *Ibid.*, Jackson to Irwin, 27 October 1927.
63. *Ibid.*, Irwin to Wilson and Stephenson, 20 October 1927.
64. *Ibid.*, Hailey to Irwin, 7 November 1927.
65. *Ibid.*, Jinnah to Irwin, 31 October 1927.
66. *Ibid.*, Irwin to Goschen, 22 November 1927. See also Telegram, Governor of the Punjab to Private Secretary to the Viceroy, 15 November 1927. This correspondence provides evidence of Hailey's surprise at developments.
67. *Ibid.*, Irwin to Hailey, de Montmorency, Montagu Butler, Innes, 17 August 1928. Field Marshal Birdwood, the six members of the Viceroy's Council and three senior officials in the Government of India, were also included in the request to the governors.
68. *Ibid.*
69. *Ibid.*
70. *Ibid.*
71. *Ibid.*
72. *Ibid.*
73. *Ibid.*, Innes to Irwin, 29 August 1928; de Montmorency to Irwin, 4 September 1928; Montagu Butler to Irwin, 17 September 1928.
74. *Ibid.*, Irwin to Hailey, 11 August 1928.
75. *Ibid.*, Innes to Irwin, 29 August 1928.
76. *Ibid.*, de Montmorency to Irwin, 4 September 1928.
77. *Ibid.*
78. *Ibid.*, Montagu Butler to Irwin, 17 September 1928.
79. *Ibid.*
80. *Ibid.*
81. Difficult problem or task.
82. Halifax Papers, Innes to Irwin,13 September 1928.
83. Harcourt Butler Papers. In a letter to Clague, Harcourt Butler had indicated 'separation is forbidden by the Government of India and federation by consent raises questions of self-determination which are difficult. Harcourt Butler to Clague, 1 November 1927. Butler himself was uncertain of the merits of separation. Harcourt Butler to Clague, 6 February 1929.
84. The Meston Settlement. Lord Meston chaired a Committee which, following the 1919 *Government of India Act*, settled the share of Provincial financial contributions to the Government of India. The Settlement was strongly criticised by the provinces.
85. Halifax Papers, Innes to Irwin, 13 September 1928.
86. *Ibid.*, Innes to Irwin, 6 October 1928. See also Simon Papers, Innes to Simon, 31 October 1928. This letter duplicated Innes' views on constitutional advance given to the Viceroy.
87. *Ibid.*, de Montmorency to Irwin, 16 September 1928.
88. *Ibid.*, Simon to Irwin, 10 November 1928.
89. Simon Papers, Simon to Hailey, 10 November 1928.
90. Halifax Papers, Hailey to Irwin, 25 November 1928.

91. Hailey Papers, Hailey to Verney, 14 August 1930. Note: It has not been possible to identify Verney.
92. Halifax Papers, Jackson to Irwin, 20 September 1928.
93. *Ibid.*
94. *Ibid.*, Stephenson to Irwin, 9 November 1928.
95. *Ibid.*, de Montmorency to Irwin, 16 September 1928.
96. *Ibid.*, Goschen to Irwin, 8 December 1928.
97. *Ibid.*, Goschen to Irwin, 13 January 1929.
98. *Simon Papers,* Hammond to Irwin, 24 July 1928.
99. *Ibid.*, Hammond to Simon, 6 January 1929.
100. *Ibid.*, Hammond to Simon, 20 August 1928.

4

The Dominion Status Declaration and First Round Table Conference

The announcement of the Simon Commission, on 8 November 1927 and the non-inclusion of any Indian component had revitalised the opponents of British rule. The Madras meeting of Congress, held in December 1927 called for a boycott of the Commission, and Jawaharlal Nehru declared India's goal was for complete independence. The Commission during its visits in 1928 and 1929 experienced intensifying boycott. The British had erred in their judgement of the likely consequence of not including Indians in the Commission. As a result, this had provoked a broad spectrum of opposition to any likelihood of its success contained in the coalescing of nationalist India, including the moderate elements and a significant portion of the Muslim grouping. This opposition found expression in an All Parties Conference held in New Delhi in February 1928, which voted for 'full responsible government'. This term was designed to incorporate the concept of Dominion Status and independence. This process culminated in the issuance of the Nehru Report in August 1928 which called for a Round Table Conference with the British to discuss its demand for Dominion Status and full responsible government. While the Nehru Report's call for the discarding of separate electorates had alienated the Muslims and greatly weakened the prospect of a united front, developments in Bardoli and the no-tax campaign presented a significant political challenge to the British. The pressure on the British to find a way through these difficulties was reinforced by Congress' call for a renewed national non-cooperation campaign if the terms of the Nehru Report had not been accepted by them by the end of 1929.

The constitutional pathway, set out under the 1919 *Government of India Act* was, of course, that defined by Simon's Parliamentary Commission process and the recommendations of its Report, presented in May 1930, to the British Government and Parliament. Irwin had formed a view, however, well in advance of the Report's publication that it would not adequately meet the political imperatives of the time, driven by the realities of Indian nationalism. Montagu Butler also identified the Report's defects, including to British interests, informing his wife Hannah: 'I am up betimes to study afresh the Simon report. Vol II is not a bit up to Vol I and is bound to cause a lot of trouble'.[1] Butler identified a number of unsatisfactory aspects, from a British perspective, including the potential undermining of the position of big landholders, British allies, by depriving them of seats in the legislatures and the introduction of income tax on them. He also noted the grave omission, from the Report, of reference to Dominion Status which was of concern to Irwin.[2] The Viceroy, on his return to England in the summer of 1929, was able to meet with the new Labour Secretary of State for India, Wedgwood Benn, armed with the knowledge that Simon and his team had effectively failed. 'Irwin had come home in possession of the prospective main recommendations of the Simon Commission a year in advance of their publication and several months before its report had been drafted'.[3] Defining the Report's failure to come up with innovative options for reform was the fact that it was not to include any reference to Dominion Status for India, a main call of the nationalists. It is remarkable that, at the time of his report's publication, Simon himself was to make the observation to Irwin.

> We have, of course, made no reference to Dominion Status (which is an expression the meaning and application of which are still obscure to me), and I am afraid I retain my opinion as to the inexpediency of the reference to it last November [at the time of the Irwin Declaration].[4]

Interestingly, it is more than likely that the source of Irwin's early knowledge of this defect, amongst others, was Colonel G.R. Lane-Fox, MP, Commission member and also Irwin's brother-in-law. The nature of the extensive correspondence between the Viceroy and Lane-Fox, during the period of the Commission, reflects this likelihood. For example, Irwin in discussing with Simon, in February 1929, the merits of a Round Table Conference in London to consider his report had requested him to 'treat the matter as confidential except, if you so desire, with George Lane-Fox who was privy to our earlier discussions'.[5]

Irwin's Declaration of 1 November 1929,[6] in which he proposed a conference to consider India's move towards Dominion Status, was therefore a preemptive attempt to regain for the British the political initiative lost by the Simon Commission, both at its formation and at its conclusion. That this should be achieved was of critical importance to the British Government and hence to the Viceroy and the governors. This chapter examines the extent to which the governors were involved in the formulation of Irwin's ideas leading to his Declaration and in the development of policy contributing to the Round Table process.

As early as September 1928, Irwin was in discussions with Sir Hugh Stephenson, during his stay at Viceregal Lodge in Simla, on the matter of how to address any transition by India to Dominion Status and prospective negotiations to this end with Indian politicians at a Round Table. On his return to his province, Stephenson prepared a four page note recording their meeting, which he sent to Irwin under cover of a letter. The note identifies the provenance of at least some of the 'theories' which were advanced in the discussions.

> I enclose a note representing roughly the theories *I advanced* in our conversation regarding the 'Prime Minister' proposal…I have not attempted to make it more than a rough note of the arguments *I put forward*.[7]

In Stephenson's note, reference is made to a general move to the left (i.e., towards extremism) by Indian politicians reflected in the decisions of the Congress held in Madras in December 1927, and also at the All Parties Conference in February 1928. The Nehru Report had also been issued in August 1928. Even so, Stephenson felt that at this time it would have been a mistake to give too much emphasis to a perception of a significant move, amongst the range of Indian politicians, particularly the moderate wing, towards extremism. However, to his mind 'the most disquieting factor is the adherence of a considerable section of "moderates" to the boycott',[8] of the Simon Commission. Very significantly, in the context of political India's call for Dominion Status and full responsible government or more extremely, complete independence, Stephenson was to observe:

> If the Commission's report leads to anything much short of Dominion status, these men [the moderates] must almost inevitably throw their whole weight against the new constitution. It will be born in the same atmosphere of hostility as the last reforms and history will repeat itself.[9]

The Governor had identified for Irwin, the risks inherent in the prospect of the final Simon Report being so defective as not to make reference to an objective of Dominion Status, a full nineteen months before the Report was issued, and indeed before the second working visit of the Commission in October 1928. Given the extensive consultations held with the Viceroy and the governors, over the seven months the Commission was in India for its second visit, it is almost impossible to believe Simon and his commissioners were not party to Stephenson's viewpoint, later acted upon by Irwin in the form of his Declaration. Stephenson went on to describe the 'Prime Minister proposal', designed to win back India's political moderates, as involving an invitation to them by the PM to a conference to consider India's constitutional issues, before the British Cabinet formulated their position in response to the Simon Report. That this 'Prime Minister proposal' was developed in India was evident to Irwin, during his 1929 visit to England, seeking Wedgwood Benn's agreement to an initiative of a Round Table Conference 'heralded by a solemn Government statement that Dominion Status and nothing less was the goal of India's political progress'.[10]

Stephenson warned Irwin of the dangers of alienating those moderate Indian politicians, who had by and large supported the British in relation to the Simon Commission, by appearing to concede the so-called extremists' call for a Round Table at which an Indian Constitution would be decided and which then the British Parliament would have to ratify.

> I feel very strongly that if the Viceroy nominates any of the extremists who have been in the forefront of the boycott, it will be construed as a surrender and an admission that the Simon Commission has been scrapped...I think that the idea of the Viceroy constituting a delegation from India irrespective of the Simon Commission is too dangerous.[11]

Stephenson suggested that a possible mechanism for identifying delegates to the Conference would be for the various legislative committees, cooperating with the Simon Commission, to elect a delegation, not from amongst themselves but, drawn from suitable candidates across the whole of India. He hoped 'that their choice might include leaders who have not hitherto cooperated, and the proposed matters for consideration would include any paper they might wish to bring',[12] and not just the Report of the Simon Commission. In the event, the December 1929 Lahore Congress was to decide that none of its membership would attend the London Round Table Conference, thus excluding the 'extremists'. Consequently delegates were effectively chosen by Irwin and the governors from the political moderates. With regard to the representation of the Princely States, at the Round Table Conference, they were assigned a quota of seats and the Standing Committee of the Chamber of Princes established the internal distribution.

Stephenson, in his 1928 discussions with Irwin had alerted him to the actual need for a Declaration and adumbrated key elements of what became known as the Irwin Declaration of 1 November 1929. These elements included that the Simon Report not be the sole policy document for consideration by the Round Table Conference, and that the Conference be held before any consideration by Cabinet and Parliament of the Report's recommendations. Irwin acknowledged the value of Stephenson's contribution in his October

1928 reply. 'It is very good of you to have taken the trouble to elaborate your views, and I recognise the force of all you say'.[13]

Within months of Irwin's discussions with Stephenson, the Viceroy embarked on a series of verbal and written negotiations with Simon on how his final report might be handled in the context of Irwin's proposal for a Round Table Conference.[14] Simon was deeply distressed by Lord Irwin's plan including any announcement of the Conference before the publication of his report. That the Viceroy and Governor Hailey had also consulted, on matters surrounding this difficult issue, is contained in a reference in Simon's correspondence to Irwin. Simon referred to Hailey's recommendation that the 'Announcement should be made as soon as the Commission had reported, and if possible should be based on a suggestion contained in the Report itself'.[15]

Simon was most concerned that Irwin's announcement not be made 'now' (i.e., early 1929) and thus 'leaving the Commission to struggle on as best it may without any mitigation of the boycott, and under the additional handicap which such an announcement involves'.[16] Irwin could see the possible benefit of an announcement before the threatened implementation of non-cooperation at the beginning of January 1930, and the November 1929 timing of his Declaration can be seen as a compromise. Hailey's recommendation that the Simon Report contains a reference to a conference of parties was taken up, even though the Report was published after the Irwin Declaration. Irwin was to advise Simon that in suggesting a Round Table Conference he was attempting to create an environment in which the likelihood of Indian opinion receiving the Report would be enhanced. Irwin acknowledged the primacy of Simon in questions of policy.

> But what I do fear is that, if nothing of the kind that I have suggested is done, the Report, whatever its merits, may be itself confronted with such a degree of unreasonable opposition in India that Parliament may find itself in a position of imposing some settlement on India which, for quite disconnected reasons, Indian opinion would set itself to oppose.[17]

However, while his Commission remained in India, Simon continued to argue his case with Irwin against the Viceroy's plans in long letters in which he set out detailed rebuttals of Irwin's logic for a conference.

Irwin had also canvassed his plans with other governors and they were not unanimously behind him. Innes of the 'inner' circle was to indicate a degree of hesitation about the Viceroy's plan.

> As you know, I am rather a sceptic about the proposed announcement. But you were good enough to give me an opportunity of expressing my views, and I am quite content to accept your judgment. But I wonder whether

> the announcement will not raise hopes which the report of the Statutory Commission will subsequently dash to the ground.[18]

However, in correspondence with his personal friend, Dawson, Editor of *The Times* of London, Irwin identified support amongst others of his principal governor advisers.

> ...it will be surely one of the strange coincidences of history if Goschen—as Governor and [acting] Viceroy—Hailey, de Montmorency, George Stanley, Sykes, all my Members of Council, and, so far as I know, the overwhelming bulk of official and non-official European opinion here, are all wrong with me, and Jix and the Daily Mail right![19]

Certainly Hailey had been closely involved in the preparation of the Declaration, a fact which Irwin acknowledged when sending him a note on the history of the statement by writing, 'you have given me such great assistance from time to time in its composition'.[20] That the construct of the final Declaration did not exactly match Hailey's drafting is indicated in a note he wrote to his friend Mr J. Gwynn, the *Manchester Guardian* correspondent in India. 'I considered that it would have been for the better if it had been made in somewhat different language'.[21] Hailey felt stronger reference should have been made to the fact 'the Preamble of the Act of 1919 still regulated the situation and that the Parliament must remain the arbiter of the stages by which India is to advance but that the ultimate objective was Dominion Status'. Lord Reading knew Hailey was in complete agreement with Irwin on the broad policy of the Declaration but, even so, he too did not agree with the Viceroy's statement and its sentiments.[22] Both Irwin's predecessor, Reading, and his successor, Willingdon, exhibited more conservative tendencies than Irwin and the governors of his era.

In the event, Irwin's Declaration did not attract the Congress and Gandhi to the first Round Table Conference. In its immediate objective of drawing the Indian nationalists into a policy debate on India's future it failed, as consequently did the Round Table Conference itself, in most of its objectives. The Declaration also 'alerted large sections of the [British] Liberal and Conservative parties to the dangers of a policy of generous constitutional reform'.[23] The concept of the Irwin Declaration, its policy objective and shape had been developed in India by the Viceroy and the key governors, and their approach was to be approved by the Secretary of State and the British Government. Once accepted as a pathway forward the role of the governors, in the period leading to the Conference, held from 19 November 1930 to 22 January 1931, was centred on complicated administrative issues, such as the composition of the British and Indian delegations and on the policy elements of what was being attempted.

An interesting insight into the contemporary attitudes of the governors is presented by their views about including Indian women at the Round Table Conference. The Labour Secretary of State had requested that this be considered, which idea Irwin had put to all of the governors. Irwin was to report back to Wedgwood Benn that the governors were unanimously opposed to the proposal, providing a summary of their extensive reasons. These included a view that Indian women generally were not politically mature and those who were would hold extreme attitudes. Also Muslims would not like women attending.[24] An indication of Irwin's own conservatism on this matter, and of his trust in the governors, is contained in his advice to Wedgwood Benn, 'that, in view of Governors' unanimous feeling, it may be accepted that women need not be included in the Conference'.[25] Wedgwood Benn did not accept the weight of advice from India on this occasion, and by the end of the month Irwin informed the governors, 'The Secretary of State is insistent that two Indian ladies should be sent to the Round Table Conference, and I am anxious to meet his wishes'.[26] The matter of the appropriateness of Simon himself attending the Conference was also under consideration. Again, Irwin used the views of the governors to reinforce his own to the Secretary of State. Irwin had been able to discuss the matter at his July 1930 Governors' Conference. He reported that all the governors strongly endorsed his view that 'the inclusion of Simon would undoubtedly be generally interpreted to mean restriction of liberty of Conference to discussion of his report'.[27] On this occasion, Simla's views were accepted.

There was much discussion, by interested parties, on what was meant by the term 'Dominion Status' within the British Empire, which had been referenced but not defined in Irwin's Declaration. Australia, New Zealand and Canada could all be seen by India as sovereign and independent dominions within the empire, but with important military, economic and political connections with Britain. This was the status which the Indian Liberals sought but was being denied them by British requirements for 'safeguards', in the key areas of foreign affairs and defence, internal security, appropriate protection of the Indian underclass and for Indian political maturity. In a letter to the King–Emperor, days after he had made his Declaration, Irwin set out as background, to what the British saw as their intent contained in the term 'Dominion Status', a series of earlier British statements making reference to India's intended future political status. All these several government public policy statements contained such phrases as 'progress to the liberty which my other Dominions enjoy'.[28] This issue was at the heart of the complexity of the political relationship between the British and political India. What did the term, Dominion Status mean and how long would it take for India to achieve the status of an agreed definition? Indian nationalists, defined by the British as extremists, required immediate and complete independence. The Round Table was designed to seek a compromise.

The difficulty the British and Indians had in defining a common view of the term 'Dominion Status' and hence the complexity facing parties to the negotiations on the issue, is reflected in the correspondence between Irwin and the governors. Lord Lytton, who was now living in England, had defended the Irwin Declaration in the British press. In a letter, at the beginning of November 1929, to Lord Lytton thanking him, the Viceroy attempted to define the confusion in British and Indian minds over the term 'Dominion Status'.

> To the English mind the phase connotes an achieved constitutional state; to the Indian mind it means the promise of a constitutional state, and thus they see no contradiction, as we do, in speaking of *Dominion Status with reservations.* And when they talk about going to the Conference to frame a Dominion Status constitution, what they really mean is to frame a constitution which should have the power of growth to full Dominion Status; but should not be incompatible with the necessity of reservations to the Imperial Government.[29]

Irwin was to identify this misunderstanding to the King as '*the* stumbling-block at the present moment'.[30] In a letter to Hailey, at the end of November 1929, Irwin had requested him to 'run your eye through this note' on Dominion Status.[31] Irwin's note had been an attempt at setting out language in relation to an objective of 'Dominion Status' suitable for inclusion in a preamble to a new Act of Parliament. In his reply Hailey indicated that he could not remember anything of recent times which had caused so much misunderstanding. Hailey believed it was partly due, on the British side, to a misunderstanding of the intent of the Act of 1919 and on the Indian side to a 'deliberate desire on the part of many to pretend the declaration meant much more than it said'.[32] Hailey also identified important divisions of attitude to the term 'Dominion Status' within the ranks of Indian leadership:

While we think objectively of Dominion Status as a state of things that can be more or less accurately described, if not precisely defined, he [Gandhi] thinks of it subjectively, as a frame of mind, which asserts itself in amnesties, suppression of police activity, and a general kind of political kiss-in-the-ring. But is this possible of others, who are mainly lawyers by profession?[33]

Reference to the importance placed on Hailey as a policy adviser, on matters concerning the Round Table, by Irwin and others and the high regard in which he was held for his abilities is scattered throughout the relevant correspondence. Hailey's name was continually used as a reference point and his views were used as endorsements for particular positions taken. In a letter to Simon in March 1930 concerning 'Dominion Status' and preparations for the Round Table Conference, Irwin opens a sentence with the term, 'One could never count upon striking a Hailey…',[34] exemplifying the Governor's capacities and the views of him held by others. Governor Innes' abilities were also highly regarded and by July 1930 the Secretary of State and Irwin were discussing the possibility of governors Hailey and Innes attending the Round Table Conference. A matter of consideration for the Viceroy was the status the governors would take at the Conference. Were they to be advisers in their own right, giving their own opinions and advice without reference to the Government of India, or were they to be under the direction of Irwin and his government? The status and standing of these two governors were such that Irwin was to advise Wedgwood Benn that 'it would hardly be right to ask heads of administrations to undertake the duties proposed, and I should have thought that proper men for this work would be men of the standing of our Secretaries to Government'.[35] Irwin probably recognised the difficulties of keeping men of such ability, energy and initiative under any semblance of his supervision from India. Pursuing the engagement of the two governors, the Secretary of State defined for Irwin the role he saw for both Hailey and Innes. Wedgwood Benn saw the two men as the governors having the widest experience of Indian affairs. The Secretary of State wanted Innes to provide advice specifically on the issue of the separation of Burma from India. As to Hailey

> …it seems to be the general opinion that he is both in ability and experience an outstanding figure. I repeat that I do not in the least want him as a possible critic of views expressed by other authorities in India or as a potential arbiter of policy, but as the ablest man to help us in developing lines on which we decide to work.[36]

The Secretary of State's second choice after Hailey was de Montmorency. Irwin agreed to Hailey and Innes attending on the basis Wedgwood Benn had proposed,[37] and Innes was to be in England on leave in any case. It is interesting to note the jealousy and chagrin with which Montagu Butler greeted these appointments, advising his wife, 'Luckily I would have hated to be sent just now…But it shows we need hope for nothing from him [Irwin] and must bide our time happily'.[38] Hailey and Innes regarded the issue of their status and role being sufficiently important to define their function in a note submitted to the Secretary of State, signed and probably written by Hailey, to which Benn agreed.[39] The main elements of the note, relating to their position on discussions of policy at the Conference, included: the governors would not make any public speech or discuss with the press any controversial questions; they would not see delegations but could discuss questions other than general policy if approached; they would have full freedom to speak to the British Government even though their views might not accord with the Government of India. This last clause indicated the governors' intent to make a policy contribution, unfettered by the Indian Government, to Conference proceedings and the fact that it had been agreed to, including presumably by Irwin, reflected the high level of trust, in their judgement and abilities, held by the British governmental hierarchy. Part of the conservative order in the India Office hoped Hailey would be able to influence the liberal policies of the Irwin/Wedgwood Benn combination: '...so if you still have influence with Irwin (and it sometimes seems to me Punch is his principal adviser!) you have great opportunity and great responsibility'.[40]

Upon advice of his participation in the Conference, Hailey began providing to Irwin his detailed policy views of what would be the key elements for consideration and of the political framework within which this would occur.[41] Hailey was comfortable with the Simon Commission's recommendation for provincial autonomy but very uncomfortable about its proposal for a federal unitary government at the Centre to evolve over time.[42] Hailey believed

> ...when the preliminary orations about Dominion Status, India's aspirations, England's responsibility and the like have worked themselves out...the statute itself has in effect to settle only two matters—the constitution of the Provinces and the constitution of the Central Government.[43]

Hailey thought that the Indian Liberals at the Conference would agree to what would be proposed, by the Simon Commission, for the provinces, and concede such matters as communal representation and special votes for landlords in order 'to secure a unanimous pressure in favour of responsibility at the Centre'. Hailey advised, if his view was correct and if the British Government had any disposition to agree to even partial responsibility in the Central Legislature, the outcome would be 'nothing short of an agreement to introduce responsibility in all departments except Defence and Foreign Relations'.[44] Hailey felt the British Parliament would accept this outcome. On the basis of these views Hailey advised Irwin of his apprehensiveness regarding the Viceroy's own proposal for a unitary system, which carried with it continuing irresponsibility at the Centre and which was dyarchical.[45] Hailey held the strong view that if the Viceroy's proposal was accepted then there would be a 'repetition of a period of struggle and antagonism, involving... constant humiliation of the administration'.[46] Hailey concluded his 'long rigmarole' modestly by stating his own 'discomfort at the prospect of facing questions for which I have in my own mind no convincing answer'. As time would continue to show there was indeed to be no answer to how Britain could grant real Dominion Status and maintain fundamental control of India.

By the beginning of November 1930, Hailey and Innes were in England preparing for the Conference. Hailey had been accommodated in the India Office and Wedgwood Benn had had a long talk with him which he reported to Irwin. Benn had advised Hailey that the government's decision

> ...was that, with all the information in our hands, that is, the Simon Report, the other Reports [such as the Butler Report on the Princes], and above all, your Despatch [the Government of India's], we should listen to the Conference and gradually make up our minds. We should then have some sort of policy; I should then be asking...[Hailey] how it was to be carried out just exactly as I should ask the same assistance from any public official.[47]

The Secretary of State, in commenting on his first meeting with Hailey, informed Irwin: 'I like him very much, and I think we shall get on famously together. He certainly has a very brilliant mind'.[48]

In the nearly three months of the first Round Table Conference, from November 1930 to January 1931, Hailey, in particular, was to provide regular reports of Conference proceedings to Irwin, reflecting his extensive policy input. Innes had a more minor role providing advice on Burma and was not consulted on the main Indian issues, which did not specifically relate to Burma. Much to Irwin's relief Innes 'rode the Secretary of State off the idea of a plebiscite on the question of Burma',[49] demonstrating the Governor's influence on an important policy matter relating to the prospect of separating the administration of Burma from India. Innes returned to Burma at the end of December 1930, before the Conference ended.[50] Not surprisingly, Hailey's series of reports to Irwin reflect not only his agreed role of 'developing lines on which we decide to work' but also the Governor's intention of obtaining results which aligned with his own views. He advised Irwin in his first report, 'Whatever I may feel about the constitution at the Centre, I am definitely on the Indian side here and have done my best to persuade others to my view'.[51] The Indian delegates, however, had suspected the governors' presence at the Round Table Conference was not in their interests. Hailey informed his friend de Montmorency that, 'The Indian delegates much resent our presence and have been to see the PM and Secretary of State about it'.[52] *New India* regarded Hailey as reactionary and 'the chief guide and authority in the higher official circles, so far as the big constitutional issues before the country are concerned'.[53] The paper saw Hailey's presence in England as a 'Machiavellian plot' and that his role was really to negotiate satisfactory outcomes, for the British Indian diehards, on India with the British Labour and Conservative parties. Hailey was indeed no benign adviser to governments but, as one would suspect, actively involved himself in obtaining and influencing, what he believed were, the best possible outcomes. He was able to do this at the highest level in London meeting with the Prime Minister, together with other officials, the Lord Chancellor and Secretary of State, on most mornings of the Conference. A senior Indian civil servant at the Conference, Harry Haig,[54] in his Conference reports, written to Irwin, reinforced the importance of Hailey's role.

> It is Hailey who is in a position to put things across. It is he who can speak to the Prime Minister and whom the other British delegates want to see... Hailey naturally and inevitably takes the lead.[55]

Hailey was to describe for Irwin the process, highlighting his pivotal function, by which the Prime Minister, dissatisfied with the generalities still surrounding the concept and scheme of federation (British India with Princely India), asked him, assisted by others, 'to draw out certain basic facts which would have to be recognised in drawing up any scheme of federation and which could not be altered by any discussion at the Conference'.[56] A further example of Hailey's influence was apparent in relation to a draft committee report, which proposed the introduction into the provinces of a purely British Constitution. Hailey informed Irwin that he, in the Cabinet Sub-Committee, advised that 'the report conveyed a wrong picture of the position that must be occupied by the Governor both as discharging the duties laid on him by Parliament and as a co-ordinating factor in his administration'.[57] Subsequently, in private the Prime Minister requested Hailey to make his own suggestions on the matter and Hailey sent him a draft of his views.[58] Hailey advised Irwin, the Chair of the Sub-Committee was consequently 'compelled' to make a number of changes to the committee's draft.

Initially, the British had been optimistic that the Conference would reach important conclusions, agreed by all parties and had tended to go as far as possible to meet Indian positions. A developing sticking point, however, was the Hindu–Muslim relationship. In this context, Hailey was to disabuse the Secretary of State of his view that special concession should be given to the Hindu position at the Conference, in relation to the communal situation, because they were numerically superior to the Muslims in India.[59] By mid-December 1930, Haig was reporting that the increasing breakdown of the Hindu–Muslim relationship was threatening the success of the Conference, and the government would almost inevitably have to decide matters for them. Haig advised Irwin that 'the Prime Minister is alive to the danger of Government making a decision in this matter which would antagonise the Muslims',[60] reflecting Hailey's advice. Haig highlighted Hailey's influence further, at the highest level at the Conference, by stating in the same note.

> Sir Malcolm Hailey's position rather is that, if the two sides cannot reach an agreement, things should be left as they are [one of the suggestions of the Simon Commission which was much resented by Muslims in India]; that, if the existing arrangements are to be torn up and a new situation created, it should be one that could reasonably be justified, and that it is doubtful whether separate electorates with a majority for Muslims in Bengal and the Punjab could really be justified.[61]

As initiatives, the Declaration and Round Table Conference enabled the British to argue their bona fides in genuinely trying to advance constitutional progression. However, their most important interlocutors, the Congress and Gandhi, were not yet ready to engage and in most respects the Conference failed. It is most likely the British realised that, without Congress and Gandhi participating, the Conference was unlikely to achieve the desired outcomes. The Round Table was held, essentially, to demonstrate British willingness to negotiate and to attract their opponents to that process in the form of the second Round Table Conference. Hailey's and Innes' participation at the Conference, was proof of the British Government's regard for the high degree of experience, policy and technical skills held at this senior level of Indian administration. By his selection to attend the Conference, Hailey in particular, had been identified as the expert on Indian affairs of the time, and had by all accounts acquitted his role as one would expect. His colleague, Governor Innes was to confirm this to Irwin.

> Hailey is looking after the Indian side of the Conference and, if I may say so, is doing the work admirably. Had it not been for him, and Stewart[62] and Haig, we should have been landed in some extraordinarily embarrassing situations.[63]

Hailey had worked extremely hard and his illness at the time would have made a demanding task even more difficult.[64]

As observed by Sapru, both Innes and Hailey continued, under other viceroyalties, to influence British policy towards liberal outcomes for India. Commenting on the Third Round Table Conference held in November 1932,

Sapru observed: 'I must say the evidence of Sir Charles Innes...[was] very helpful and made the die-hard element pause a little. Then came...Sir Malcolm Hailey...and I should think Sir Malcolm cast his influence altogether on the side of progress'.[65]

The governors, the Viceroy and the metropolis had failed, in the period 1926 to 1931, effectively to find a constitutional way forward to solve their Indian problem. However, they had prepared the way for further exploration of possible avenues forward in the search for agreement, with the nationalists on constitutional advancement. The next chapters will examine how the governors responded to the direct threat, largely aggravated by this failure, presented to British rule by the Indian nationalist and other critical challenges.

Endnotes

1. Montagu Butler Papers, Butler to his wife, 26 June 1930.
2. *Ibid.*, Butler to his wife, 16 July 1930.
3. Campbell Johnson, *Halifax*, p. 218.
4. Halifax Papers, Simon to Irwin, 16 May 1930.
5. *Ibid.*, Irwin to Simon, 16 February 1929.
6. The Dominion Status Declaration was actually made by Irwin on the evening of 31 October 1929 but became more widely circulated and known the next day, 1 November.

   > In view of the doubts which have been expressed both in Great Britain and India regarding the interpretation to be placed on the intentions of the British Government in enacting the Statute of 1919, I am authorized on behalf of His Majesty's Government to state clearly that in their judgment it is implicit in the declaration of 1917 that the natural issue of India's constitutional progress, as there contemplated, is the attainment of Dominion Status.

7. Halifax Papers, Stephenson to Irwin, 25 September 1928. Enclosure. My italics.
8. *Ibid.*
9. *Ibid.*
10. Campbell Johnson, *Halifax*, p. 219.
11. Halifax Papers, Stephenson to Irwin, 25 September 1928. Enclosure.
12. *Ibid.*
13. Halifax Papers, Irwin to Stephenson, 4 October 1928.
14. *Ibid.*, Irwin to Simon, 16 February 1929.
15. *Ibid.*, Simon to Irwin, 26 February 1929.
16. *Ibid.*

17. *Ibid.*, Irwin to Simon, 27 February 1929.
18. *Ibid.*, Innes to Irwin, 27 October 1929.
19. *Ibid.*, Irwin to Dawson, 21 January 1930.
20. *Hailey Papers*, Irwin to Hailey, 21 November 1929.
21. *Ibid.*, Hailey to Gwynn, 10 April 1930.
22. *Ibid.*, Reading to Hailey, 26 March 1930.
23. Tomlinson, *The Indian National Congress and the Raj*, p. 16.
24. Halifax Papers, Telegram, Viceroy to Secretary of State, 11 August 1930.
25. *Ibid.*
26. *Ibid.*, Telegram, Viceroy to Governor of Madras, 25 August 1930.
27. *Ibid.*, Telegram, Viceroy to Secretary of State, 23 July 1930.
28. *Ibid.*, Irwin to the King-Emperor, 6 November 1929.
29. *Ibid.*, Irwin to Lytton, 9 November 1929.
30. *Ibid.*, Irwin to the King-Emperor, 6 November 1929.
31. *Ibid.*, Irwin to Hailey, 26 November 1929.
32. *Ibid.*, Hailey to Irwin, 4 December 1929.
33. *Ibid.*
34. *Ibid.*, Irwin to Simon, 13 March 1930.
35. *Ibid.*, Telegram, Viceroy to Secretary of State, 2 July 1930.
36. *Ibid.*, Telegram, Secretary of State to Viceroy, 1 September 1930.
37. *Ibid.*, Telegram, Viceroy to Secretary of State, 5 September 1930.
38. Montagu Butler Papers, Butler to his wife, 16 September 1930.
39. Halifax Papers, Innes to Irwin, 6 November 1930. Enclosure.
40. Hailey Papers, Hirtzel to Hailey, 19 June 1930.
41. Halifax Papers, Hailey to Irwin, 26 September 1930.
42. *Report of the Simon Commission*, Volume II, p. 146.
43. Halifax Papers, Hailey to Irwin, 26 September 1930.
44. *Ibid.*
45. See earlier detailed discussion on Irwin's proposal at p. 152 of Chapter 3.
46. Halifax Papers, Hailey to Irwin, 26 September 1930.
47. *Ibid.*, Wedgwood Benn to Irwin, 4 November 1930.
48. *Ibid.*
49. *Ibid.*, Irwin to Innes, 6 October 1930.
50. *Ibid.*, Innes to Irwin, 19 December 1930.
51. *Ibid.*, Innes to Irwin, 20 November 1930.
52. Hailey Papers, Hailey to de Montmorency, 13 November 1930.
53. *New India*, 11 December 1930.
54. Sir H.G. Haig. ICS, 1904. Member of the Governor-General's Executive Council. Later to succeed Hailey as Governor of the United Provinces from 1934 to 1939.
55. Halifax Papers, Haig to Irwin, 27 November 1930.
56. *Ibid.*, Hailey to Irwin, 4 December 1930.
57. *Ibid.*, Hailey to Irwin, 9 December 1930.

58. *Ibid.*
59. *Ibid.*
60. *Ibid.*, Haig to Irwin, 18 December 1930.
61. *Ibid.*
62. Sir S.F. Stewart. India Office. Permanent Under-Secretary of State for India. Secretary to the Simon Commission. Adviser at the 1930 and 1931 Indian Round Table Conferences.
63. Halifax Papers, Innes to Irwin, 19 December 1930.
64. Cell, *Hailey*, p. 178.
65. *Sapru Papers*, Sapru to Sir Mohammad Ahmad Sa'id Khan, K.C.S.I, Governor of the United Provinces, 14 August 1933.

5

Communal Tensions and the Detenu Issue

This chapter will explore two major, interconnected matters of ongoing concern to the Secretary of State, Viceroy and the governors. These were communal tensions and the detenu (or revolutionary prisoners) issue. This will allow an examination of the development of the overall British approach towards these matters and the nature of the respective governors' contributions to the policy processes involved. Inter-communal tensions based on religious prejudice, but partially precipitated by the constitutional reforms of 1909 and 1919, were a significant challenge to Irwin and the governors. The reforms of 1909 had introduced communal electorates, and the reforms of 1919 had extended the religious electoral division. The role of these reforms in aggravating ill-feeling between the major religions is reflected in the fact that between 1900 and 1922 there had been sixteen communal riots, but between 1923 and 1926 there had been seventy-two.[1] The Congress, Gandhi and other nationalist politicians recognised the risks to their goal of independence presented by the communal problem and attempted to allay it; the Congress by encouraging communal harmony, and Gandhi by attempting to encourage the unity of the Indian people through his policy of non-violence. The problem of communal hatred proved intractable and some blamed the British for deliberately aggravating tensions, which had previously largely simmered below the surface, in introducing separate electorates based on religion in order to maintain their political supremacy.[2]

Upon his arrival in India, Lord Irwin was to face the most serious of the forty communal riots that he had to confront in the first twelve months of his viceroyalty.[3] Irwin's first and worst experience of communal rioting occurred in Calcutta, under the jurisdiction of the Governor, Lord Lytton, where the communal situation had been further aggravated by economic decline, terrorism and communist activity. The trouble began on 2 April

1926 over the issue of playing of music by Hindus in front of mosques.[4] By 15 April, Lytton was reporting to Irwin the occurrence of serious street fighting and looting of shops with a large number of people killed.[5] By 25 April, Irwin was reporting to the Secretary of State that armoured cars were being used and that there was a need for the military to act as police sergeants.[6] Showing his sensitivity to the disruption of British commercial interests in Calcutta caused by the disturbances, Irwin advised Lytton of the need for 'the comprehensive scope of the measures taken to suppress disorder'.[7] In the same vein Birkenhead informed Irwin 'that utmost firmness should be shown by the authorities in repressing violent disorders by whatever means may be necessary for the purpose'.[8] The necessity of this approach was duly passed on to Governor Lytton. In dealing with the disorders, and responding to the Secretary of State's concerns, Irwin advised him that 'further emergency powers may be required, as the Goondas Act[9] is not very suitable for emergent measures', and that Bengal was being asked to define what emergency powers might be required. Further, that the Governor considered that incitements to violence appearing in the press and in leaflets needed to be stopped.[10] Lytton had been taking legal advice on aspects of prosecuting the press, and Irwin advised Birkenhead if existing legal power in this area proved ineffective the Governor might ask for further power. Irwin informed Birkenhead that in his view, at the current juncture of the emergency, 'we do not anticipate any question of suspension of control of civil authorities is likely to arise. The present situation demands merely firm and effective action by the Civil Government'.[11]

Despite Irwin's view from Delhi of the relatively moderate degree of response required to deal with the situation Bengal was to ask for emergency powers, to expel bad characters, in the form of an Ordinance. Irwin informed Birkenhead that the Governor of Bengal had advised him that

> Goondas Act is deficient in two respects for dealing with the present emergency: Firstly, procedure is too slow and cumbrous; secondly, the Act does not enable Government to deal with new comers who are potentially a great danger in present state of affairs. Government of Bengal have decided to summon meeting of Legislative Council at once in order to take fresh powers for use only in emergency…But powers are required at once. Bengal has asked that Governor-General should make Ordinance to cover period till Council has met.[12]

As previously indicated Ordinances were only normally issued in situations of emergency and carried with them significant political sensitivity both in India and in Britain. Lytton was to prove not to be particularly attuned to this factor. An examination and comparison of the Bengal, Delhi and Home Government's approach to dealing with the Calcutta riots, including through the emergency measures contained in the Bengal request for an Ordinance, will illustrate their various approaches to how an evident situation of emergency might be dealt with, and the nature of their policy relationship.

Irwin's and his Council's measured response to Lytton's request for an Ordinance is reflected in the Viceroy's advice to Bengal that the Government of India was not 'satisfied such a state of emergency now exists as would justify Ordinance but if satisfied would issue with concurrence of Secretary of State'.[13] To satisfy themselves, the Indian Government requested further information including advice as to when the Bengal Legislative Council was to meet, and the extent to which Bengal would be hampered in dealing with the emergency in the interim. They also put before Lytton a view that a previous issue of an Ordinance might prejudice the chances of securing assent in the Legislative Council to the envisaged Bill and that certification would be unfortunate. It is a consistent theme throughout Irwin's viceroyalty that the use of the power held by a Governor, contained in the 1919 *Government of India Act* (Section 72), to override a majority decision of his Legislative Council to pass legislation by certification, had to be avoided wherever possible. The British wanted to be seen to be complying with their own principles of democracy, at least to deny their opponents an opportunity for criticism.

Irwin advised Lytton:

> ...it is clearly undesirable, unless it is absolutely necessary, that a position should be created, where after I had passed an Ordinance the Bengal Legislature could impliedly condemn my exercise of my discretion by a refusal to implement it by regular legislation of a similar character.[14]

Irwin, no doubt, had taken into account the possible attitude of a swarajist dominated Legislative Council which had engaged in obstructing legislation related to ministers' salaries, and the Bengal Criminal Law Amendment Bill. Although the Government of Bengal had advised that the Governor of Bengal in Council had decided to drop the idea of an Ordinance and to proceed with legislation, they were to reinforce their view that a state of emergency did in fact exist. In the local view, circumstances satisfied the requirements of the 1919 *Government of India Act* for issuance of an Ordinance.[15] However, the Government of India in contrast believed that some calm had been restored in Calcutta at this time[16] and Irwin advised Birkenhead that the situation in Calcutta had returned to normal and all the shops in the disturbed area were open.[17]

The Government of Bengal had already provided Delhi and London with a draft of their proposed Ordinance[18] and advised that their draft of the Bengal Presidency Area (Emergency) Security Bill was substantially identical to the draft Ordinance. On the basis of this draft, the Government of India approved the Bill on 8 May 1926 and it was copied by letter, for information by Bengal, to the Secretary of State on 10 May,[19] and by telegram by Irwin on 15 May.[20] Birkenhead informed Irwin that he had a number of suggested amendments to make to Delhi and Bengal, and that he was particularly sensitive to any possibility of the Governor of Bengal moving to certify the legislation.

> ...it is important that Bill should be so framed that I may be in a position to defend it and deal convincingly with all reasonable criticisms of it in this country. If it is not intended to certify, I should not be disposed to press these points if after consideration they are not adopted.[21]

Birkenhead listed four points for consideration principally related to ensuring the Bill was seen, particularly in the British Parliament, as not draconian. He wished that orders under the future Act be always reviewable, be appellable, have a fixed time limit and be used only against 'hooligan types'. Birkenhead had set out, for both Irwin and Lytton, the wider political framework they had to take into account and within which the governors were required to work. Irwin also asked Bengal whether it was proposed that their Bill be submitted to a Select Committee in this tight time frame and Irwin reinforced the need for Bengal to obtain Birkenhead's specific approval if there was any intention of certification.[22] In the prevailing circumstances of India and of British politics, legislation within the available democratic framework was preferable, for the British, to the extreme measure of an Ordinance. Bengal responded that the Secretary of State's suggested amendments had either already been taken into account or would be included, but there would be no reference to a Select Committee. Lytton had earlier advised Irwin that the Swarajists had decided to oppose the Bill,[23] and if the Bill was refused or if there were any unacceptable amendments then it would be certified by him.[24] The Swarajists had a change of heart, as the Bill was passed by the Council without amendment, except those accepted by the government, and the Governor-General's assent was duly given.[25] In fact Lord Irwin had correctly predicted this result when he advised his friend Geoffrey Dawson, the editor of *The Times* of London that, 'My own anticipation is that having howled for drastic action when the crisis was on they (the Swarajists) will run away from it all; but we shall see'.[26]

While Lytton had requested what might be regarded as extreme measures to deal with emergency, the Viceroy and the Secretary of State were well attuned to the political implications of proceeding to grant them in the form of an Ordinance. This was so despite the seeming contradiction of Birkenhead's reputation as a hard line Conservative. In effect the severity of measures contained in the Bengal Presidency Area (Emergency) Security Act may have varied only by degree from the intended Ordinance. However, presentationally for the British, it was preferable that the Bengal Legislative Council had agreed to laws to combat the emergency situation in Calcutta, within the democratic process available to it. The moderating influence of Irwin and the central government on Bengal was further demonstrated by their approach, towards the sensitive matter of detenu policy, as will be seen, even in the face of emergency. Irwin, at this early stage of his viceroyalty, was contending with difficult matters with little background knowledge, but with the benefit of the support of the experienced ICS, which will be seen further in this chapter.

The matter of the communal problem, principally existing between Hindus and Muslims, not only in Bengal but also across India, was one which drew the concern of Irwin and the governors during the entire period of Irwin's viceroyalty. Communal differences, which also existed between other groupings such as the Sikhs and Muslims, complicated British attempts to solve the Indian political situation.[27] While communal competition may have suited any policy of divide and rule, actual violence contradicted the concept of the *Pax Britannica* and any view that the British were a civilising influence. Communal disharmony also gave opportunity to people regarded as terrorists by the British, which in turn provided further complication to a resolution of the detenu issue.

Having been in India only a matter of weeks, Irwin had sought advice from the experienced Governor of Burma, Sir Harcourt Butler, as to the appropriateness of the Viceroy making a personal appeal to the two major communities for peace, the content of any speech and its timing.[28] Butler agreed it would be useful for the Viceroy to say something, even though it might not be in the overall interests of British political advantage and advised, 'The communal situation is always difficult…I agree with your Excellency that on a suitable occasion something should be said'.[29]

Irwin was to follow Butler's advice, less than a month later on 17 July 1926, when he found an appropriate occasion at the Chelmsford Club, in Simla, to address representatives of all the communities of India in an appeal for peace between them. Interestingly Pandit Madan Mohan Malaviya was present to listen to the Viceroy just a few days before experiencing the wrath of the Bengal Government. This event will also be discussed.[30] In his speech, Irwin indicated that the responsibility for communal peace lay in the communities, but where trouble arose it would be dealt with as appropriate by local authority. He did not reveal any role he was likely to take, personally, in directly influencing and determining the degree and the nature of local action towards disorder and emergency, as had occurred in Bengal. Alexander Muddiman, at that time Home Member in the Government of India, recorded in his file note:

> H.E. the Viceroy in his recent speech at the Chelmsford Club, Simla made it clear…the remedy…is not to be sought in legislation but in an improvement in the mutual attitude of the leaders and the members of the communities at variance.[31]

The important elements of the Viceroy's speech matched the advice on the communal issue which Hailey had earlier sent to de Montmorency, then the Viceroy's Private Secretary. Hailey had stressed the importance of communal leaders taking the initiative themselves, without viceregal intervention, and 'the impossibility for the Government of India to develop an all-India policy because there are too many variables'.[32] Hailey later observed Irwin's approach had 'really done some good' because his speech had been delivered with a 'high and serious tone…[which] appealed to the Indian imagination, and delivered on this plane, has managed to put them in the wrong without provoking the usual recriminations'.[33]

During 1927 the problem of a solution to the communal difficulties in India continued to exercise the Viceroy's mind. In June, Irwin had circulated to five of the governors a detailed proposal, including for a joint conference between Hindu and Muslim leaders, which he acknowledged had been developed by de Montmorency, his Private Secretary who was to become Governor of the Punjab in August 1928, and Hailey.[34] The proposal's objective was to convince the leaders 'to compose their more virulent differences'. It suggested a complementary and simultaneous approach could be made to the major religious leaders and the heads of great sects and shrines. Indeed historically '…in linking the power of the state to rural hierarchies of mediation, the British had developed a structure for incorporating local authorities and cultures into their empire'.[35] For example, in the case of the Muslims of the Punjab, this had occurred through 'the hereditary custodians of the *sufi* [Muslim ascetic mystic] shrines, men known usually as *sajjada nishins* [literally, those who "sit on the prayer carpet"]'.[36]

In considering the proposal, Irwin acknowledged the difficulty in separating religious and political motives in the Indian communities which may have 'become inextricably mixed in the political discord'. Hailey and de Montmorency had identified three practical considerations to be examined in the context of how to address the problem of allaying communal differences. First, the need for the British to identify the attitude of the two major religious groups towards communal electorates, in order to be properly prepared for the Simon Commission.[37] Second, whether there was anything the Viceroy could do, from an administrative aspect, to prevent communal disturbance? Third, apart from constitutional or administrative matters was there anything else which could be done? [38]

As to the first consideration the governors were aware that the terms of the 1916 Lucknow Pact between Congress and the Muslim League, which had recognised separate electorates, was again under current discussion between the parties. There were, therefore, disadvantages in the Viceroy's offering a conference in circumstances where the government might be asked to agree to an outcome reached between the communities, which the government could not support in the context of the Simon Commission. As regards administrative measures, which might be taken, the proposal pointed out the complexity presented by the diversity of the religious composition of different provinces. Certain administrative measures might provide a solution in one province but not in another. 'For example, for the Punjab it might suffice to have it generally accepted that…a Muslim could sacrifice a cow in a Muslim quarter of town…'.[39]

The governors' proposal pointed out it was only in a reduced communal temperature that 'administrative tonics can be calmly discussed and administered'. They underlined that Indian politicians would be of little assistance as 'they are generally accused by the public of having accentuated the communal view point in order to strengthen individual parties or personal followings'. The proposal identified, however, one class of Indians which did not concern itself with politics, secular advantage or preferment but only on 'the purely religious side of religion as opposed to its communal and practical aspects in the mass of the people'.[40] The two governors saw the heads of the great sects and shrines as the men of real eminence, whom the British had appealed to in the past in relation to the suppression of Sati, the building of the Ganges canal and the enlistment of Muslims in the First World War to fight the Turks.

> Among those of eminence we can bank on religious grounds on some feeling of respect for the King-Emperor as semi-divine according to Hindu ideas and as entitled to obedience as head of State for the time as enjoyed by Muslim scriptures.[41]

It was on this pivot that Hailey and de Montmorency believed that the representative of the King-Emperor in India could do something to improve communal relations. As these important religious leaders were seen as too sacrosanct to leave their establishments for a conference the proposal recommended that they would have to be addressed by a formally delivered message from the Viceroy. His letter would set out the background to the communal problem and to the king's view of the impact of religious disharmony in India. It would include reference to the monarch's sentiments set out in the Royal Proclamation, announcing assent to the *Government of India Bill* on 23 December 1919, such as the 'need for mutual forbearance between all sections and races of my people in India'. Reference would also be made to the Instrument of Instructions to governors in which they were required to encourage religious toleration, cooperation and goodwill, and to Queen Victoria's Proclamation which identified religious toleration as a keystone of British policy. The letter would incorporate a personal message from the Viceroy appealing to the revered religious leaders of India, asking that they use their special influence to achieve communal peace and harmony.

In response to the ideas of Hailey and de Montmorency, Montagu Butler advised Irwin that an appeal to religious leaders would have too many practical difficulties basically because the test of religion in India was not personal conduct. 'I doubt if there are many holy men of eminence who regard it as their mission to influence conduct, nor do people look to them for guidance in this respect'.[42] Butler was not in favour of a direct appeal but believed references to the matter in the Viceroy's speeches, such as at the Chelmsford Club, did great good. An additional smaller complication, indicating some governors' sympathies in the Punjab for the communities had also been identified by Butler. He informed his wife that a leading Hindu had written him 'a hint that the Hindus feel they will not be safe in the Punjab so long as Hailey and de Montmorency are in league with the Muslims'.[43] Governor Stephenson also believed the direct result of an appeal by the Viceroy in his province would be small, and a conference would provide too many complications. Again Stephenson was to refer to the benefit of the Viceroy's Chelmsford Club speech.[44] Sir Leslie Wilson, in Bombay, advised, 'in any discreet enquiries which I have made, I find a great diversity of opinion as to the best course to adopt to deal with the communal differences between Hindus and Muhammadans'.[45] He also felt a conference had fundamental difficulties and that the likely adverse reaction of Indian political leaders to any attempt to elicit interference by India's religious heads would further complicate matters.

Taking these viewpoints into account, Irwin informed all the governors that 'after much consideration I have decided to address the two houses of the Legislature on 29 August upon the communal question...'.[46] As a consequence of the governors' advice, Irwin dropped the idea of approaching religious leaders. He indicated to the governors that he would suggest in his speech his willingness, nevertheless, to convene a conference if the responsible leaders of the great communities thought it useful. Marris responded with a view doubting that any conference would be of use in achieving religious harmony.[47] Harcourt Butler from Burma, perhaps faced with a different communal situation, was to congratulate the Viceroy on his intent.[48] Jackson does not appear to have responded to the consideration of the communal issue.

India's ingrained communal difficulties continued in the future to complicate British rule and were beyond the powers of Irwin and the governors to resolve. Interestingly Lord Lytton does not seem to have contributed to the development of the initiative to resolve the communal problem at the broader level. In an environment of communal antagonism, terrorism and revolution were more easily able to flourish, as Lytton was to experience. It was also often difficult for the British to distinguish between these elements of challenge, particularly in the context of an appropriate response to each of them as they tended to overlap.

Before the Government of India had reported to London in early May 1926 that the communal troubles in Bengal were largely over, Lytton had suggested to Irwin that they should meet, as soon as possible, to discuss the Calcutta situation and also other policy issues concerning Bengal and Delhi.[49] Against the background of the controversy[50] caused by Lytton's absence from Calcutta in Darjeeling, his hill station retreat, for a considerable period during the height of the rioting, Irwin agreed subject to Lytton's being confident that the emergency had passed.[51]

Lytton prepared a memorandum of their discussions, held in Simla from 8 to 10 May, which Irwin cleared before the Bengal Governor copied it to Lord Birkenhead.[52] The two headings in the note which concern this chapter are: The Calcutta Riots and the Emergency Bill proposed by the Government of Bengal, and the Bengal Detenus. Discussion in relation to the Calcutta communal riots was dealt with quickly and was essentially an explanation by Lytton of why he had decided to drop the request for an Ordinance. His request had related to the complication of the police, under Section 55 of the Criminal Procedure, having no power to detain the large numbers of men arrested for more than a day or two unless an Ordinance had been issued. In the event, Bengal had been able to bluff these men into leaving Calcutta and thus the problem had been solved by a far less stringent method than the use of an Ordinance.

By far the most extensive matter discussed, in the context of communalism and revolution aggravating and feeding one off the other, was the question of policy towards the so-called detenus or revolutionary prisoners. Around 100 were held in Bengal jails and a similar number were under restricted movement. British intelligence had identified three distinct and overarching terrorist groups in Bengal and with connections to communism.[53] The New Violence Party, the Anushilan Samiti, and the Jugantar Party, were dedicated to the violent overthrow of British rule. Their numbers were very small with no 'more than 3,000 active members of all Bengal terrorist parties at any one time'.[54] The death toll inflicted by the terrorists was also relatively small with eleven British officials and ten non-officials killed in 1930.[55] However, while the threat of terrorist attack remained the British were forced 'to be more conciliatory to the non-terrorist nationalists [i.e., Congress]',[56] and thus terrorism influenced 'Congress policy in an increasingly activist and demanding direction'.[57] In other words Congress was able to take advantage of the British position by increasing the pressure of their political demands.

At his meeting with Lytton the Viceroy advised that the question of the detenus needed to be considered against a background of the Secretary of State's having given assurances, to a deputation of Labour Members of Parliament, that he would have Irwin review the question upon arrival in India. The matter of policy relating to the holding of large numbers of prisoners arrested in Bengal for revolutionary activity, and the renewal of the Bengal Criminal Law Amendment Act (BCLAA),[58] under which they were held, became a major area of difference between Irwin and his Bengal governors. These imprisonments had been effected without trial under Section 11, (1) (f) of the BCLAA, 1925, which was even possible where there was only suspicion of terrorist intent. In their first exchange on the matter Irwin advised Lytton he was bound to be guided by Bengal, but wished to improve their tactical position given the Act was temporary, might not be renewed and would expire in early 1930. Lytton was asked whether it was Bengal's intention to keep the men in custody for the full five years of the Act and if not to identify the circumstances in which they might be released. Lord Lytton explained it was only under the most overwhelming proof of conspiracy to murder that he, the previous Viceroy Lord Reading, and Ramsay Macdonald, the Prime Minister at the time, had agreed to imprisonment without trial. The Governor advised it was his desire to release all those who could reasonably be believed would refrain from revolutionary activities but that he would require a guarantee from them to this effect. Lord Lytton advised the Viceroy it would only be in the context of the formation of a strong nationalist party within the Legislative Council, with which it would be possible to negotiate, following the November 1926 Indian elections, that a settlement leading to release might be achieved. This might occur in the circumstances of a swarajist victory and an offer to take office on certain terms, or a swarajist defeat and a non-swarajist ministry being sworn in, although in the latter situation a settlement might be more difficult.[59]

In a further attempt to resolve the matter, the Viceroy again sought policy advice, in August 1926, on the subject of the detenus from Sir Hugh Stephenson, who was acting Governor of Bengal during Lytton's absence on leave in England at that time. Stephenson was a member of the Bengal Governor's Executive Council and was to be appointed Governor of Bihar and Orissa in 1927. He was to suggest

> ...that Government should make a formal announcement that we are willing to release any of the detenus who will give an explicit undertaking—with or without sureties—that they will abstain from revolutionary activities, provided that Government is satisfied with the sincerity of the undertaking given.[60]

However, Stephenson was to go on to advise Irwin of the essential impracticality of this proposal. First, in reality the detenus, for a number of reasons, would be very reluctant to give any explicit undertaking. Second, in Bengal there really was or would not be any party or party leaders with whom a deal could be done. Third, there was no possibility of the Legislative Council passing a permanent measure, in relation to the detenus, of however restricted a nature. Finally, such an agreement would be regarded as being extremely one sided and in favour of the government. Stephenson advised Lord Lytton's proposal, that a deal could be done as the result of the emergence of a strong party, foundered in his view as in fact it would be most unlikely there would be any political entity, after the Indian elections, with which to achieve an accommodation. Stephenson was reduced to admitting:

> I confess I see no immediate solution and the communal tension has given added strength and opportunities to the revolutionary party. I can only pin my faith to individual bargains with detenus and to a general improvement of the situation economically and politically when the communal tension dies down.[61]

That Irwin continued to mull over his Bengal governors' policy advice is evidenced by Irwin's request, at the end of November 1926 referring to their May discussions, to Lytton, returned from England, to keep him closely advised of any decisions on the approach to detenus before commitments were made.[62] Days later Irwin was to request another meeting in Calcutta with Lytton, in company with Alexander Muddiman, Home Member and his senior ICS adviser. The meeting was called to discuss the BCLAA, the issue of the detenus held under that Act and under Regulation III (of 1818), proposals of the Bengal Government for further press legislation, and conditions in Bengal jails.[63] By then Irwin was informing Sir Stanley Jackson, who replaced Lytton in March 1927, that 'I suppose Bengal is probably the most difficult of all the governments out here and you will have a great many tiresome things to handle'.[64] Irwin confirmed to Jackson that the most 'tiresome' matter was the question of the Bengal detenus.

Irwin and Muddiman met Lytton and his officials, to discuss Bengal problems and proposals on 10 December 1926, but it wasn't until after their next meeting, in January 1927, that their continuing tensions on detenu policy really emerged. However, at the beginning of August 1926, Acting Governor Stephenson in Council, had taken a decision, in relation to the communal situation in Bengal, which must have contributed to Irwin's view that Bengal was indeed the most difficult of provinces. On 3 August Stephenson was to advise that, in the face of the gravity of the communal situation then existing in Bengal, new powers were necessary to deal with the circumstances. The Government of India was informed that 'full powers to restrain communal incitement by the Press and secondly, restraint of dangerous leaders',[65] were required. Bengal advised also that, in pursuance of their policy, orders had been obtained, under Section 144 of the Code of Criminal Procedure, prohibiting Malaviya and Moonje [66] from entering Calcutta where they intended to give, what was feared would be, inflammatory speeches on 4 August. Bengal also requested a warrant under Regulation III of 1818 against Sahid Suhrawardy [67] and measures against the press along the lines of the 1910 Press Act.

The Bengal Government's policy approach towards Malaviya, Moonje and Suhrawardy, drew separate responses of reprimand both from the Viceroy on 8 August, and senior officials of the Government of India on 10 August.[68] Delhi was most concerned that there had been no reference to them before action, particularly given the all-India implications for other provinces and on the general political situation, even though the Viceroy recognised 'that this matter technically was within the discretion of your Government'. Stephenson was to apologise for the Bengal Government's actions in not previously consulting the central government.[69]

The file record of how senior British officials of the Government of India regarded Bengal's approach is particularly illuminating in a number of respects. James Crerar was to record, 'I am entirely opposed to the use of

Regulation III as a general means of dealing with communal disturbances. Suhrawaddy is a non-entity...we should be using a sledge hammer to deal with a worm'.[70] He felt the proper approach was for the police to keep him under surveillance and make an arrest under the ordinary law. The objectivity of Crerar's judgement, in relation to the severity of the measures used, is contained in his words.

> ...much as I regret not to be able to support the recommendation of a Government presided over by an administrator who is a personal friend and for whom I have the greatest respect, I cannot do other than endorse the view taken in the Home Secretary's able note.[71]

Muddiman, the Home Secretary (member) felt that Bengal's need to consult was obvious

> ...from the fact that the use of Regulation III of 1818 against a Muhammadan was to be pendant to the order under Section 144 of the Criminal Procedure Code against a Hindu and of course the action under the Regulation could be only carried out by the Government of India. Did I not know Sir Hugh Stephenson too well to entertain the idea I should have been suspicious that the Bengal Government were trying to force our hand by precipitate action under Section 144.[72]

Muddiman believed there was a need for a sufficient police and military force, and that the ordinary law should be steadily and fairly enforced to assist conciliation and resist violence. Charles Innes, then a member of the Governor-General's Council was a little more acerbic.

> The Malaviya incident...seems to have been a blunder of the first magnitude... quite intolerable that it [an order under Section 144] should have been issued without prior consultation...What we ought to aim at is the creation of conditions in which confidence will be restored and in which a spirit of toleration has some chance of growing up. These conditions can be created in my opinion only by the steady pressure of patient, firm, impartial Government.[73]

The tone and nature of these comments by Crerar, Muddiman and Innes, as senior ICS advisors, the latter two to become governors, can be seen as a good indication of their moderate and generally conciliatory influence on all-India policy making, and including on the approach adopted generally by Lord Irwin towards Indian nationalism. Their views and policy approach reflected a culture, in the senior reaches of the ICS, of acting within the law of the time and concern for an appropriately moderate response to extremism, reinforced by an awareness of the need to nurture Indians who would collaborate with the Raj. The senior ICS, headquartered in Delhi (and elsewhere) and Irwin thus had essentially complementary approaches to these issues and problems. Evidently, they were also not inclined to any sympathetic bias towards members of their own cadre, even those in difficulties. It is not unreasonable to assume they would carry these attitudes and principles into their governorships.

Crerar's acknowledgement of the need 'to avoid any unnecessary irritation to a local government who, we must allow, has been severely tried throughout the hot weather' to some degree differentiates the operating circumstances of Calcutta from Delhi and Simla. But there was no acknowledgement of the provincial government being better placed, perhaps, to judge the appropriate reaction to their local circumstances. In the case of Malaviya and Moonje, Stephenson had advised the Viceroy, emphatically of a very strong local view held by 'law abiding citizens and trade and commerce that the provincial government should prevent wire pullers using inflammable material to further their political and personal ends'.[74] Malaviya had after all given an inflammatory speech in Calcutta on 30 June to the Durwan Association whose members had taken part in the Calcutta riots.[75] However, a demonstration of the importance of the central government's acting in a coordinating role for local governments, to ensure an all-India view and response, is contained in a communication on Malaviya and Moonje from Montagu Butler. The Governor advised Irwin, on 12 August, his 'old friend' Malaviya had been in his province on his responsive cooperation tour and, but for the events in Bengal, he would have invited him to stay at Government House. Butler also expressed astonishment at the 'extraordinary' action taken by Bengal against 'Dr Munje', which 'is hardly calculated to encourage others to join in cooperating with Government in working the constitution'.[76] This comment is a clear indication of the British policy of maximising the opportunity for collaboration, and for nurturing friends in the Indian political class, within a moderate and conciliatory approach to political provocation. It was only within this peaceful environment that the constitution could be properly worked. Developments in Bengal had also exasperated the India Office. 'That ass Lytton defends himself for having remained at Darjeeling...the Bengal Government are making an even greater hash of things in his absence'.[77]

Further evidence of the nature of the relationship existing between the senior echelons of the British administration and some leading Indian nationalists is identified by Nanda. 'High British officials enjoyed Motilal's [Nehru] company and were recipients of his hospitality; one of them, Sir

Harcourt Butler...claimed in 1920 "a friendship of thirty years standing" with him'.[78] It was also claimed that Butler 'had provided him [Nehru] with maple furniture and champagne in gaol'.[79] Butler also knew Gokhale,[80] and had recommended him as Education Member.[81] Given the nature of the governors' role it is perhaps not surprising that they developed personal relationships of varying degree with their nationalist interlocutors over the years. These associations would have been likely to have moderated reciprocal attitudes and actions between them.

Central government intelligence had understood the importance of nurturing friends to ensure cooperation and for support for measured constitutional advance, and thus of Malaviya and Moonje to British interests. In the face of the attitude of the Viceroy and central government to what they regarded was Bengal's mistaken policy towards Malaviya and Moonje, reinforced by both provincial and central government legal advice that the Bengal prosecution was likely to fail, the Bengal Executive Council was to withdraw the prosecution of the two men, but only by a majority of one.[82] This narrow majority can be seen as indicative of an underlying provincial view that strong action had in fact been necessary in their circumstances.

As previously referenced, Irwin and Lytton were to meet again in Calcutta, at the beginning of January 1927 to discuss detenu policy, and a first point of difference emerged shortly thereafter. When commenting on a draft speech Irwin intended to make to his Assembly, which contained reference to the detenu question, Lytton advised him that if he could not accept his amendment then all reference to detenu policy should be dropped. 'I cannot agree to release men whom we still believe to be dangerous merely because other people, however influential, have expressed the opinion that there would be no danger'.[83] Lytton's security advisers, Moberly and Tegart, had strongly put to him their view that there should be no reference in the Viceroy's speech to detenu policy. Even so, Irwin was to advise the Secretary of State that he would restate detenu policy in his speech in general terms,[84] and reminded Lytton.

> I do feel very strongly that the policy of wider arrest ought to proceed simultaneously with the policy of cautious release, and I don't think that we should very easily, in the face of the apparent improvement of conditions, defend the position of greatly extended arrest with no movement in the direction of release.[85]

Lytton's unhappiness with the Government of India was emphatically advised, towards the end of January 1927, with the words 'I have been disturbed recently by several circumstances regarding our policy towards the Bengal detenus'.[86] These 'circumstances' related to telegrammed advice received from the Government of India that Bengal's proposed policy had failed to carry the understanding arrived at in the January conference with the Viceroy in Calcutta. In response Lytton informed Irwin:

> ...it was agreed between us that the fresh arrests and the conditional releases were inseparable items of the same policy, and I further agree with you that it would be unwise for the arrests to precede the releases by more than a short interval. The Government of India telegram proposed that the releases should precede the arrest. Our letter had proposed that the arrests should precede the releases. I think the solution is to be found in the words of your letter to me of January 19, namely, that the two should proceed simultaneously...[87]

The Irwin/Lytton policy, although not entirely agreed between them, was being driven by British and Indian public opinion and politicians who found it odious that men could be held indefinitely without trial. The policy of arrest and release meant that the government could argue that overall prisoner numbers were not increasing, prisoners were being released and terrorism was being controlled. Lytton was most concerned to be able to act on his own judgement, making the point to Irwin, 'you will agree, I am sure, that our discretion in such use of the powers of the Bengal Criminal Law Amendment Act should not be fettered by the Government of India'.[88]

The relationship between the Governor of Bengal and the Government of India was to be further tested by Irwin's decision, despite Bengal's 'grave reluctance', to release unconditionally five of the Regulation III prisoners. Also, Irwin was to advise Birkenhead 'we have declined to agree to a system of conditional release and residence in remote Provinces recommended by Bengal for certain Regulation III prisoners'.[89] Lytton's extreme irritation with Irwin's Regulation III policy, which was strictly within the Viceroy's field of authority, was advised in the strongest terms.

> I was greatly disturbed by the receipt of a letter from the Government of India ordering the immediate release of Jiban Lal Chatterjee [90] and release of four other Regulation III detenus within a short time. I must protest strongly against these, and if they are insisted on, I cannot be responsible for consequences. It is useless to talk of resignation on the eve of my departure, but if the Government of India had taken this line at any time during the last three years, I should have felt compelled to resign.[91]

Lytton had once again revealed his penchant for threatening resignation in the face of difficulties. He indicated that these Regulation III men were the terrorist leaders and the first to be arrested and should be the last to be released. Lytton informed Irwin that since their January meeting in Calcutta there had been a net reduction of twelve detenus in prison, and that he would accept a direction to accelerate releases if progress was not regarded as satisfactory.

> ...but I must protest against claim of Government of India to select individuals. Jiban is a most dangerous man...I beg of you not to impose unwelcome instructions on us in a matter so vitally affecting the maintenance of order in this Province.[92]

In his response, Irwin reminded Lytton that action under Regulation III was taken on the sole responsibility of the Governor-General in Council, and therefore he had statutory obligations to fulfil, but he had paid the most careful attention to Bengal's views. Replying, Lytton referred to another layer of difficulty which, he believed, existed between them on the detenu issue, namely the role of their civil services in complicating matters: '...when we meet and talk we seem to be in complete agreement, but as soon as we are at a distance our respective Governments seem to be carried further away from each other by every communication which passes between them'.[93] Nevertheless, Lytton was to indicate forcefully that the unexpected demand of the Government of India for the immediate release of individuals was a departure from agreed policy, but despite his earlier threat to resign, Lytton was not irreconcilable, acknowledging the strong tenor of his earlier letter, indicating:

> I know you will not judge me by the term of a phrase and will forgive any fault in the tone of my letter by remembering that I am writing under difficulties and have been most profoundly disturbed by the latest communication we received from the Government of India. I do trust that with your help matters can still be adjusted agreeably to both of us.[94]

Before responding to Lytton, advising that he was unable to change his policy, Irwin was to set out the full history of the situation before the Secretary of State, which he copied to Bengal, seeking his rhetorical assurance 'that our policy and attitude in this matter towards Bengal has your support'.[95] Consequently, in a statement, setting out progress in relation to the detenus, made to the Legislative Assembly in early March 1927, Irwin committed himself, as it turned out prematurely, to releasing four of the five Regulation III prisoners who were of concern to Lytton.[96] He was to indicate also that the release of one other of the Regulation III prisoners was still under consideration on medical grounds. Even in the face of London's strongly implied endorsement of Irwin's policy, Lytton continued his emphatic opposition to the release of the five Regulation III prisoners and in particular Jiban Lal Chatterjee, who Bengal regarded as most dangerous. Surprisingly, at this stage, Lytton introduced a new but very important consideration, namely that of the real prospect of the releases endangering the British security network in Bengal.

> ...we could not agree to their being set free in Bengal when we have good reason to believe that their immediate object would be the murder of our agents. We are bound to protest in the strongest manner possible against our being forced to take such action...[97]

Lytton was receiving, verbally, highly sensitive information from his police adviser Tegart, and also Moberley, in relation to detenus, including the Regulation III prisoners in question. The information because of its highly sensitive nature had not been in the correspondence with Irwin. In the case of Chatterjee, the intelligence indicated that if he were released then an important police agent would be placed in serious risk. In this situation Lytton repeated his hope 'you will feel yourself able to leave to our discretion the actual selection of individuals in applying any policy which may be agreed from time to time between our respective Governments'.[98]

Irwin was to give way and advise the Secretary of State

> ...in deference to his [Lytton's] very strong remonstrance we have agreed that these [four Regulation III prisoners who Irwin had wished to release unconditionally] should be transferred to the operation of the Bengal Criminal Law Amendment Act, by which means, if the Bengal Government can establish a case for further detention, it will be possible for the Government to release them conditionally, which of course is not possible under Regulation III... We are still arguing about one individual in regard to whom Lytton seems to be taking rather an exaggerated view.[99]

That Lytton won the argument on Chatterjee also, is contained in a telegram to Lytton from Irwin advising 'we are accepting your views and are communicating officially agreeing that he (Jiban) should be placed under the Bengal Criminal Law Amendment Act'.[100] The sting from Lytton on the detenu issue, in an otherwise pleasant and friendly farewell letter to Irwin, written from on board the *S.S. Genoa* in early April 1927, is contained in the words 'I hope if a similar situation develops in the future that you will get the local people up to talk to you before you decide to overrule them on a matter on which they feel so strongly'.[101]

This episode reveals the Viceroy's willingness to bend under strong representation from the governors. It may also be reflective of Irwin's consistent personal tendency towards reasonableness and conciliation in his dealings with interlocutors, both difficult British colleagues and Indian nationalists. The differing approaches of the Governments of India and of Bengal to the various security and emergency issues facing them, including the communal riots, terrorism and detenus, and the amplification of these difficulties in the press is explained at least to some degree by the different perceptions they had of their own responsibilities towards these problems. There is little doubt that Bengal's early attitude was flavoured by Lord Lytton's unusual character but it can be said that his approach, taking the part of a man who saw his responsibility as being for the peace and tranquility of his province, on the face of it, was not unreasonable. Again, it was odd, given his position on the need to share sensitive information face to face that he had not advised Irwin of this concern earlier. In Lytton's favour it may be said he had also been consistent, across viceroyalties, on his approach to security matters. His posture towards Irwin was not simply derived from his jaundiced view of Indian affairs, and the fact that he could see the date of his imminent departure. He had taken almost the same position on terrorism much earlier in his governorship with the then Viceroy, Lord Reading. Lytton had, before Irwin's time, advised Birkenhead of a strong difference with Reading in relation to the Mirzapur Street bomb case over the issue of the re-trial of the accused who had been acquitted. Lytton had decided not to proceed with a re-trial for fear of compromising his intelligence network. Lytton had also had differences with Reading over requests for an Ordinance which he (Lytton) intended to use instead of Regulation III, to give him the power to imprison without trial on the basis of secret evidence of guilt.[102] Interestingly, there is no evidence Lytton had used his privilege of communicating direct with the Secretary of State, during his governorship, to actively or directly seek to influence him against Reading's or Irwin's approach and decisions on Bengal security or other policy matters. Rather he had used the avenue, in his interests, to raise issues of mainly personal concern such as leave and emoluments.

It must be said that Irwin's attitude, to these matters of difference with Lytton was also understandable. There was clear need for the Centre to coordinate policy towards terrorism and other emergency and security issues in India. Given his view across all of India, Irwin was obviously better placed to develop and coordinate approaches which maximised benefit and minimised complication to the range of British Indian provinces on these matters. Importantly, Irwin was also conscious of the need for Indian administrators to comply with the standards of public opinion, in relation to the treatment of offenders, expressed in the British Parliament and press and relayed to him by secretaries of state. Irwin had to take account of both British and Indian politics in adequately dealing with emergency in India and it was not just a security issue for him. Irwin's firmness in dealing with Bengal on security matters, given his relative lack of experience at the beginning of his viceroyalty, is noteworthy. Even so he could display flexibility when presented with good arguments.

Sir Francis Stanley Jackson replaced Lord Lytton on 28 March 1927 with only a fifteen minute conversation with his predecessor to assist the handover.[103] However, Irwin was to make up for this by setting out for Jackson, in very clear terms and against the background of previous disagreements with Lytton, the need for the closest cooperation between them on security matters in Bengal. In informing Jackson that he was ready to consider fully the views of the Bengal Government, Irwin set out the parameters of their future relationship by advising Jackson.

> ...it has struck me...the Government of Bengal were not always content with stating fully and forcibly their views, but have been disposed some times to put their case so high that their views were in danger of overlooking the responsibility that attaches to the Government of India.[104]

Without any reference to any personal role Lord Lytton may have had in contributing to the often difficult relationship which had developed between their governments, Irwin identified his view to Jackson that senior Bengal police had had a disproportionate influence on Bengal policy.[105] Irwin then set out for Jackson their governments' respective responsibilities for the administration of the BCLAA and Regulation III, which had created such differences of opinion. While indicating no wish to interfere unnecessarily in decisions on the treatment of individuals held under the Bengal Act, there were certain prisoners such as Subhas Chandra Bose[106] and Satyendra Chandra Mitra,[107] 'whose importance extends beyond the limits of Bengal'. Irwin indicated in the case of such men that Bengal and the Government of India needed to cooperate in the closest way, to avoid the embarrassment caused to his Government and the Secretary of State by the Bengal Government's recent offer of terms to Bose without consultation. That the Viceroy and the Government of India also sometimes erred is evidenced by an apology from Irwin to Birkenhead for not consulting with London on the conditions of release for one Jadu Gopal Mukharjee,[108] a Regulation III prisoner, involving him residing in England.[109]

Birkenhead had chosen the same day as Irwin to provide his own advice to Jackson on how affairs should be run in Bengal.[110] Birkenhead first made reference to the 'severe wigging' he had given Bengal for their mishandling of the Bose case and suggested to Jackson that the balance of advantage was in freeing Bose, and that it should be done promptly. Birkenhead then advised he had been shown a letter, which he copied to Jackson in quotation marks, from a Bengali Hindu politician to a friend, which was self-explanatory in its implications for Jackson and his rule. The letter indicated that Bengal was almost in a hopelessly chaotic condition, the Governor's Executive Council was weak and self-interested, and that no one had had any regard for Lytton. The letter's pertinent advice to Jackson was contained in the words:

> The next Governor, if he wants to bring back normal conditions in Bengal will have to rule...and give his immediate attention to (1) the Muslim question, (2) the rural problem of the scarcity of drinking water, (3) malaria and Kalaaza,[111] (4) primary education, (5) development of local self-Government including the affairs of the Calcutta Corporation. In order to achieve this, the new Governor will have to gain the confidence of officials and non-officials, take Cabinet into his confidence, infuse energy, repose trust in his well-wishers and take help and advice from the Europeans. He should spend more time in Calcutta and less in Darjeeling.[112]

Birkenhead closed his letter without comment, after the quoted text, leaving one to wonder whether Birkenhead himself had had any role in composing or directing the preparation of such a set of explicit and pertinent instructions. Jackson could not have had any doubt that the Secretary of State agreed with the letter's contents, and the need for him to work hard to compensate for Lytton's failures. Jackson, in response to Irwin's 'guidance' on how their two administrations should interact, informed Irwin 'I will do my best to assure that in future, when the Government of Bengal are called upon to state their case, it is as near as possible in accordance with the actual facts of the position'.[113]

Birkenhead, Irwin and Jackson were then to focus on how best to deal with Bose, who was then imprisoned, on Bengal's behalf, in Burma. Birkenhead advised Irwin his

> ...own instinct was to release him unconditionally of our own accord before we are driven to do so by his increasing illness and by public opinion, but whatever is done must be done quickly and I should like to be able to announce a definite decision in Parliament next Monday.[114]

Irwin was to ask for Jackson's views 'in regard to policy of Secretary of State's suggestion'. Jackson responded that a critical point was to determine the true state of Bose's health and he was sending his surgeon, Major Hingson, for this purpose. 'If the report about his health is unsatisfactory, as I expect it to be, I should recommend that he be released. My inclination is that on balance it would be well worth the risk'.[115] Jackson indicated he had overruled his police advisers in their view that Bose should be deported out of India to recover his health, which was worsening. He requested the Viceroy's approval of Bose, who was being transferred to Calcutta, being released unconditionally. Irwin advised Jackson of his agreement, that he would be seeking Birkenhead's concurrence and that the Governor should make the announcement of any release.[116] Birkenhead was to agree and to repeat that the release must be done quickly, and not be seen as coming as the result of Parliamentary pressure as then no-one would receive credit for the decision.[117] Jackson confirmed Bose's serious condition and he was duly released, to his family in Calcutta.

Jackson soon afterwards advised Irwin he was considering further releases given the prevailing good atmosphere but the police were rather 'sticky'. He had asked them for a list showing the order in which they thought prisoners might be freed.[118] Jackson asked for Irwin's approval for a policy of faster release and specifically for the release of Satyendra Mitra, the Assembly member. He advised Irwin he had told Sakar, the Swarajist whip in the Bengal Legislative Council, it would help if his party 'would get up and declare *emphatically* against any sort of violence'.[119] Jackson also indicated that Tegart believed the terrorists were still well organised in Dacca and Chittagong and the Governor felt the arrest of terrorist gangs there would demonstrate 'our power and vigilance, and also that the activities of the police are approved'. Irwin informed Jackson of his 'complete agreement on the policy to be pursued',[120] including with respect to Regulation III prisoners, and that there should be no general amnesty but a policy of continuing steady release. Irwin was able to advise the Secretary of State that on 17 June 1927 there were 38 men in jail, down from 72 on 15 January, with 11 held under Regulation III.[121] The British practice was to release prisoners first into home or village domicile and then, depending on their good record, to unconditionally free them. Part of Jackson's policy was to find jobs for these men to assist them avoid becoming recidivists. Jackson, revealing his sensitivity towards his relationship with his police, informed Irwin, that it was his preference, for example with Satyendra Mitra, to carry the security men with him, in the application of their agreed policy, and not to overrule them.[122] By 25 July Jackson had evidently succeeded in reaching agreement with his police, and advised Irwin of Bengal's intention to release Mitra in time for an announcement at the opening of the Bengal Legislative Council on 23 August.[123] Irwin suggested Jackson should capitalise on the admirable effect his decision on Bose had had in Bengal by

> …emphasising the fact that you have come with a new mind to these difficult problems and have personally been examining and deciding, &c. I emphasise the importance of your making it as personal as you can, as I am sure that tells in this country, and you are very favourably placed at the moment for doing it.[124]

Further signs of tension on the detenu issue, between Jackson and his government, appears at the end of 1927, in a telegram when the Governor advised Irwin.

> I am a little agitated in my mind regarding detenus. I am not satisfied with the rate of progress respecting release and feel that the Political Department [in the Government of Bengal] have not fully appreciated the policy I wished to be pursued…[125]

In the face of opposition from the Bengal Political Department and the police to the rate of release of the more dangerous prisoners, Jackson turned to the Viceroy for help. Irwin, acknowledging the rate of release had slowed, assured the Governor there had been no change of policy and that 'we should be glad to see the process of release accelerated'.[126] By 31 December 1927, Jackson, in pursuit of the agreed policy, had reduced the prisoners held under Regulation III to 5 and under the Bengal Act to 16, down from 8 and 31 respectively at 31 August 1927.[127] However, the Governor was compelled to advise Irwin that despite the endorsement of the Secretary of State, the Viceroy and his Assembly to the agreed detenu policy of release, Moberly, the political member, had adopted 'what appears to be a definite obstructionist attitude'.[128] In the face of this, Jackson advised that he had been forced to take the matter to his Executive Council. Jackson's problems in relation to the detenu issue were to continue into 1928, particularly as the men held on the shortened list were the more difficult cases and the position of the Bengal police inevitably hardened. Jackson was finding it more difficult to bring his police advisers, who were most concerned with practical rather than political problems, along.

Complications presented by the attitude of the Bengal police to the speed of release of Bengal detenus, and related matters were of sufficient concern for Jackson and Irwin to meet, in New Delhi, in early February 1928.[129] This meeting coincided with the arrival, for its first visit to India, of the Simon Commission. Prior to their meeting, further difficulties had been presented by an article in the Bengal newspaper, *The Statesman*, which had prompted rumours that a general amnesty would be given to the remaining detenus, in order to improve the reception given by the Commission.[130] Even given the concerns surrounding the intended boycott of the Commission, Irwin made it clear to Jackson that the question of the policy regarding the detenus should be kept separate from that of the Commission, and that there should be no concession or change in approach.[131]

Jackson had attempted to involve the Simon Commission in a consideration of his detenu policy, at this time, when he wrote to Simon suggesting the Commission might wish to examine, during its return visit, 'the methods adopted at arriving at a decision for release or continued restraint of these detenus after they had served varying terms of detention'.[132] Jackson's approach clearly indicated his wish for the Commission to endorse his policy of 'accelerated release' and demonstrated a degree of misunderstanding of the Commission's function and agenda. Simon's reply is not surprising. 'The Commission is not appointed either to pronounce judgement on the statute law of Bengal, or as to the exercise by the Government of Bengal of the discretionary power which the statutes placed in its hands'.[133] However, Simon hinted at the value to him if Jackson's policy of accelerated release 'has been carried to a point which leaves only a small residuum of undoubtedly dangerous characters'.[134] The approach, of keeping the Simon Commission completely separate from detenu policy, was to change at the end of March 1928 when Jackson informed Irwin, 'I shall feel justified in pressing for a reasonable release, which should enable us, before the Commission returns to India, to reduce the number of men still under restraint to small proportions'.[135] The importance of moving on the detenus as some concession to obtaining peace in relation to the Simon Commission had replaced Irwin's earlier view, conveyed in January, in relation to detenu policy.[136]

Against the background of the attitude of Lord Lytton and his relationship with the Government of India on the detenu issue, and both Irwin's and Birkenhead's counseling of Jackson on his expected performance and on the matter of detenus, it is perhaps not surprising the Governor approached the matter of the release of the detenus with a certain alacrity. One Governor had sided loyally with his professional police advice, the other had discounted this to some degree and accepted the overriding importance of all-India policy in making his decisions. Governor Jackson successfully achieved the outcome the Viceroy, the Secretary of State and by extension the one British and Indian public opinion also sought. It is also noteworthy, in terms of all-India policy and Indian public opinion, that the complete release of the detenus had been achieved by the date of the return of the Simon Commission in October 1928. This development was not coincidental given Simon's letter in which he had informed the Governor 'it would be of great assistance to them if they could find when they came to Bengal that only a small number of detenus remained under restraint'.[137] Even so, the achievement of complete release did little to placate Indian sentiment against the all-British Parliamentary Commission.

The detenu issue had been a significant challenge for both Lytton and Jackson and, as will be seen in the next chapter, Bengal would have other concerns for Jackson during his tenure, until March 1932, as Governor of the Presidency.

Endnotes

1. Gopal, *Irwin*, p. 8.
2. See Page, *Prelude to Partition*, for a detailed analysis of various strategies identified as used by the British to offset the nationalist challenge in order to perpetuate Imperial control. The strategies identified included the establishment of representative institutions, offsetting rural interests against urban, and aggravating tensions between Muslim and non-Muslim.
3. Gopal, *Irwin*, p. 16.
4. Lytton, *Pundits and Elephants*, p. 167.
5. Halifax Papers, Telegram, Viceroy to Secretary of State, 23 April 1926. Between 22 and 29 April, 56 people had been killed and 365 injured. Telegram, Viceroy to Secretary of State, 30 April 1926.
6. *Ibid.*, Telegram, Viceroy to Secretary of State, 25 April 1926.
7. *Ibid.*, Telegram, Viceroy to Governor of Bengal, 24 April 1926.
8. *Ibid.*, Telegram, Secretary of State to Viceroy, 26 April 1926.
9. The Goondas Act was designed to cover the infiltration of 'bad characters' or *goondas*, into Bengal and Calcutta, who were largely paid by extremists to involve themselves in insurrection.
10. Halifax Papers, Telegram No 788-S, Viceroy to Secretary of State, 30 April 1926.
11. *Ibid.*, Telegram No. 796-S, Viceroy to Secretary of State, 30 April 1926.
12. *Ibid.*, Telegram, Viceroy to Secretary of State, 3 May 1926.
13. NAI, Home/Political, file 123/11/1926, Telegram, Government of India to Government of Bengal, 3 May 1926.
14. Halifax Papers, Telegram, Viceroy to Governor of Bengal, 3 May 1926. Note the validity of an Ordinance was for a period of 6 months. If an extension of powers was judged necessary the British preferred that appropriate legislation be passed through the Council process to avoid political criticism.
15. NAI, Home/Political, file 123/11/1926, Letter, Government of Bengal to Government of India, 5 May 1926. Note the *Government of India Act* 1919 defined in Sections 71–72 the procedures applying to the approval of Ordinances, including their disallowance.

16. Halifax Papers, Telegram, Government of India to Government of Bengal, 3 May 1926.
17. *Ibid.*, Telegram, Viceroy to Secretary of State, 6 May 1926.
18. *Ibid.*, Telegram, Viceroy to Secretary of State, 3 May 1926.
19. NAI, Home/Political, file 123/11/1926, Letter, Government of Bengal to Government of India, 5 May 1926.
20. Halifax Papers, Telegram, Viceroy to Secretary of State, 15 May 1926.
21. *Ibid.*
22. *Ibid.*, Telegram, Government of India to Government of Bengal, 15 May 1926.
23. *Ibid.*, Lytton to Irwin, 12 May 1926.
24. *Ibid.*, Telegram, Governor of Bengal to Viceroy, 16 May 1926.
25. *Ibid.*, Telegram, Viceroy to Secretary of State, 25 May 1926.
26. *Ibid.*, Irwin to Dawson, 18 May 1926.
27. Hailey Papers, Hailey to Muddiman, 7 May 1927. Hailey reports on communal rioting in Lahore between the Sikhs and Muslims.
28. Halifax Papers, Irwin to Harcourt Butler, 12 June 1926.
29. *Ibid.*, Harcourt Butler to Irwin, 28 June 1926.
30. Birkenhead, *Lord Halifax*, p. 223; Lord Irwin, *Speeches*, Volume 1, 1 April 1926 to 24 June 1929, Simla, 1930, p. 24 (see also pp. 110–112 of this chapter).
31. NAI, Home/Political, file 57/XXVII/26, 16 August 1926.
32. Hailey Papers, Hailey to de Montmorency, 10 June 1926.
33. *Ibid.*, Hailey to Vincent, 23 August 1926. Sir W.H.H. Vincent. ICS, 1885. Served in Bengal, Bihar and Orissa and the Government of India. Member of the Council of India, 1923–1931.
34. Halifax Papers, Irwin to various governors (Wilson, Jackson, Marris, Stephenson and Montagu Butler), 13 June 1927.
35. Gilmartin, *Empire and Islam*, p. 46.
36. *Ibid.*, p. 42.
37. Thus, taking the communities' views into account the Simon Commission might have been expected to identify a solution to this problem.
38. Halifax Papers, Irwin to various governors, 13 June 1927.
39. *Ibid.*
40. *Ibid.*
41. *Ibid.*
42. *Ibid.*, Montagu Butler to Irwin, 27 June 1927.
43. Montagu Butler Papers, Butler to his wife, 4 August 1927.
44. Halifax Papers, Stephenson to Irwin, 19 June 1927.
45. *Ibid.*, Wilson to Irwin, 21 June 1927.
46. *Ibid.*, Irwin to various governors, 23 August 1927.
47. *Ibid.*, Marris to Irwin, 31 August 1927.
48. *Ibid.*, Harcourt Butler, 30 August 1927.
49. *Ibid.*, Telegram, Governor of Bengal to Viceroy, 29 April 1926.
50. In common with a number of Indian newspapers, the *Forward* of 4 May 1926, Calcutta, strongly criticised Lytton's absence in Darjeeling.

51. Halifax Papers, Telegram, Viceroy to Governor of Bengal, 30 April 1926.
52. *Ibid.*, Lytton to Irwin, 5 June 1926.
53. Lytton Papers, Intelligence Report on file titled; 'The Terrorist Conspiracy in Bengal', 1 July to 31 December 1926.
54. Laushey, *Bengal Terrorism and the Marxist Left*, p. 135.
55. *Ibid.*, p. 76.
56. *Ibid.*
57. *Ibid.*, p. 137.
58. Hereafter BCLAA.
59. Halifax Papers, Lytton to Irwin, 5 June 1926.
60. *Ibid.*, Stephenson to Irwin, 9 August 1926.
61. *Ibid.*
62. *Ibid.*, Irwin to Lytton, 22 November 1926.
63. *Ibid.*, Irwin to Lytton, 27 November 1926. Note that Regulation III of 1818, could only be used in the case of (a) Communist conspiracy, (b) actual rebellion such as the Moplah (Revivalist Muslim rebellion in 1921, in Kerala on the Malabar coast of South West India, against the British and Hindus), (c) anarchist or revolutionary conspiracy and crime. Use of the Regulation was not appropriate in the case of communal disorder. Cases under the Regulation had to be submitted to two judges and approved by the Viceroy. NAI, Home/Political, note on file 209/26.
64. Halifax Papers, Irwin to Jackson, 30 November 1926.
65. NAI, Home/Political, file 209/26, Telegram, Governor of Bengal to the Government of India, 3 August 1926.
66. Dr B.S. Moonje. Political Responsivist in the Central Provinces and prominent member of the Hindu Mahasabha.
67. S. Suhrawardy (1892–1963). Bengal politician. Member of the Swaraj Party and later the Muslim League. Jinnah favourite. Prime Minister of Pakistan, 1956–1957.
68. Halifax Papers, Telegram, Viceroy to Governor of Bengal, 8 August 1926. NAI, Home/Political, file 209/26, Telegram, Government of India to Government of Bengal, 10 August 1926.
69. Halifax Papers, Telegram, Governor of Bengal to Viceroy, 9 August 1926.
70. NAI, Home/Political, note on file 209/26, 12 August 1926. Note Crerar is not being personally disparaging to Suhrawaddy by using this language. He is merely using a common English colloqualism or saying. He could have also used for example '...a sledge hammer to break a nut'.
71. *Ibid.*
72. *Ibid.*
73. *Ibid.*
74. Halifax Papers, Stephenson to Irwin, 9 August 1926.
75. *Ibid.*, Telegram, Viceroy to Secretary of State, 15 August 1926.
76. *Ibid.*, Montagu Butler to Irwin, 12 August 1926. Note Moonje spelt Munje by Butler in this case.

77. Harcourt Butler Papers, Hirtzel to Harcourt Butler, 29 August 1926.
78. Nanda, *Three Statesmen*, p. 253.
79. *Ibid.*
80. G.K. Gokhale (1866–1915). Moderate Indian leader and President of the Congress in 1906.
81. Nanda, *Three Statesmen*, p. 233.
82. Halifax Papers, Telegram, Viceroy to Secretary of State, 15 August 1926; Telegram, Acting Governor of Bengal to Viceroy, 17 August 1926.
83. Halifax Papers, Lytton to Irwin, 11 January 1927.
84. *Ibid.*, Telegram, Viceroy to Secretary of State, 20 January 1927.
85. *Ibid.*, Irwin to Lytton, 19 January 1927.
86. *Ibid.*, Lytton to Irwin, 26 January 1927.
87. *Ibid.*
88. *Ibid.*
89. *Ibid.*, Telegram, Viceroy to Secretary of State, 20 February 1927.
90. Chatterjee was ill following a hunger strike and Irwin will have not wished him to get worse or die in prison.
91. Halifax Papers, Lytton to Irwin, 22 February 1927.
92. *Ibid.*
93. *Ibid.*, Lytton to Irwin, 25 February 1927.
94. *Ibid.*
95. *Ibid.*, Telegram, Viceroy to Secretary of State, 1 March 1927.
96. *Ibid.*, Telegram, Viceroy to Secretary of State, 12 March 1927.
97. *Ibid.*, Lytton to Irwin, 5 March 1927.
98. *Ibid.*
99. *Ibid.*, Irwin to Birkenhead, 16 March 1927.
100. *Ibid.*, Telegram, Viceroy to Governor of Bengal, 26 March 1927.
101. *Ibid.*, Lytton to Irwin, 3 April 1927.
102. Birkenhead Papers, Lytton to Birkenhead, 11 December 1924.
103. Halifax Papers, Jackson to Irwin, 29 March 1927.
104. *Ibid.*, Irwin to Jackson, 7 April 1927.
105. *Ibid.*
106. S.C. Bose (1897–1945). The future ally of the Axis powers in the Second World War. In the 1920s a revolutionary leader in Bengal advocating violent resistance.
107. S.C. Mitra (1888–1942). Arrested under Regulation III of 1818 and detained without trial until 1927 in Burma. Elected to the Legislative Assembly in 1926 as a member of the Swaraj Party, and on release became its Chief Whip.
108. J.G. Mukharjee (1886–1976). An eminent Bengali anti-imperialist and nationalist.
109. Halifax Papers, Telegram, Viceroy to Secretary of State, 10 April 1927.
110. Birkenhead Papers, Birkenhead to Jackson, 7 April 1927.
111. A chronic and potentially fatal parasitic disease of the internal organs (black fever).

112. Birkenhead Papers, Birkenhead to Jackson, 7 April 1927.
113. Halifax Papers, Jackson to Irwin, 18 April 1927.
114. *Ibid.*, Telegram, Viceroy to Governor of Bengal, 5 May 1927.
115. *Ibid.*, Telegram, Governor of Bengal to Viceroy, 6 May 1927.
116. *Ibid.*, Telegram, Viceroy to Governor of Bengal, 7 May 1927.
117. *Ibid.*, Telegram, Secretary of State to Viceroy, 9 May 1927.
118. *Ibid.*, Jackson to Irwin, 1 June 1927.
119. *Ibid.*
120. *Ibid.*, Irwin to Jackson, 11 June 1927.
121. *Ibid.*, Telegram, Viceroy to Secretary of State, 17 June 1927.
122. *Ibid.*, Jackson to Irwin, 18 June 1927.
123. *Ibid.*, Telegram, Governor of Bengal to Viceroy, 25 July 1927.
124. *Ibid.*, Irwin to Jackson, 17 August 1927.
125. *Ibid.*, Telegram, Governor of Bengal to Viceroy, 2 December 1927.
126. *Ibid.*, Telegram, Viceroy to Governor of Bengal, 5 December 1927.
127. *Ibid.*, Irwin to Jackson, 11 January 1928.
128. *Ibid.*, Jackson to Irwin, 31 December 1927.
129. *Ibid.*, Telegram, Viceroy to Governor of Bengal, 20 January 1928.
130. *Ibid.*
131. *Ibid.*
132. Simon Papers, Jackson to Simon, 24 March 1928
133. *Ibid.*, Simon to Jackson, 31 March 1928.
134. *Ibid.*
135. *Ibid.*
136. *Ibid.*, Telegram, Viceroy to Governor of Bengal, 20 January 1928.
137. Halifax Papers, Jackson to Irwin, 4 April 1928.

6

Communism, Terrorism and Countermeasures

Together with the increased political and security pressure presented by Congress and their volunteers, during Irwin's rule, more dangerous challenges to the British in India came in the form of communism and labour disputes and the continuing threat of terrorism. These challenges were mainly centred in the presidencies. The nationalists were happy to exploit the very difficult circumstances presented by these emergencies. This chapter will explore, through the available sources, the governors' approach to communism and terrorism, the need for emergency measures, and the kind of pressure they collectively mounted against this challenge. The chapter throws additional light on the governors' role and influence on the Viceroy and the Secretary of State, and on the nature of the working relationship between them, under the great pressures of emergent circumstances. While the lines between communism, terrorism and the Civil Disobedience Movement were blurred for the governors their interaction with civil disobedience will be addressed more specifically in chapter eight.

There had been one or two references, during 1927, in communications between the governors and Irwin on communism in India and the influence of the Soviet Union. But it was not until 1928 that communism, and how to deal with its consequences on labour, and on the politics of India became a consistent theme in their correspondence. By April 1928 both Bengal and Bombay were reporting the presence and influence of British Communists on strikes in their presidencies. Bengal was experiencing strikes in connection with the East Indian Railway Workshops at Lillooah and at large engineering firms.[1] Sir Stanley Jackson was to inform Irwin

> ...that gentleman from Bombay—Phillip Spratt[2]—is here and he is being closely watched. I am informed he has done nothing for which we could limit his activities, but he is a dangerous Communist and as such I wish he could be precluded from leading astray these ignorant men.[3]

Sir Leslie Wilson, in Bombay, advised Irwin of serious strikes in his presidency involving some 50,000 workmen in about 22 textile mills. Wilson identified the strikes as 'a political and communist stunt which is a new element in the labour question in Bombay'.[4] Like Jackson, the Governor was to report the involvement of a Briton (named Bradley) and that he had given instructions that he be carefully watched with a view to prosecuting him under the Criminal Penal Code.

Governing from his summer capital Mahableshwar, Wilson found his problems were amplified by the strike situation in Bombay city. It had become sufficiently serious for the Governor to involve himself directly in meeting the mill owners, and with the only organised and registered trade union of mill operatives. While Wilson acknowledged that the government had no statutory right to interfere at all, he was to assure the mill owners that his administration had no intention of allowing the workers to be 'led astray by communist leaders'.[5] Wilson informed Irwin the mill owners had not been advised of the grievance which had caused the men to strike. He advised 'he had got an undertaking from them that they would be prepared to consider any such grievances when they were put before the Mill Owners' Association by the representatives of any registered trade union'. He had assured the trade union he would not meet with extreme leaders and 'I look to them and to no one else to put forward the legitimate grievances of the men'.

While Wilson had informed Irwin that the strikers' grievance was not clear, the mill owners were to acknowledge a background of general economic depression in the industry, with 25 per cent of the spindles and 10 per cent of the looms having shut down over the previous four months. In these circumstances the mill owners had asked the Government of India for protection from cheap imports. If agreement to protection was not forthcoming, the owners had informed Wilson they would have to announce a reduction in wages. The Governor

> ...urged them very strongly to do nothing of the sort at present, and pointed out that any such announcement would be...a grave tactical blunder, as it would immediately throw the blame for the strike from the shoulders of the communists on to them.[6]

Lord Birkenhead regarded the influence of the British Communists and of 'imported money' as being of such importance in maintaining the strikes in Bombay and Bengal, as to suggest to Irwin 'that you [should] consider whether action should not be taken immediately to prevent import of funds from political sources in Europe'.[7] Birkenhead believed it was difficult to draw a distinction, in India, between legitimate industrial disputes and those incited for subversive purposes, as the Communists' avowed aim was to use legitimate economic and political circumstances for illegitimate ends. However, Birkenhead was sure any movement with which Spratt and Bradley were associated was clearly subversive and he suggested that an Ordinance, on the analogy of the British Emergency Powers Act of 1920, should be introduced as soon as possible. In response, Irwin advised Birkenhead that his government had been 'already examining possible methods of preventing receipt of funds from Russian communist sources…and have also been watching closely the activities of the communists in connection with the various strikes'.[8] Irwin believed the strike situation was

> …developing fairly favourably. Present tendencies, if they continue, suggest that the Lillooah strike [in Bengal] may peter out soon…The position of the extremists in Bombay has been appreciably weakened…[they] are likely to lose ground steadily if things follow their present course for another week or two.[9]

That Irwin was sanguine of the outcome and sensitive to the politics of the situation is seen in his advice to Birkenhead 'that here as in England we have to be careful to carry public opinion with us…and it would be a mistake to proceed by ordinance'. Irwin wished to avoid any risk of giving the agitators a 'martyr's halo instead of as I hope leaving them in a position of leaders discredited by an expensive halo'.[10] On this occasion Irwin's confidence was misplaced as the workers' strikes, Communist influence and the governors' concern with how to deal with these threats were to be a consistent theme throughout the balance of his viceroyalty. In fact differing views between the Viceroy, the secretaries of state, and the governors of Bombay and of Bengal in particular, on the appropriate policy approach to worker unrest, communism and terrorism were a source of real tension in the administration of India at this time. Reflecting troubles to come, within three days of Irwin's buoyant response to Birkenhead of 9 May, Wilson was advising that Bradley's influence had spread to the railways in Bombay, and the workmen had passed a resolution putting forward their minimum demands to be conceded within eight days.[11] Wilson was to indicate:

> …at the moment, one can only watch events carefully, and give every assistance to the police to maintain law and order, and to protect property…and I feel sure of all your support in anything we can do to stamp out this Communist element.[12]

Shortly afterwards in Bengal, Jackson sent a message to Irwin, reflecting an apparent lack of coordination on behalf of the central and presidency governments.

> My Government is seriously embarrassed by lack of information as regards policy of Railway Board in connection with strike of their servants at Lillooah. It is not possible for my Government to deal with it as if it were an ordinary industrial dispute as the Government of India through the Railway Board are involved as a party...I should be glad to hear your views.[13]

Irwin responding indicated that the Lillooah strike had not been justifiable, had been carried on under the influence of extremist agitators and that the general labour situation had become even more complicated by new mill and threatened railway strikes.

> Any weakening in our attitude in the Lillooah strike, after it had lasted for ten weeks, would affect the position elsewhere most unfavourably...I am sorry if the difficulties of the Bengal Government have been increased by doubt as to our policy [of not agreeing to any concession so long as the men remained on strike].[14]

Jackson informed Irwin he was much obliged for his reply but matters had been further complicated with another strike in connection with the jute presses in Bengal,[15] involving a very large number of men.

> I am afraid that Labour is very restless throughout our industrial area at the moment, and they go out in a body at the least provocation. One must believe that the cause of this is propaganda by a much larger number of ill-disposed individuals—more numerous than we have hitherto appreciated... the members of the Provincial Congress Committee are active and are doing a great deal of harm—their object obviously being to impress Labour that they are their true champions.[16]

Jackson had identified the political component of an economic problem. It had become apparent that the Congress and the Communists were in competition for the support of labour, and again Jackson advised 'we must make all the necessary arrangements for the maintenance of law and order'. He was later to indicate to Irwin his desire 'for some method...to prevent these outsiders like Spratt deliberately attempting to create unrest and trouble'.[17] Jackson informed Irwin of a further example of Congress infiltration of unions in the form of a sweepers' strike in Calcutta influenced by Congress and of connected arrests.[18]

Wilson felt his hands tied in Bombay when at the end of May, advising the mill strike remained deadlocked, he informed Irwin 'I wish very much that it were possible for some legislation to be passed to enable us to deport Communists from outside who are deliberately stirring up trouble in industry with the help of money from Moscow'.[19] By June 1928 Irwin's mind had changed on the issue of the appropriateness of an Ordinance to control remittances from Communist sources outside India, and he and the Secretary of State had under consideration appropriate draft legislation on that matter as well as on effecting the deportation from India of British subjects engaged in Communist agitation.[20] In the face of the deadlocked mill strikes in Bombay, Wilson was to suggest a new policy approach from government, involving a sort of industrial tribunal.

> If a further deadlock is arrived at because of definite points at issue between the owners and the men with regard to facts, either in respect of profits, wages, hours of labour, or similar questions, it may be desirable for Government to set up some impartial committee with power to enquire into statements made by both sides, and give a decision as to which side is correct. Government has not any power to do more.[21]

Irwin agreed this would be a good idea and indicated he had some similar conciliation mechanism in mind in a Labour Bill, which he hoped would be put to the Assembly in September 1928.[22]

Communist activity, in the presidencies, principally related to strikes on the railways and in the mills continued in 1928 with Lord Goschen in Madras reporting the arrest of Communist leaders, following violence, had improved the strike situation in his presidency.[23] Goschen had earlier confirmed an interconnection between the Communists and Nationalists when he advised Birkenhead, 'Undoubtedly politics loom largely behind the strikes as for electioneering purposes various parties are anxious to secure this part of the workforce'.[24] (Governor Hailey had long been aware of the dangers of this connection to the British position. 'The great danger to my mind is not the direct Communist teaching so much as the gradual infiltration of the doctrine of unrest'.)[25] Hirtzel, in the India Office, informed Goschen that the Secretary of State was 'very much impressed…by your firm prompt and effective handling of the railway strike…I hope you will get convictions against the two Communists'.[26] The emergency situation in Bombay was escalating, and Wilson was to seek appropriate measures from Irwin to deal with the 'serious position of mill strikes and activities which Communists are now showing'.[27] Jackson in Bengal asked for Irwin's approval to certify or overrule his legislative council's rejection of increased pay for the Bengal and Calcutta police.[28] Irwin replied to Wilson that his request, given that it involved the Government of India taking all-India action, must necessarily involve central government consultation with all local governments. Irwin informed him 'you recognise fully the difficulties of Government action against Communists who are engaged in labour disputes and the danger that the Government may be led into measures which seem to be not merely anti-Communist but anti-Labour'.[29] Pending consultation with other governments, Irwin was to suggest action in Bombay under the ordinary law. With Jackson, Irwin agreed, in an exception to the general rule, that certification by the Governor of the necessary legislation increasing police pay was appropriate especially given the likely positive effect on police morale.[30] While acknowledging the generally undesirable nature of certification, Irwin and the Governor could point to the 'unreasonable and perverse' action of the Bengal Legislative Council in rejecting the salary increase. The Government of India was always conscious of the need to be able to argue their case from a position of political strength both within India and to those in Britain, while the local governments were primarily and understandably motivated by their more immediate circumstances. Delhi's decision and that of Bengal would have been motivated by the need to ensure the interests of the Bengal police force were safeguarded.

In dealing with the serious nature of the mill strikes in Bombay, Wilson had decided to try and set up 'some form of committee of enquiry…consisting of three independent people'.[31] The mill strike, contrary to Irwin's earlier views had now lasted over four months. Wilson reported that he had been successful in obtaining agreement between the mill owners and workers as to the terms of reference and the personnel of the committee, but no agreement had been reached on the matter of the men returning to work forthwith.[32] Wilson informed Irwin he was counseling the mill-owners not to give in to the Communists, and had asked them to keep him closely advised. He also indicated there was a very real risk of a general rail strike greeting the Simon Commission on arrival in his presidency. In fact Commission related strikes were to cost India thirty million working days in 1927–1928.[33] In the context of the Government of India's exploring what action was possible against the Communists in Bombay, a senior security officer, Isemonger,[34] had been sent there to investigate the situation. Wilson advised Irwin that Isemonger had told him in Bombay

> …that he [Isemonger] is quite sure that Bengal and Madras will have sufficient evidence against the Communists in those places to enable sufficient proof to be found of their connection with the Third International,[35] and then the leaders…can be arrested on the same day and sent to some place, to be selected by the [Central] Government for trial [for subversion under the Indian Penal Code].[36]

After discussions with his security man, Irwin informed Wilson, 'we are very willing here to explore the possibilities of running a big conspiracy case',[37] but it would take time. Irwin warned Wilson of the dangers, in talking to the mill-owners, of prejudicing the Bombay Government's position as impartial arbiters. The Viceroy advised him of the agreed policy decided by the Government of India, which had been developed together with the other presidencies and Bombay, against the Communists.

> (1) We shall introduce our Communist Deportation Bill and Trades Disputes Bill in this Assembly. (2) We shall proceed as rapidly as we may with examination of the possibilities of a general conspiracy case on the lines you suggest. (3) We shall look forward to receiving from all Local Governments considered replies to our circular letter that we sent some ten days ago, inviting their views as to general legislative action against Communists. (4) If any grave emergency blows up before we have been able to take any action, as indicated above, or arm ourselves with new powers, we shall be fully prepared to consider proceedings against dangerous individuals under the Regulation [III of 1818].[38]

The influence of both the Patel brothers over British policy was evident when Irwin reported to the governors at the end of September that the Public Safety Bill 'was defeated in the Assembly by the President's [Vithalbhai Patel] casting vote'.[39] Irwin informed the governors that he did not intend to certify the legislation as no real emergency existed at that time, and would re-introduce the legislation at the next opportunity in early February 1929. Sir Frederick Sykes, who had been in place as Governor one month, was to receive a clear and early enunciation of Irwin's approach towards Communist extremists in January 1929. The Viceroy advised him:

> ...my own feeling is that these extremists are quite definitely out for trouble, and that we ought to seize the first and every opportunity of prosecution and of checking them in any way that may suggest itself...my present idea was to reintroduce our Public Safety Bill in the Assembly next Session...and to consider very carefully, if it can be done within the four corners of a law, taking direct legislative action against Communists as such.[40]

During 1929, contradictions emerged between this early expression of intent and what action the Viceroy came to deem as possible in practice, frustrating the relationship between Irwin and Sykes on policy towards extremism.[41] The Viceroy's advice, in January 1929, of his intended approach with regard to Communists, to both Sykes in Bombay and Jackson in Bengal, was to elicit their views of appropriate policy responses to the activities of the Communists in their presidencies. Irwin had reiterated to them his intention of re-introducing the Public Safety Bill, giving power to deport Communists, who had been defeated, in September 1928, by Vithalbhai Patel in the Assembly, and of including in it provisions for forfeiture of funds remitted to India for Communist purposes.[42] After considering the views of local governments, Irwin had decided also that a conspiracy case would be launched against existing Communist agitators in about April 1929.[43] In the Viceroy's view, this would be more effective than special legislation which he advised he was not in favour of introducing. Pending the conspiracy case and the introduction of the Public Safety Bill in March, the Viceroy asked both Sykes and Jackson, against a background of continuing labour agitation in their presidencies, whether 'you think anything more could be done to try and enforce respect for the ordinary law'.[44] He acknowledged the difficulties presented to Jackson by an inefficient court and judicial system in Bengal, which failed to secure convictions promptly.

Jackson responded that he was pleased with the Viceroy's advice and 'I am personally convinced that the present communist activity in India should be checked and at once'.[45] He advised that he had removed a particularly inefficient Sessions Judge and had considered the prosecution of Sen Gupta,[46] in connection with an inflammatory speech he had recently delivered to Congress. After consideration of the implications, he and his Council had decided not to prosecute, to avoid any possibility of consolidating a currently divided Congress party. Jackson informed the Viceroy of his view

> ...that the foundation of policy must be to enforce rigidly the ordinary law, especially those sections of it which deal with seditious utterances. This should be the view in every Province in India and that there should be complete unanimity of action.[47]

The Governor acknowledged that this being the policy

> it would appear to be necessary to apply the law equally to speeches in Congress with those which are made outside. We will do all we can in Bengal to avoid the feeling that the law is impotent to deal with those who break it.

Governor Sykes, in an extensive reply to the Viceroy's letter, indicated 'that the Bombay Presidency, whose prosperity primarily depends upon a concentrated industry, might be selected as the first area for a trial of strength'.[48] Sykes informed the Viceroy that the industrial situation in Bombay was poised on a knife's edge and there was a real risk of the labour leaders calling a general strike in addition to the ongoing mill-strikes. As this action could involve the railways, municipal workers and the intensification of an oil transport strike the situation was very serious, and it was further aggravated by a hostile press. About this time Sykes was to receive a visit from Sir George Rainy,[49] on the suggestion of Hailey, to discuss 'Sykes' anxieties in Bombay'[50] and a summons from the Viceroy to visit him by the end of the month. The Governor had received deputations from the mill owners who had requested 'drastic action against the labour leaders and the prohibition of strike meetings and picketing'.[51] Sykes wrote to the Viceroy that

> ...two of the greatest difficulties which seem to me to be fundamental are that, on the one side, there is an atmosphere of widespread suspicion and antagonism. The mill-owners, at the present time, are not united as to the policy which they ought to follow, and they do not yet seem to appreciate the fact that sound political action can only follow sound economics, and that the things that matter are that there should be good wages, good conditions of work and good discipline.[52]

The Governor had developed a view, a matter of weeks into his governorship, that the workers of Bombay did indeed have valid grievances, and that this was fertile ground for Communist activity. That the British were aware of the need to address the causes, and not just the symptoms of labour unrest through coercive action, was demonstrated by the Fawcett Committee's[53] attempt in March 1929 to address worker grievances in Bombay. The Committee failed, in the face of the industry leaders' unwillingness to give concessions and their insistence on tariffs and other government measures, to overcome industry problems.[54] The Committee's failure brought on a general strike in all Bombay mills on 24 April, organised by the Communist Union, the Girni Kamgar. Continuing labour unrest in India and a British recognition of the importance of addressing its causes, was to precipitate the Royal Commission on Labour appointed in July 1929 'to examine and report on the existing conditions of industrial labour in India on the health, efficiency, and standard of living of workers, and the relations between employers and employed'.[55] The Commission's Report, issued in 1931, while not entirely efficacious, led to a number of improvements in the industrial relations area in India and reduced labour unrest in the ensuing years. The influence of communism on mill-workers was to decline.[56]

While the underlying causes of labour unrest in Bombay were still being examined by the Fawcett Committee and the Commission on Labour was yet to be appointed, Sykes continued to review his existing legal options for action against the Communists. His conclusion expressed to Irwin was:

> I think the suggestion that we have ample powers already to deal with the Communists will have to be considerably modified. Regulation III of 1818 does not apply here in Bombay, and while it is true that Regulation XXV of

> 1827[57] can be used...it does not apply to European subjects...the necessity for the Public Safety Bill, so far as this Presidency is concerned, can be fully made out.[58]

Sykes went on to identify a requirement for legislation to entirely prohibit or at least control picketing, both at the mills and at the homes of the workers. The Governor was to advise against the prohibition of meetings, convened by labour leaders, as he believed such a step would be merely provocative. The recognition of the serious situation in Bombay by the Viceroy was evidenced by Sykes receiving his prompt, although reluctant approval to employ Regulation XXV of 1827. 'If circumstances make this imperative... you and your advisers are really the only people who can gauge the situation from hour to hour, and I have no doubt that your people will not employ the Regulation unnecessarily'.[59]

Following the Governor's letter to Irwin of 26 January, copied to Lord Peel, the Secretary of State was to also respond to Sykes' need for support. In his letter Sykes had indicated that the British communist, Bradley, was doing a lot of work 'behind the scenes', and 'the Indian communists derive a great deal of moral support from the fact that a European is permitted to spread Communist propaganda without interference from government'. Peel reacted by advising Irwin of the

> ...deep misgivings with which I regard the Government of India's proposals [regarding Indian Communists]...In the circumstances described by him [Sykes] it seems to me impossible to leave Spratt and Bradley at large, while legal authorities pursue their lengthy deliberations to a doubtful conclusion. I would beg you to consider this matter further to give the Public Safety Bill priority over all other business, and to rid yourselves of Spratt and Bradley before Bombay again becomes a shambles. But, of course, I appreciate that responsibility for the decision lies with you.[60]

Peel, on the same day, sent a message direct to Sykes advising him of the need for him and the Viceroy

> ...to evolve the means of checking this movement before it becomes serious. I need hardly say that you can rely on my support for any reasonable measures you may take or propose in order to achieve this, whether it is in the Cabinet here or in discussion with the Government of India that my support may be required.[61]

This was a rare example of a Secretary of State indicating a willingness to, in effect, go over the head of the Government of India in developing policy with a presidency governor. Given the strong degree of support proffered by

Peel, Sykes, in the face of future developments in Bombay, was probably to regret the transfer of power to the Labour Party in June 1929. Sykes in his autobiography, *From Many Angles*, was to note 'One of my chief difficulties throughout my term of office was to get the Government of India to support me promptly in a crisis'.[62] Given the capacity of the Secretary of State to direct the Government of India, Sykes may have been unhappy also with the consistency of support given to him from London.

By the end of March 1929, and in consequence of the powers then available to move against the Communists, including under the Public Safety Act, which had been passed, arrests of leading activists had occurred. These included Spratt and Bradley who were charged with conspiracy 'to deprive the King of the sovereignty of British India'.[63] The policy of arrest did not immediately solve Sykes' difficulties as he was to report, at the end of April.

> Situation resulting from Bombay mill strike is giving some anxiety. At present only 17 mills are working and about 110,000 mill operatives are idle, mostly Hindus, who attend meetings convened by strike leaders in very large numbers. The feeling between Hindus and Muhammadans is becoming strained, as bulk of Muhammadans do not support the strike.[64]

At this time the issue of terrorism and policy towards the previously imprisoned detenus arose with the murder of Saunders, a police inspector at Barisal in Bengal Province, and reports by the Bengal police of an increased likelihood of violence by the released terrorists. Irwin wrote to Jackson of Bengal asking for his views on the matter and reminding him of his support in applying their previously agreed policy of re-internment of re-offenders under the BCLAA.[65] Irwin also referred to the recent increase in terrorism in the Punjab and the United Provinces. Jackson advised Irwin that he had consulted with Tegart and Lowman, the heads of the Bengal Police Service and the Intelligence Branch, respectively. They had informed him there was indeed increasing concern regarding the activities of ex-detenus and of Congress volunteers. Jackson indicated:

> I shall not hesitate to use the Act if necessary…I feel that I shall be able to depend upon your approval of any action I may take in this respect. We do not at all like the prospect of being without the powers under this Act which will disappear in the ordinary course next March.[66]

Irwin wrote back advising Jackson that he had informed the Secretary of State he wished to discuss the matter of the expiry of the Bengal Act, with him, on his return to England later that year.[67]

Irwin also wrote to both Hailey and de Montmorency indicating he wished to discuss with them in Simla the policy to be pursued on the BCLAA ceasing to be operative.[68] One can suspect that it was not only because of increasing security concerns in their provinces that Irwin sought out these two governors, but also to use their expertise and experience to prepare himself for his forthcoming meeting in England with the Secretary of State. In his letters to the governors he informed them the Bengal

> ...police view is that the [terrorist] organisation is still in existence and... they are merely waiting until the powers lapse to renew their policy of assassination...it might be well to consider whether those powers should be renewed for Bengal only or whether they should be continued by an all-India enactment which would enable the powers to be applied to other Provinces by notification if the circumstances justified this.[69]

Irwin, Hailey, de Montmorency and senior officials, including Sir Charles Tegart met at Viceregal Lodge in Simla, on 8 June 1929, to discuss the policy approach to the Bengal Act. The record of discussion, contained in a file note[70] reflects the two governors' low-key and considered approach to the problems at hand. After descriptions of relevant background to the issue by the participants, including the implications of Congress' stated intentions of non-cooperation after 1 January 1930, Hailey stated his view 'that special powers should not be invoked until there was clear evidence that the police could not carry out their functions under the ordinary law'. He did not think existing conditions justified or demanded the extension of the powers of the Bengal Act. Governor de Montmorency had the same view as Hailey that an all-India measure was not appropriate.

Not surprisingly Tegart's view, and that of the Bengal police, was that unless the Act was renewed on its expiry at the beginning of 1930 it would be impossible to keep the terrorist movement in check. Sir David Petrie[71] believed renewal of the Act was essential to keep the strong possibility of a terrorist campaign in check. Hailey's fellow Governor developed the argument in favour of local legislation, advising that he would approach his Legislature for powers similar to the Bengal Act if the need arose.[72]

Security matters, including industrial agitation, were of continuing concern in Bombay, Bengal, the United Provinces and the Punjab during the second half of 1929, and were the subject of continuing exchanges of communication between the respective governors and the Viceroy. The security situation faced by the British at this time was a blend of labour unrest aggravated by communism and extremist nationalism in the form of terrorism, further inflamed by Congress activity. This emergency threat was met by a British response formulated in concert by the governors, Viceroy and Secretary of State, developed from positions of their own various perspectives.

In Bombay the level of intimidation, particularly in relation to the continuing mill strikes there and terrorism, had induced Governor Sykes to indicate he would be seeking an Ordinance, pending the preparation and introduction of appropriate legislation, to deal with the situation.[73] Sykes observed 'we have throughout been most anxious to hold scales even and to take no action adverse to legitimate activity of Trades Unionism'. Sykes began drafting legislation to control picketing and intimidation on the lines of British law and a bill for safeguarding life and property in times of emergency. The Governor had intended the scope of the picketing legislation should extend to the whole presidency.[74] Sykes had been under some local criticism that his government had failed to deal firmly with the emergency situation in Bombay.[75] The *Times of India*, reporting on the serious nature of the mill strikes, indicated that Sykes had set about sounding out 'public opinion as to the measures best calculated to bring about a settlement of the deadlock'.[76] Public opinion included newspaper editors and the representatives of important public bodies in Bombay city who had suggested to Sykes the introduction of an immediate Ordinance, a Court of Enquiry and punitive local legislation against picketing and hooligans.

Lord Irwin rejected Sykes' request for an immediate Ordinance to deal with picketing and intimidation on the basis that the scope of effect sought by the Governor had been too broad, and would have ceded too much power to Bombay. However, Irwin was to seek approval from the Secretary of State, with some amendments, for Bombay's legislative programme, which included the Picketing Bill, the Criminal Intimidation Bill and the Public Security Bill, intended to safeguard life and property. Wedgwood Benn gave his approval to the introduction of the Criminal Intimidation Bill provided its application was restricted to the presidency area, it was not confined to intimidation in connection with trade (labour) disputes, and its currency was limited to five years. He also approved the Bill for Public Security but could not agree with the Picketing Bill.[77] The Secretary of State also made it clear that, in the event of the legislation not being passed by the Bombay Legislative Council, there would be no question of his agreeing to the legislation being certified by the Governor, overriding the Council under the *Government of India Act*. Once again, the powers sought by the Governor, as those he had judged as necessary to deal with the serious security situation which he held existed in his presidency, had been diluted at least partly on the basis of British domestic politics, by both the Viceroy and the Secretary of State. The Viceroy had judged Sykes' request for an Ordinance as too extreme and unnecessary. Wedgwood Benn had identified with, to him, the more important and overriding political considerations connected with Labour Government politics, which were fundamentally sympathetic to trade union concerns.

At the beginning of November 1929 Jackson visited Irwin to discuss the likely situation in Bengal from 1 January 1930, when Congress had indicated that it would mount a renewed campaign of non-cooperation, which would turn out to be intensified by Gandhi's Salt March later in the year. Jackson advised that while the security situation in his presidency had improved, there was still a need to prepare for any contingency that might arise. In that context Bengal had prepared a provisional draft measure for emergency purposes modelled on a 1924 Ordinance. This draft Ordinance was intended to provide stringent powers. It was to have a life of six months and would permit the Government to try any case without a jury. There would be no right of appeal and suspects could be detained without trial.[78] Irwin informed the Governor that his

> Ordinance was quite unsuitable in its present form, in as much as besides seeking to regulate everything between heaven and earth in the same Ordinance, it did this by inviting the Government of India to make a complete surrender of its powers to the Local Government by authorising them to make rules on all these various topics.[79]

Irwin advised Wedgwood Benn that he and Jackson had also discussed the BCLAA at their meeting

> ...but he [Jackson] was unwilling to commit himself at this stage beyond saying he recognised the difficulties, in view of the comparatively tranquil record of the last months, of asking for its extension...I asked him what he would think of the possible line that you and I discussed together [in England] of saying that it was hoped not to renew the Act, but that, if there was any recurrence of the causes that had led to its original sanction, there would be no hesitation in taking the same course again...he thought this was worth considering.[80]

Lord Lytton was still involved in the politics of India, and wrote to Irwin reporting discussions in London with Wedgwood Benn over dinner, the main topic being the renewal of the Bengal Act. It is not surprising that the former Governor also pressed for the renewal of the Act. He reported that the Secretary of State was extremely reluctant to incur the odium, of both Indian nationalists and his own supporters in England, of re-enacting the Bengal Act if it could be avoided.[81] Lytton had argued his case extensively and informed Irwin 'he [Benn] admitted the force of my argument but I fear he will feel the political situation at home too difficult unless he is strongly pressed by you—in which case I think he might give way'.

Against this background of unrest in India, the Secretary of State advised Irwin that Fenner Brockway, a British MP, was to move a motion in Parliament calling

> ...attention to prosecution of political opinion in India...the general line to be taken is that to prosecute merely for expression of political opinion is unnecessary and bad policy, though prosecutions may be necessary in definite cases of violence or incitement to violence.[82]

Wedgwood Benn sought the Viceroy's comments. Irwin responded that he and the governors entirely agreed it was bad policy to prosecute merely for expression of political opinion and, emphatically, that this had not been the policy of local governments or the Government of India's approach.[83] Irwin provided, in a detailed response, observations by those local governments which had experienced serious security difficulties, to assist Wedgwood Benn with the Brockway motion. These had been submitted by Madras, Bombay, Bengal, the United Provinces and the Punjab. The views of the United Provinces were representative.

> ...there is no justification for allegation that people are being prosecuted merely for expression of political opinion. Altogether since January 1, 1929, only seven men have been prosecuted under (relevant legislation). In all these cases there was either incitement to violence or its justification implicit or explicit. Government's action has been rigidly limited to minimum necessary to prevent growth of disorder. All possible forbearance to free expression of opinion has been shown consistently with responsibility for preservation of tranquility. It is unnecessary to emphasise, in view of past history of non-co-operation movement that serious disturbances can be caused by appeals to racial, religious or class feeling, while ostensibly avoiding direct incitement to violence.[84]

In a period when the Government of India was pursuing a conciliatory policy towards Congress, in an attempt to obtain their agreement to participate in the first Round Table Conference, local governments were particularly careful not to provide provocation for anti-government behaviour. Their comments reflected a consistent intention by the various jurisdictions to be careful and discriminatory in their actions, even in the face of considerable incitement, including to violence. Irwin reinforced with his governors the importance of not aggravating Congress.

> At a time like this I think it is clearly to our advantage if it can be avoided not to provoke feeling, whether in extremist or more moderate circles...the

> general situation suggests the policy of going slow at the moment with fresh prosecutions for sedition.[85]

Governor Jackson in Bengal was at the same time to inform Irwin of discussions he had held with his Council and ministers to consider the BCLAA, following which he had concluded, 'I cannot personally see that anything which has happened at Lahore or since calls for any alteration in procedure which we have been following'.[86] He also informed the Viceroy that there were 'signs of a little more activity' amongst terrorist organisations in Bengal but the atmosphere had been generally calm. Even so, the issue of terrorism and how to deal with it in Bengal, including the appropriateness of renewing the BCLAA, continued to be of concern to the Bengal Governor.[87] The process through which the Secretary of State, the Viceroy and the Governor of Bengal were to reach a conclusion on how the Bengal Act should be dealt with is a further useful illustration of how important policy decisions were decided between them.

Jackson informed Irwin his political department had put before the Government of India their view 'that the Act [expiring on 23 April 1930] should be retained on the Statute Book, but *not* to be brought into force except by notification by the Governor-General in Council'.[88] Jackson advised Irwin the main problem with this proposal was that it meant the Act would have to be reintroduced into the Legislative Council, and as it was unlikely to be approved by his ministry or passed by the Council, there would be a need for his certification. Jackson acknowledged the political problem of certification which could alienate the Moderates, but advised that the Bengal police were willing to risk any political consequences. Oddly, Jackson was to think 'it best to allow the proposals of his political department to go up to India', in the face of his personal view that it would be sufficient deterrence to terrorism merely to make a public statement that the Act would be again brought into force in case of need. Irwin in acknowledging the Governor's comments was to indicate 'I am rather concerned to know that your own view differs from that which your Government have officially expressed…it may put us in a certain difficulty'.[89] After consideration by his Government, Irwin advised the Secretary of State that the Governor of Bengal had been informed his Government's proposal

> …was open to objection on point of form and also to the serious practical objection, that it would not seem reasonable to revive the powers under such an Act save for comparatively short periods strictly limited to the immediate emergency, and consequently the Government might be continually faced with the difficult problem of deciding whether the powers should be continued.[90]

Irwin advised Wedgwood Benn that the Bengal Government had informed him that it would have preferred to continue the Act on a permanent basis, but in deference to political considerations they had not put this forward.[91] In a meeting with Irwin to discuss the BCLAA, which included Moberly, Bengal's Home Member, in Delhi on 3 March 1930, Jackson had indicated the political difficulties of making the powers of arrest and detention without trial permanent. He believed such action would play into the hands of the Extremists. The Governor favoured a course which would let these powers lapse, 'but there should be a definite announcement that, as soon as necessity arose, there would be no hesitation in re-enacting the powers'. The Governor expected a definite guarantee that the Viceroy and Secretary of State would approve an Ordinance, to be followed by local legislation, when judged necessary and recommended by him. He also held that 'the special procedure [the use of tribunals to expedite prosecutions] for trial of cases provided for in the earlier sections of the Act should be retained without a break', and that he would, if necessary ensure this by certification in the Council. Moberly was opposed to allowing the powers of arrest and detention to lapse, under the Act, even under the suggested guarantee, citing the need to encourage the police and discourage the terrorists. Moberly believed any delay in approval of satisfactory measures would need cover by the use of Regulation III of 1818. Jackson was later to provide the Viceroy with a record of their discussions.[92]

Irwin advised the Secretary of State that the matter of BCLAA had been discussed in his Council and 'we are clearly of the opinion that it is impossible to propose permanent continuance of the Act or to support the proposal made'[93] by the Government of Bengal. The Government of India had identified the two effective alternatives to be

> ...(a) to allow the provisions regarding detention without trial to lapse, accompanied by a strong and definite announcement, [that there would be no hesitation in re-enacting the powers of the previous Act], and the re-enactment probably for five years of the special procedure sections; or (b) the continuance of the whole Act for a period of five years.[94]

These alternatives had been put to Bengal, and Irwin informed Wedgwood Benn that, in the light of differences on the issue within the Bengal Government, it would be necessary to request his final decision at short notice. In response to these views, Governor Jackson indicated his government now favoured the adoption of alternative which would appear to involve a definite lapse of the BCLAA. If so Bengal would require any new legislation to include provision for 'special' procedures involving the use of tribunals to expedite prosecutions, which in effect would reduce the need for detention without trial.[95] Irwin informed Jackson 'it is essential that [his] Bill should in fact continue certain sections of the existing Act', and unless he disagreed 'we shall inform the Secretary of State officially the proposal of your Government is certain sections of the existing Act should be continued'.[96] After further communications on the refinement of the legislation and of the related statements to be made, including amendment by the Secretary of State to avoid threatening language, the BCLAA (Part Continuance) was passed, without serious opposition, by the Bengal Legislative Council on 1 April 1930. Jackson informed Irwin, 'I never dreamt that we should get it through so easily as up to the last moment considerable opposition was threatened'.[97] The Secretary of State was to make a statement in the British Parliament advising of the passage of the Bill and of its intent, including the option of the granting of executive powers of arrest and detention without trial if emergency recurred.[98] The Viceroy was to congratulate the Governor on his success.[99]

The security situation in Bengal was to deteriorate shortly afterwards to the point where the 'special' procedure contained in the new Act of expeditious trial by three judges was to be utilised. The fundamental underlying intent of the Secretary of State to win over public opinion in Britain and India by responding to extremism by restraint and moderation, is reflected in a personal letter on the matter to Lord Irwin.

> I was bitterly disappointed at the necessity for the revival of the first part of the BCLAA...we have always worked in order to enlist at any rate the silent support of public opinion on the side of public security; and in this regard I believe that extraordinary powers and severity of punishment only, in the end, accentuate the difficulties we are trying to overcome.[100]

On the other hand, Jackson, reacting under the reality of local circumstances, was to report:

> The arrest of known terrorists throughout Bengal under the Bengal Criminal Law Amendment Act was carried out with marvellous efficiency...We are all very grateful for the prompt manner in which you [Irwin] responded to our appeal.[101]

The various policy perspectives of the layers of participants involved in the decision process relating to the Bengal Act were indicative of their particular operational frameworks. The Government of Bengal and its police force drew their attitude, to the Act's renewal, from their practical in-field experience of violence and intelligence of terrorist intent. The Governor of Bengal, while sympathetic to the views of his operatives, was required to assimilate the practical politics and opinion of his constitutional regime; the Bengal Legislative Council and his ministers and Executive, as well as those of the Nationalists. Importantly, he was also required to take into account the practical realities of the Viceroy's own political situation, both with respect to Indian public opinion, including that expressed through his Assembly and the domestic press and that of metropolitan opinion, conveyed by the Secretary of State. The Viceroy and Government of India, at a distance from the immediate practical pressures of Bengal terrorist activity, were able to assess available policy options more dispassionately. The Secretary of State, far removed from the immediate tensions of India, inclined to the exercise of more ideological principles and politics. It is noteworthy that in the process of the interplay of the perspectives brought by these various layers of authority, conclusions and decisions were arrived at through courteous consultation, concession and consequent agreement. The record does not reflect, at any level, peremptory autocratic direction. In this environment the governors' views and perspectives were assimilated, to lesser or greater degree, into final decisions and outcomes.

Despite the measures available under the renewed BCLAA, the security situation in Bengal continued to deteriorate. In response, Acting Governor Stephenson informed Irwin that the security situation in Bengal demanded, in addition to the BCLAA, the more stringent measures of the old Bengal Criminal Law Amendment Ordinance (BCLAO)[102] in the form of legislation. Irwin agreed to this view and sought the concurrence of Wedgwood Benn. The Secretary of State's liberal attitude, and that of the British Cabinet, was again confirmed by their initial rejection of Irwin's request for legislation to replace the BCLAO. '...introduction and possible rejection at this juncture of proposals for permanent legislation will worsen situation. I must therefore press you to be content with the meeting of situation by re-enacting Ordinance when the time comes.'[103] Irwin had earlier informed Wedgwood Benn of details, drawn from advice from Bengal, of the extreme likelihood of an increase in terrorist activities there, as the Civil Disobedience Movement declined and that legislation was essential and should be permanent.[104] In the face of Benn's decision, Irwin responded, 'I am grateful to you for what you say over the Bengal Ordinance. I was sorry to have to be insistent, but I am quite certain that Stephenson is broadly right'.[105] Governor Stephenson, rebutting Benn's view admitted to Irwin 'I have written strongly, but I have been personally concerned in this revolutionary fight since 1916 or even before, and do know something of the revolutionary and of the outlook of the police'.[106] Wedgwood Benn had, in addition, been approached by Governor Jackson, in London, who had also strongly pressed the necessity for permanent legislation,[107] aligning with his representations to Irwin in November 1929. Irwin, having received Stephenson's representations again reinforced with Benn the British Indian view of what was necessary in Bengal. 'I am of opinion that his [Stephenson's] judgment in a matter like this is one it would be a grave error to disregard.'[108] In the face of this strong representation, and overriding his concern he was approving another Rowlatt Act,[109] Wedgwood Benn capitulated: 'I feel bound to accept your strong objections to a procedure by Ordinance'.[110] He insisted, however, that the legislation would have to have a time limit and be passed without certification.

It would seem the Secretary of State's and Cabinet's final decision had been precipitated by the Viceroy's strong views, based on the judgement of a highly regarded Service Governor. A strong element of this action would seem to reflect the importance of the personal factor in the decision making process at the most senior governmental levels, and even at the level of the British Cabinet. This decision making pathway may not have been available, in similar circumstances, to governors such as Montagu Butler or indeed to Jackson himself, who Irwin and Birkenhead evidently had not held in the highest esteem.[111] Sykes had also complicated his relationship with his seniors and their negative responses to his requests for security measures may have been based on a view that Sykes lacked judgement. Lytton had also been in this category. Despite Benn's concession, Irwin and Stephenson continued to press for a ten year duration for the Bengal Act against the Secretary of State's view that five would be appropriate.[112] On this time frame, Benn stood firm. In the event the Bill was passed, in the Bengal Legislative Assembly, by 61 votes to 15, without the need for certification,[113] and Benn admitted that it may have got through with a ten-year time frame.[114] He was to ask Irwin to 'convey to Stephenson (his) thanks for his action and congratulations on its success'. Jackson reported, from London, it was in fact the Prime Minister (R.J. MacDonald) who had upset the Cabinet's initial decision not to agree to the Bill and had agreed to legislation.[115]

From Bombay, Governor Sykes continued to argue for Ordinances and additional powers, along the lines of a Defence of the Realm Act (DORA),[116] to deal with the activities of the Civil Disobedience Movement. Irwin advised Bombay that his Government's 'general view is that local governments should take all measures necessary to counter the civil disobedience movement regardless of the Sapru conversations',[117] which were then occurring with Gandhi. Irwin also pressed Sykes to prosecute all members of the Congress

Working Committee, who had attended a recent meeting in Bombay,[118] and advised him again that he doubted whether the Governor was using his existing powers to the full.[119] The Viceroy was not convinced of the necessity of a forfeiture of property Ordinance requested by Sykes or of a DORA Ordinance, and also indicated his dissatisfaction at the rate of police recruitment in the Bombay Presidency.[120] In the case of the Ordinance to deal with local bodies, which had been drafted, Irwin advised, as it dealt with a transferred subject, action under it would require the concurrence of the relevant minister, unless the Governor was to exercise his overriding powers. Irwin stressed to Sykes 'I do not wish to issue an Ordinance and then to find that no action is taken under it'.[121] Irwin, while acknowledging the situation in Bombay was more difficult than in other provinces, reiterated his consistent policy view, derived from Hailey, 'that a great deal can be done at the moment by steady and unremitting pressure exercised through existing powers'.[122] Even so Irwin had, in fact, offered consistent support of the governors' security situations through the issuance of Ordinances, which Hailey had noted: 'We cannot complain that the Government of India has been inactive. The Viceroy has issued more Ordinances than I remember in the course of the last twenty years'.[123]

The contrast between Irwin's support and confidence in Stephenson and other governors, and his evident view that Sykes was not managing the crisis in Bombay as well as he could, is quite notable. Following a pattern, Irwin had strongly endorsed the policy approach of an experienced and trusted Service Governor, while finding a presidency governor's performance and approach wanting. It is significant, in this context that Stephenson had been only acting as Governor of the Presidency of Bengal during his representations, on the BCLAO, to Irwin and Wedgwood Benn. While Irwin also had not been entirely confident of Jackson in Bengal, Stanley had not really been tested to the extent of his other presidency colleagues and was still reporting all was quiet in Madras.[124]

At this time the Viceroy was to argue the case also, on behalf of de Montmorency, for measures, along the lines of the BCLAA of 1930, to combat terrorism in the Punjab. The terrorist movement was, with the exception of Bengal, 'better organised and more dangerous there [the Punjab] than in any other Province',[125] and during the previous twelve months there had been more than thirty terrorist attacks. Irwin was able to use the precedent of his recent dealings with Wedgwood Benn on the BCLAA and BCLAO, seeking his approval for 'drastic' legislation but shaped its form to what he knew would be more acceptable, by only requesting a duration for the legislation of five years. In the event, Wedgwood Benn agreed to

Irwin's request stressing again the importance of securing passage of the Bill without certification,[126] which de Montmorency was able to achieve.[127] De Montmorency's sound reputation may have, once again, assisted Irwin's approach to the Secretary of State on the matter.

The considerations, which the layers of Indian Government—Secretary of State, Viceroy and governors—took into account in relation to policy towards terrorists and the Civil Disobedience Movement at the end of 1930, are further exemplified by their examination of the aspects of renewal of four critical Ordinances which were expiring at the time of the Round Table Conference. These were the Press and News-Sheets Ordinances, expiring on 27 October 1930, and the Intimidation and Instigation Ordinances expiring on 29 November. The Viceroy was to ask his governors three questions in relation to the renewal of the Ordinances. First, were the Ordinances of real value in combating emergency? Second, whether the powers should be renewed at once or could be delayed? Third, did the existing powers in the light of experience need modification?[128] Having considered the replies of the local governments with respect to the Press and News-Sheets Ordinances, Irwin informed Wedgwood Benn

> ...that on the question of policy they [the Governors] are entirely unanimous that in combating the civil disobedience campaign, principally by checking malicious propaganda and incitement to sedition, powers have been of definite value and that powers should be renewed with no interval between lapse and renewal.[129]

Some minor amendments to the Ordinances were also suggested. The Viceroy agreed with the governors that 'removal of control over press would give an impetus to subversive movements at a very critical time and would gravely prejudice the progress achieved by the unremitting effort during the last few months'.[130] However, Irwin informed Wedgwood Benn that for legal reasons there would have to be a lapse of the existing Ordinances, and the establishment of clear grounds for action as created by civil disobedience. Accordingly, Irwin was to suggest a draft measure, combining the Press and News-Sheets Ordinances, would be prepared and held in readiness. Irwin sought the Secretary of State's approval to promulgate the Ordinance when the Governor-General (Irwin and his Executive Council) saw fit. Benn agreed to the text of the Ordinance and to Irwin's suggested procedure but asked Irwin to consider 'whether in order to avoid the assumption of these very strong powers which for example enable the arrest of children selling newspapers in the streets some other means of dealing with the case could not be devised'.[131] Later the Secretary of State asked for Irwin's views on how a Press Ordinance would be likely to react on the Round Table Conference, to be advised that he (Irwin) had written 'personally to all Governors emphasising our desire to carry on without resort to special powers if we could do so without jeopardising the position'.[132] However on balance the view held by the Indian administration was that the risk of a serious deterioration in the situation in India of not renewing the Ordinance outweighed any likely impact on the Conference. Irwin advised:

> So far as India is concerned I do not think the Press Ordinance will materially affect the Conference. We shall of course, have the usual criticisms about repression in India being inconsistent with conciliation in London...I hope that reactions on the delegates would not be more than ephemeral.

Governor Stephenson had written to Irwin in quite unequivocal terms on the subject of the Ordinance and the Conference.

> The Round Table Conference has not the slightest influence on the decrease in civil disobedience. It is decreasing because the Congress know they are beaten and because people in general are getting weary of it, but the Round Table Conference is a factor only in keeping it going. To my mind the only hope of any Round Table agreement, if reached, being accepted out here is for us to keep the ring meanwhile. If we can enforce law and order and keep the peace, we are creating an atmosphere in which agreement is possible.[133]

Stephenson did not like the prospect of having to prove a deterioration in circumstance before a renewal of the Press Ordinance would be approved and did not 'share what seems to me to be the pathetic trust of the Government of India in the Criminal Law Amendment Act', as a substitute for Ordinances. Sykes was to suggest the 'examination of the possibility of including all Ordinances required in one comprehensive Ordinance of the nature of a D.O.R.A.'.[134]

With regard to the Intimidation (against picketing and boycott) and Instigation (against non-payment of taxes) Ordinances, Irwin advised Wedgwood Benn that local governments had all agreed 'on the necessity of constant vigilance and the danger of a relaxation of effort. Congress leaders have shown no sign of any suspension of programme...we cannot count on such rapid improvement as will permit abandonment of powers'.[135] Irwin again sought Benn's approval to the principle of the renewal of the Ordinances' powers if the circumstances required, and after the current Ordinances had expired. Local governments had also been asked whether it would be possible to 'introduce provincial legislation for this purpose and whether that would require certification',[136] but opinion was generally opposed to local legislation. Taking into account the various views he had received on the matter of the renewal of the Ordinances under consideration, Irwin wrote to all his governors to inform them of 'the way we are inclined to look at the question'.[137] Irwin felt if it were possible it would be better 'to carry on without the powers...[to avoid an impression] that the powers we may take are in excess of the requirements of the situation'. Therefore, Irwin believed, before there was any resort to the powers of the Ordinances 'we ought to be quite sure that the necessity in fact exists'. Even with the prospect of losing ground, Irwin felt there was more to gain 'by allowing a probationary interval' before any renewal. Irwin also alerted the governors to his continued sensitivity to the need not to complicate the Round Table Conference process or to offend Wedgwood Benn.

> I am thinking a good deal of my obligation to the Secretary of State...He has been very good in sanctioning the measures we considered necessary, and in the present instance he has approved of the policy of renewal of powers on the sole condition that we are satisfied that the situation requires them.[138]

Irwin concluded by indicating 'I should be glad to hear how all this strikes you, if there are any points not covered by our respective official communications'. In response the governors of the Punjab, Assam, Madras, and the United Provinces,[139] were all to advise that in their circumstances they had no need at the present to seek the powers of the Intimidation and Internment Ordinances. Within days Irwin informed the governors he had

> ...finally decided on the Press Ordinance in the light of rather pressing information from Bengal and the Punjab as to the influence the Press was having in the direction of violent crime...[and] the Secretary of State has agreed to the Instigation Ordinance,[140] [but further consideration was to be given to the Intimidation Ordinance.][141]

Having considered the advice received from Bengal and the Punjab and the effect of the renewal of the Ordinances on the outcome of the Round Table, Irwin had decided on balance 'that failure to renew immediately Press Ordinances will favour revival of civil disobedience movement'.[142] The Viceroy was to issue the Ordinances with special instructions to the governors that their powers should not be abused.

This chapter reveals again the nature of the working relationship between the governors and the Viceroy and Secretary of State. While tensions were evident in the relationship, consequent on the strains presented by nationalism and emergency, the governors were required to engage in what was a difficult process of policy development with the Centre, to meet the challenge of insurgency. The provincial governors engaged in this process more easily. The policy outcome was a firm and measured response to the threat presented by emergency which was developed by the parties in a detailed and considered way. The next chapter will explore the governors' response to the complicated circumstances of the Bardoli land tax assessment.

Endnotes

1. Halifax Papers, Jackson to Irwin, 4 and 18 April 1928.
2. P.A. Spratt. British Communist agitator; as was a Mr Bradley. These men 'had arrived in India with specific instructions to organise the Workers' and Peasants' Party as a legal cover for the Communists and to infiltrate the labour unions'. See Laushey, *Bengal Terrorism*, p. 91.
3. Halifax Papers, Jackson to Irwin, 4 and 18 April 1928.
4. *Ibid.*, Wilson to Irwin, 23 April 1928.
5. *Ibid.*, Wilson to Irwin, 28 April 1928.
6. *Ibid.*
7. *Ibid.*, Telegram, Secretary of State to Viceroy, 2 May 1928.
8. *Ibid.*, Telegram, Viceroy to Secretary of State, 9 May 1928.
9. *Ibid.*
10. *Ibid.*
11. *Ibid.*, Wilson to Irwin, 12 May 1928.
12. *Ibid.*
13. *Ibid.*, Telegram, Governor of Bengal to Viceroy, 14 May 1928.
14. *Ibid.*, Telegram, Viceroy to Governor of Bengal, 16 May 1928.
15. See D. Chakrabarty, *Rethinking Working Class History*, for a detailed analysis and history of the jute industry in Bengal, and of the plight of workers in the uneven power relationship with mill owners. See pp. 119–120 for the economic basis of the 1929 general strike in Calcutta.
16. Halifax Papers, Jackson to Irwin, 19 May 1928.
17. *Ibid.*, Jackson to Irwin, 6 June 1928.
18. *Ibid.*, Jackson to Irwin, 30 June 1928.
19. *Ibid.*, Wilson to Irwin, 22 May 1928.
20. *Ibid.*, Telegram, Viceroy to Secretary of State, 22 June 1928; Telegram, Viceroy to Secretary of State, 13 July 1928.
21. *Ibid.*, Wilson to Irwin, 20 June 1928.
22. *Ibid.*, Irwin to Wilson, 25 June 1928.
23. *Ibid.*, Goschen to Irwin, 27 July 1928.
24. Goschen Papers, Goschen to Birkenhead, 15 June 1927.
25. Hailey Papers, Hailey to Hirtzel, 15 March 1926.

26. *Ibid.*, Hirtzel to Goschen, 16 August 1928.
27. Halifax Papers, Telegram, Governor of Bombay to Viceroy, 9 August 1928.
28. *Ibid.*, Telegram, Governor of Bengal to Viceroy, 9 August 1928.
29. *Ibid.*, Telegram, Viceroy to Governor of Bombay, 13 August 1928.
30. *Ibid.*, Irwin to Jackson, 14 August 1928.
31. *Ibid.*, Telegram, Governor of Bombay to Viceroy, 22 August 1928.
32. *Ibid.*
33. Keith, *Constitutional History*, p. 289.
34. F.C. Isemonger. C.I.E., C.B.E. Indian Police Service 1898. Director, Intelligence Bureau, Home Department, Government of India.
35. The Third International was a Communist organisation founded in Moscow in 1919, and designed by all available means to overthrow Capitalism and the international bourgeoisie.
36. Halifax Papers, Telegram, Governor of Bombay to Viceroy, 22 August 1928.
37. *Ibid.*, Irwin to Wilson, 29 August 1928.
38. *Ibid.*
39. *Ibid.*, Irwin to various governors, 28 September 1928.
40. *Ibid.*, Irwin to Sykes, 2 January 1929.
41. See Sykes, *From Many Angles*, p. 370, for an example of Irwin, in mid 1929, refusing Sykes powers of an Ordinance to deal with picketing and intimidation, and Wedgwood Benn only conditionally assenting to emergency legislation.
42. Halifax Papers, Irwin to Sykes, 18 January 1929; Irwin to Jackson, 18 January 1929.
43. *Ibid.*, Telegram, Viceroy to Secretary of State, 19 January 1929.
44. *Ibid.*
45. *Ibid.*, Jackson to Irwin, 26 January 1929.
46. Gupta, Sen. Chairman of the Congress Reception Committee in 1929.
47. Halifax Papers, Jackson to Irwin, 26 January 1929.
48. *Ibid.*, Sykes to Irwin, 26 January 1929. It is interesting to note this 10 page policy letter, with attachments, had been 'blind' copied to the Conservative Secretary of State, Peel, without evidence of this to the Viceroy. It drew a response from Peel to the Viceroy, indicating an immediate need for action. See Telegram, Secretary of State to Viceroy, 21 February 1929. See footnote number 59, this chapter.
49. Sir G. Rainy. ICS, 1898. Member of the Governor-General's Council.
50. Hailey Papers, Irwin to Hailey, 10 January 1929.
51. Halifax Papers, Sykes to Irwin, 26 January 1929.
52. *Ibid.*
53. A Committee under Sir Charles Fawcett, Chief Justice of the Indian High Court, which at the beginning of 1929 conducted an enquiry into the mutual relations of employers and employed in Bombay.
54. Sykes, *From Many Angles*, p. 361.
55. *Report of the Royal Commission on Labour in India*, London, His Majesty's Stationery Office, 1931.

56. Sykes, *From Many Angles*, pp. 371–372.
57. An old Statute of the East India Company which could be used to arrest and deport communists from India.
58. Halifax Papers, Sykes to Irwin, 26 January 1929.
59. Sykes Papers, Irwin to Sykes, 10 February 1929.
60. Halifax Papers, Telegram, Secretary of State to Viceroy, 21 February 1929.
61. Sykes Papers, Peel to Sykes, 21 February 1929.
62. Sykes, *From Many Angles*, p. 363.
63. Halifax Papers, Telegram, Viceroy to Secretary of State, 19 March 1929.
64. *Ibid.*, Telegram, Governor of Bombay to Viceroy, 30 April 1929.
65. The BCLAA provided for internment without trial and arrest on suspicion of terrorist intent. It was politically sensitive in Britain and India.
66. Halifax Papers, Jackson to Irwin, 10 May 1929.
67. *Ibid.*, Irwin to Jackson, 18 May 1929; Telegram, Viceroy to Secretary of State, 17 May 1929.
68. *Ibid.*, Irwin to Hailey and de Montmorency, 1 June 1929.
69. *Ibid.*
70. NAI, Home/Political, Secret note on file 155, 8 June 1929.
71. Sir D. Petrie. Indian Police Service 1900. Director, Intelligence Bureau, Government of India.
72. No decision on the matter was recorded on the file. It is interesting to note Irwin did not, according to the record, contribute to the lengthy discussion beyond asking two straightforward questions relating to whether the detenus had reformed their ways, and what Congress' reaction would be to a reasonable Simon Commission outcome.
73. Halifax Papers, Telegram, Governor of Bombay to Viceroy, 24 June 1929.
74. *Ibid.*, Telegram, Viceroy to Secretary of State, 16 July 1929.
75. *Ibid.*, Telegram, Viceroy to Secretary of State, 11 July 1929.
76. *Times of India*, 19 June 1929.
77. Halifax Papers, Telegram, Secretary of State to Viceroy, 24 July 1929.
78. Laushey, *Bengal Terrorism*, p. 28.
79. Halifax Papers, Telegram, Viceroy to Secretary of State, 6 November 1929.
80. *Ibid.*
81. *Ibid.*, Lytton to Irwin, 28 November 1929.
82. *Ibid.*, Telegram, Secretary of State to Viceroy, 26 November 1929.
83. *Ibid.*, Telegram, Viceroy to Secretary of State, 6 December 1929.
84. *Ibid.*
85. *Ibid.*, Viceroy to various governors, 12 December 1929.
86. *Ibid.*, Jackson to Irwin, 9 January 1930.
87. *Ibid.*, Jackson to Irwin, 20 January 1930.
88. *Ibid.*
89. *Ibid.*, Irwin to Jackson, 26 January 1930.
90. *Ibid.*, Telegram, Viceroy to Secretary of State, 5 March 1930.
91. *Ibid.*

92. *Ibid.*, Jackson to Irwin, 10 March 1930.
93. *Ibid.*, Telegram, Viceroy to Secretary of State, 5 March 1930.
94. *Ibid.*
95. *Ibid.*, Telegram, Governor of Bengal to Viceroy, 8 March 1930.
96. *Ibid.*, Telegram, Viceroy to Governor of Bengal, 11 March 1930.
97. *Ibid.*, Jackson to Irwin, 2 April 1930.
98. *Ibid.*, Telegram, Secretary of State to Viceroy, 25 March 1930.
99. *Ibid.*, Irwin to Jackson, 5 April 1930.
100. NAI, Home/Political, file 350/1930, private letter, Wedgwood Benn to Irwin, 22 April 1930.
101. Halifax Papers, Jackson to Irwin, 25 April 1930.
102. Hereafter BCLAO.
103. Halifax Papers, Telegram, Secretary of State to Viceroy, 30 July 1930; Wedgwood Benn to Irwin, 1 August 1930.
104. *Ibid.*, Telegram, Viceroy to Secretary of State, 25 July 1930.
105. *Ibid.*, Irwin to Wedgwood Benn, 5 August 1930.
106. *Ibid.*, Stephenson to Irwin, 2 August 1930.
107. *Ibid.*, Wedgwood Benn to Irwin, 1 August 1930.
108. *Ibid.*, Telegram, Viceroy to Secretary of State, 4 August 1930.
109. *Ibid.*, Wedgwood Benn to Irwin, 1 August 1930. The Rowlatt Act, passed in 1919 to counter terrorism, caused considerable Indian resentment. Its powers were never used.
110. *Ibid.*, Telegram, Secretary of State to Viceroy, 5 August 1930.
111. Birkenhead as Secretary of State in 1929 had passed over Jackson, the senior Governor, as acting Viceroy in favour of Lord Goschen. Presumably Irwin had concurred in this decision.
112. Halifax Papers, Telegram, Viceroy to Secretary of State, 8 August 1930.
113. *Ibid.*, Telegram, Viceroy to Secretary of State, 23 August 1930.
114. *Ibid.*, Wedgwood Benn to Irwin, 28 August 1930.
115. *Ibid.*, Jackson to Irwin, 27 August 1930.
116. Hereafter DORA.
117. Halifax Papers, Telegram, Viceroy to Governor of Bombay, 9 August 1930.
118. *Ibid.*, Telegram, Governor of Bombay to Viceroy, 13 August 1930.
119. *Ibid.*, Telegram, Viceroy to Governor of Bombay, 16 August 1930.
120. *Ibid.*
121. *Ibid.*
122. *Ibid.*
123. Hailey Papers, Hailey to Irwin, 2 June 1930.
124. Halifax Papers, Stanley to Irwin, 25 August 1930.
125. *Ibid.*, Telegram, Viceroy to Secretary of State, 4 October 1930.
126. *Ibid.*, Telegram, Secretary of State to Viceroy, 10 October 1930.
127. *Ibid.*, de Montmorency to Irwin, 8 November 1930.
128. *Ibid.*, Telegram, Viceroy to Secretary of State, 4 October 1930.
129. *Ibid.*, Telegram, Viceroy to Secretary of State, 7 November 1930.

130. *Ibid.*, Telegram, Viceroy to Secretary of State, 8 October 1930.
131. *Ibid.*, Telegram, Secretary of State to Viceroy, 25 October 1930.
132. *Ibid.*, Telegram, Viceroy to Secretary of State, 20 December 1930.
133. *Ibid.*, Stephenson to Irwin, 2 December 1930.
134. *Ibid.*, Sykes to Irwin, 3 December 1930.
135. *Ibid.*, Telegram, Viceroy to Secretary of State, 14 November 1930.
136. *Ibid.*, Viceroy to Secretary of State, 7 November 1930.
137. *Ibid.*, Irwin to various governors, 9 December 1930.
138. *Ibid.*
139. *Ibid.*, de Montmorency to Irwin, 12 December 1930; Hammond to Irwin, 12 December 1930; Stanley to Irwin, 15 December 1930; Lambert (acting) to Irwin, 18 December 1930.
140. *Ibid.*, Irwin to Lambert (and other governors), 21 December 1930.
141. *Ibid.*, Irwin to Stephenson, 18 December 1930.
142. *Ibid.*, Telegram, Viceroy to Secretary of State, 20 December 1930.

7

The Challenge of Bardoli and Lessons Learnt

Developments in Bardoli were to be recognised by the British as a complex and dangerous challenge, as the event struck at a fundamental pillar of British rule, namely the collection of land revenue. Any failure in Bardoli would strike not only a political blow but also potentially at the orderly collection of revenue across India and thus at the whole Indian (and British) economy, at a time when the world economy was already precarious. Of course the protagonists had selected their Bardoli strategy for these reasons. This chapter will explore how the governors responded to the grass roots resistance of the Bardoli farmers or *ryots*, and the threat that the situation posed to British rule across India. It will also identify the decision-making process applied by the British Indian rulers to find a solution to this difficulty.

The Governor of Bombay, Sir Leslie Wilson, was to make to the Viceroy a first and relatively minor reference to Bardoli, in March 1928 when he advised him the Swarajists in his Legislative Council had been defeated by nine votes over support for the Government's Bardoli policy.[1] The crisis in the Bardoli *taluka*[2] of the Surat district of Bombay Presidency had arisen over a scheduled thirty year re-assessment of land tax, increasing the amount to be paid by the farmers, an amount which was being refused by them. Wilson assured Irwin 'I have been into the case most carefully and very minutely checked the figures before the orders were issued, with the result that I am convinced we are right, and that no hardship whatever is put on the ryots of the taluka'.[3] In another note, shortly afterwards, Wilson informed the Viceroy:

> I have satisfied myself that we are acting absolutely fairly; in fact, are erring on the lenient side. It is a remarkable fact that they have chosen the Bardoli Taluka for their agitation, when there is another taluka quite close where the re-assessment is even higher, and nothing is said about that. Bardoli is always considered the most fruitful place to start these negotiations.[4]

Wilson, no doubt was to regret his early confidence, as Bardoli was to become the principal matter to absorb his and the Raj's energies in 1928. Bardoli had a certain sensitivity in British eyes as it was the place Mahatma Gandhi had chosen, in 1922, to lead a non-violent mass civil disobedience campaign which included the non-payment of taxes. This campaign had collapsed as the result of Gandhi's withdrawal at the repugnance he felt over the murder of Indian policemen at Chauri Chaura in the United Provinces. While Gandhi was to become associated with the 1928 Bardoli campaign led by Vallabhbhai Patel,[5] the actual and underlying causes of the movement were to be debated by the Viceroy and the governors, as shall be noted.

By the end of April 1928, Wilson had begun to see the implications of the developments in Bardoli but continued to believe that the

> ...agriculturalists really have no grievance...this non-payment of land revenue is purely a political stunt, and one which must be defeated. If we give in, in any way, over this, the result would be very serious in other parts of the Presidency where re-assessments have been, or are being put in force.[6]

Consequent upon his belief that the farmers had no real grievance, Wilson was to reject a request, by the eight Gujarati members of the Bombay Legislative Council, to set up an independent enquiry as to the merits of the agriculturalists' case. These councillors represented the Bardoli *ryots*, and were threatening to resign. Wilson affirmed to Irwin that 'this is purely a Congress movement up there...and it is absolutely impossible for us to give in an inch when fighting a question of principle like this'.[7] By this time the government had increased its pressure on the agitators by selling land forfeited because of non-payment of tax and was continuing to resist calls for an independent enquiry. Irwin advised Wilson of his full support for the Governor's Bardoli policy, where 'matters are no direct business of mine and obviously lie within your province'.[8] To this point Irwin had seen no need to intervene to direct policy regarding Bardoli but he was soon to become actively involved.

Even though Irwin had stated that Bardoli matters were not his direct business, he was to remind Wilson of the predominant concern of the Government of India to coordinate important policy matters across the provinces of British India. Irwin had read articles in the *Times of India* revealing Wilson was now considering an independent official enquiry into Bardoli matters. He was to inform the Governor, 'I trust you will let us know before any important action is taken which might have reactions elsewhere'.[9] It was fortunate, perhaps, Irwin had picked up the newspaper references as the Secretary of State had also done so and informed Irwin:

> I am seriously perturbed by newspaper reports of what is going on in Bardoli. Altogether apart from its bearing on the situation as regards the Simon Commission it is surely impossible to tolerate the sort of unofficial government which seems to have been set up and to which subsidy from the President of the Legislative Assembly [Vithalbhai Patel] must seem to people as much an official sanction.[10]

The vernacular press had also picked up on the sensitivity of Bardoli. The official translation and summary of vernacular newspapers in the United Provinces noted: 'Newspapers generally vehemently condemn what they call a policy of terrorism on the part of officials…and pay a tribute to the tenants of Bardoli as pioneers in the fight for Indian independence'.[11]

In his first intervention on Bardoli, Birkenhead acknowledged to Irwin he had received communications from Wilson on the matter but in his view it was 'imperative before things go any further to demonstrate unmistakably that Government can and will govern'.[12] While formally indicating 'the responsibility is yours' Birkenhead was by strong implication to put before Irwin the level of response to developments in Bardoli he now thought necessary.

> I shall of course give you the fullest support in any measures you and Wilson think necessary to take such as the arrest of leaders under the Bombay Regulation 25 of 1827 if there are no other means of dealing with them, or intensive campaign of distraint for non-payment under protection of troops. This may not improve prospects of co-operation with Simon, but re-assertion of Government authority seems to me even more important at the moment.[13]

In response Irwin copied by telegram, a letter dated 1 July he had received from Wilson, which set out the latest situation in Bardoli. Wilson had advised there had been no serious change since 9 June, and the land forfeitures he had imposed continued. Citing an unparalleled misrepresentation of facts the Governor had indicated 'if it is at all possible Governor in Council considers no stone should be left unturned to conciliate public opinion'.[14] A meeting of the Governor's Council and ministers had been held on 29 June and the

> Opinion of majority was that Government, in view of need of conciliating public opinion should make an offer to cultivators, substance of which is that Government will next cold weather appoint an officer to enquire into settlement and, if necessary, make proposals for modification provided they first pay up the revised settlement for the current year. Stress is laid on condition that before enquiry is made revised revenue must be paid in full.[15]

Given the all-India implications Wilson had sought Irwin's approval for this course. After a general discussion of a range of considerations, Irwin informed Wilson that the Government of India

> ...would be reluctant to dissent from considered judgement of Governor in Council and Ministers; but feel strongly that any such offer if made should be accompanied by statement that Government would be obliged to consider further action to secure compliance with the law if offer of Government is not instrumental in securing settlement. Such further measures might include issue of Ordinance.[16]

Irwin asked Birkenhead to defer any public statement in Britain, on a policy approach to Bardoli, until Wilson's response to the Viceroy's view had been received. Irwin had now reached a point where Bardoli had assumed such importance in his mind that he was to suggest to Wilson sending Secretary Haig, Home Department, to Bombay to ensure the necessary level of coordination between the two governments.[17] The Viceroy also advised Wilson he himself should 'visit Bardoli or the Headquarters of the District, with the expressed object of informing yourself at first hand of the situation... [and] exercising some direct personal influence'.[18] In the same message Irwin asked Wilson whether he had considered the possibility of what might be seen as a more impartial non-official re-enquiry, which might be conducted by a senior legal or judicial person assisted by an expert Revenue Officer. Some perception of Irwin's own behaviour, its influence on the development of policy advice and an indication of his innate good manners were reflected in the concluding paragraph to a telegram to Wilson, in which he had further developed these ideas. 'I beg you not to think me either presumptuous or interfering—I only desire to help you in any way I can. But I am apprehensive of the reactions of this business inside and outside your Presidency...'.[19] Wilson's immediate reply was to indicate that the key issue continued to be the payment of enhanced land revenue before any enquiry, and if this could be achieved by the appointment of a judicial person he could agree to this. However, 'I do not think it of any use my going to Bardoli unless agreement about payment of land revenue is reached'.[20] But Wilson thought an Ordinance enabling the expulsion of undesirable persons from Bardoli would be very useful.

At this stage Birkenhead judged he had all the information on Bardoli necessary to make a very strong intervention to Irwin.

> I must however make my own position plain; it is with some anxiety that I note the weakening in the attitude of the Government of Bombay...I do

not accept what seems to be the view of the Governor and his Ministers that primary consideration is conciliation of public opinion...the primary consideration is to break this movement [Congress non-cooperation] before it has gone any further, and to show the whole of India unmistakably that no such attempt can succeed.[21]

Birkenhead made the observation that 'the enemy have chosen their ground badly, because the Bombay Government's case appears to be unchallengeable on its merits and I can see no grounds for weakening in their attitude or in departure...from their policy'.[22] Birkenhead went on to note the activities of Congress in the agitation and its connection with communism both in Britain and in India, and to remind Irwin that Congress should consequently, in accordance with the British 'friends and enemies policy'[23] be cold shouldered. Irwin immediately suggested to Wilson they should meet quickly to discuss matters, and in place of the intended visit by Haig.[24] By 12 July Bardoli had become of sufficient importance in British politics to reach consideration by the British Cabinet.[25]

Irwin reported his meeting with Wilson to Birkenhead on 16 July.[26] Irwin pointed out that due

...to the skilful use of remarks made by the Settlement Commissioner and the disparaging conclusions of the Settlement Officer...moderate opinion is ranged very strongly against the Government...There is a genuine belief that the settlement has not been a fair one to the cultivators and requires to be re-examined. It was in this context that Wilson and his Ministers felt that public opinion needed to be conciliated.

The Viceroy advised that a number of issues had been agreed with Wilson.

The immediate policy should be to urge on with the measures of forfeiture, sale and warning, as it is evident that we shall have succeeded in discrediting the movement instead of making martyrs of its leaders, if these measures produce the result we want.[27]

It had been agreed Wilson would visit the district, making it clear the government was determined, if need be, to enforce payment stressing the first conditions of any settlement must be cessation of agitation immediately, the payment of the revised assessment and the abandonment of the claim for a non-official enquiry. Only then could government 'agree to grant an official enquiry into any alleged errors of calculation or fact affecting the whole or individual assessments...[but not] into the principles of land revenue settlement'.[28] If no agreement could be reached:

> ...then it is proposed by Leslie Wilson to state in opening his Legislative Council on the 23rd instant what Government of Bombay had been and indeed still would be ready to do provided they received a clear assurance within a fortnight of the termination of the movement...[if this course was rejected] Government will take all necessary measures to enforce compliance with the law and to crush the movement by direct action.[29]

Birkenhead's impatience with conciliation was revealed in his advice to the Viceroy and Wilson that if he were the Governor, 'I should allow no further time for palaver, but should announce on the 23rd what Government intend to do as from that date and do it'.[30] Irwin responded, 'I think we must leave management of tactical situation to Wilson who has throughout contemplated imposition of a time-limit',[31] which Wilson saw as essential so the effect of his speech would have time to sink in.[32]

Prior to Wilson's departure for Surat and Bardoli, Birkenhead reinforced with him, through the Viceroy.

> I trust you will make it plain that you are there to announce decision of Government and not to negotiate and will bear in mind that it is not our policy to save Patel's face, but on the contrary to discredit him and his supporters by all possible means and even at the cost of some prolongation of the struggle...Subject is arousing great interest here not only in Cabinet but also in Conservative party where apparent supineness of Government has come in for much criticism. I shall do my best to dispel it, for I am satisfied that you are doing and intend to do all that authority and prestige of Government require.[33]

On 19 July the Viceroy informed Birkenhead:

> Leslie Wilson telegraphs from Camp that on the 18th he had meetings all day, but arrived at no agreement. Vallabhbhai Patel appears to have spoken for the other side and claimed that payment of new assessment should be suspended pending result of enquiry.[34]

Wilson was, in the event, to address his Legislative Council in the terms agreed with Irwin and largely with Birkenhead. Next day, the Governor advised Irwin, 'it is impossible to say much at the moment as to the effect which my speech will have',[35] but felt that, owing to the influence of Patel, coercive measures might have to be introduced to meet the situation.

To add to his woes at this time, Wilson informed Irwin of further developments on the labour front in Bombay Province. 'The communist strike leaders are embarking on an attempt to force a general strike on the Great Indian Peninsula Railway system...[and] it may paralyse our activities in Gujerat [Bardoli]'.[36] The success of the Communists would have impacted on the ability to move police and troops by rail if drastic action had to be taken in Bardoli. Pressure seemed to be mounting on Wilson when the following day he informed Irwin 'I understand that Gandhi is now active and advising Patel',[37] and of Patel's former connection with railway workers when he had earlier been Chairman of the Railway Workers Union in Ahmedabad.

Despite his concerns, but in accordance with his judgement that Patel and his supporters should be given a fortnight to consider, Wilson was able to inform the Viceroy, and through him the Secretary of State, on 6 August 1928,

> ...the Revenue Member has received a letter signed by all members of the Legislative Council who represent cultivators in Bardoli stating that they are now in a position to inform Government that the conditions laid down by me in my opening speech to Council on July 23rd will be fulfilled...Patel and Gandhi will of course try and save their faces.[38]

Wilson's ability to judge the prevailing and immediate circumstances of the volatile Bardoli problem had produced a favourable outcome for the British, which had belied Birkenhead's more reactionary preference. Irwin had maintained confidence in Wilson's capacity to achieve a breakthrough, and had deferred to the Governor's preferred policy approach. In a long note[39] to Birkenhead copied to Irwin, Wilson set out the issues relating to the settlement of the Bardoli crisis, including the preparations he had made in the event that the government's ultimatum had not been accepted. These included arrangements for the arrest of the *Satyagraha*[40] participants under the Criminal Law Amendment Act, the removal of the Collector who had been incompetent and the drafting of police and troops. The Governor had been very concerned with the possibility of the Communists bringing the railways to a standstill, which almost certainly would have occurred, considerably escalating the crisis, had Patel and Gandhi rejected Wilson's conditions. While the Governor did not, in his note, directly set out an analysis of why his policy in Bardoli had succeeded for the British, the inference carried was that perceptions of government firmness and strength had prevailed. There was no acknowledgement, by Wilson, that Gandhi may have played a role in calling off a non-violent movement, which had been conducted previously within his definition of *Satyagraha*, and which now threatened violence.[41] Both sides claimed victory.

In trying to resolve the difficulties in Bardoli, over the six months of the campaign, Governor Wilson had refused to negotiate with Patel and had been ordered by Birkenhead not to have anything to do with the Mahatma. Wilson had attempted to negotiate, in a constitutional way, through the members of the Bombay Legislative Council representing the Bardoli ryots. In his note to Birkenhead he advised him that these members had indicated that 'however willing they could not give a reply accepting my conditions without the consent of Patel'.[42] Wilson

> ...reminded them of my own responsibility as laid down in my Instrument of Instructions[43] in paragraph 2, where it says that I should bear in mind that it is necessary for me to see that those who are returned to the Council shall look for the redress of the grievances of their constituents to the work of representative institutions. I explained to them that they were the proper representatives of the Bardoli peasants...,[44] [and not Patel.]

In 1928, Parliamentary principles were still not working, to British advantage as fully as intended by them, in Bombay Presidency.

Irwin was to give his friend Dawson, of *The Times* of London, his succinct and confidential view of why there had been serious trouble in Bardoli.

> ...between ourselves, he [Wilson] was badly let down in the earlier stages of the business (a) by the people who did the assessment and by his own Revenue Department, who ought, at the early stages, to have got out of the business, as they easily could have, by ordering a re-enquiry, and (b) by his local officials who, whether inadvertently or by design, gave little hint of the potential dangers of the position.[45]

Following the settlement reached by Wilson on Bardoli on 6 August, Irwin had written to him seeking his advice of lessons learnt in order to inform other governors. Wilson responded that the first lesson was undoubtedly the need

> ...to take into consideration, when there is any hint of a dispute about a re-assessment, the political history and condition of the taluka or district concerned, with particular reference to the fact as to whether or not there has been any evidence of teachings there of the policy of civil disobedience. On the first warning given to the Collector he should inform the Commissioner and issue public warnings of the steps the Government would take in the face of refusal to pay taxes.[46]

Wilson advised that 'the most important lesson, however, which has been taught [to] me is the difficulty, under the law as it stands, of dealing with an organised campaign for non-payment of taxes'. He strongly urged that local governments should have the powers to make non-payment of taxes definitely illegal. This was particularly the case 'as the organised non-payment of taxes is a definite plank in Gandhi's platform of civil disobedience'. Interestingly, in the face of this advice Irwin informed the governors that he did not feel 'fresh powers are necessary',[47] and the powers of the current Land Revenue Code and the Criminal Law Amendment Act were sufficient, to cope with situations such as Bardoli, as long as the emergency was dealt with quickly .[48] Birkenhead also advised his views of the need for decisive action to Irwin. 'The immediate success of Goschen's prompt grasping of the nettle in the Madras railway strike seems to show that the moment we really assert ourselves opposition collapses',[49] and, even in the face of the Governor's success, to reject Wilson's justification for delay of allowing 'a political movement to come to a head'. Consequently, Irwin informed the governors of the need for the earliest action where land revenue assessments could cause opposition.[50]

Following Wilson's analysis, Irwin turned to all the governors for their views on how incidents such as the one that occurred at Bardoli might be prevented.[51] He advised them, he believed a fundamental issue and weakness in the existing system was that, while land tax payers had only the executive to appeal to for redress of grievances, which was not seen as an independent arrangement, income tax payers could appeal to the High Court. Irwin suggested the importance of putting 'our heads together over the matter' in joint deliberations at a Revenue Conference.

Governor Hailey, the first to reply, agreed with the growing importance of questions connected with the assessment of land revenue: '...the danger of the future lay less in the urban agitation to which we have been accustomed, than in the possibility that the minds of the rural population may be unsettled by agitation regarding land revenue and similar issues'.[52] He had also informed the king about this view,[53] and that 'The United Provinces Government was alarmed by the propagation of communist ideology in the course of the peasant agitation',[54] again identifying the link between communism and nationalist activity. Hailey advised Irwin that, in the United Provinces, they were about to bring forward a Land Revenue Bill which would address a number of important matters, such as the length of settlements and the rate of maximum increase, but which did not provide for an independent avenue of appeal. Given the sensitivities surrounding his Bill, Hailey suggested a Revenue Conference could complicate its passage and that the issues be dealt with by correspondence or unannounced informal conference.[55] While a number of governors agreed that a Revenue Conference would be worthwhile Irwin was to postpone regretfully the Conference on the 'heavy preponderance of opinion from the Punjab, United Provinces, Madras and Central Provinces',[56] that such a conference would complicate their legislative programmes.

Events in Bardoli had highlighted the importance, for the stability of British rule, of ensuring efficient and equitable land revenue assessment and implementation. These considerations were referred to in a request by Irwin to several governors for them to assess urgently a Land Revenue Bill submitted to him by the Punjab Governor for clearance.[57] Irwin pointed out:

> ...de Montmorency and his Government are most anxious that assent should be given, and given as soon as possible. They assure me that refusal to give assent will give a handle to possibly dangerous agrarian agitation in which extremist politicians as well as zamindars may join.

Irwin warned of the possibility of the introduction of a system of revision of land revenue settlements by judicial tribunals if the current Bill did not become law. The key elements of the Bill, of relevance in other jurisdictions, related to the percentage of net assets which the government could claim as land revenue, the percentage of enhancement or increase of tax and the period of settlement. While Irwin was seeking to ensure proper coordination across provinces, in a politically volatile situation, the complexity of the land revenue system across British India was revealed by the diversity of considerations set out in the responses from the governors.

Governor Hailey indicated 'the normal percentage of assets taken in the United Provinces is 40 under the Bill passed last December. But methods of calculation in the two provinces [United Provinces and the Punjab] are entirely different and no direct comparison is possible'.[58] The Governor of Bombay informed Irwin that land revenue assessment in his presidency included irrigated land but not in the Punjab, so comparisons would be difficult.[59] The Governor of Madras advised that 'the Punjab Land Revenue system appears to be based on calculation of rental value, while it is not so in Madras. Therefore adoption in Punjab of rule of percentage proposed could not affect Madras save by false analogy'.[60] Reinforcing the importance of land revenue matters to stable government, Montagu Butler, in the Central Provinces, reminded the Viceroy, that these issues

> ...have always been strictly controlled by the Government of India with a view to as much uniformity as possible on land revenue matters in all Provinces... other Local Governments concerned should be consulted formally [not by private and personal communication]. The issues concerned are so grave, particularly in a Province like this which has no stable source of revenue, that full enquiry is necessary before a decision is taken.[61]

Butler's suggestion was to be followed in May 1929.

Despite some difficulties with Vallabhbhai Patel over personnel[62] and his threat to boycott the Bardoli official re-enquiry,[63] Wilson was able to inform on 23 October 1928 'that all outstanding questions with regard to the Bardoli re-enquiry are now settled'.[64] He was very pleased to have cleared the way for his successor, Sir Frederick Sykes, who was to arrive, in Bombay, at the beginning of December, to face his own assortment of administrative challenges. Governor Sykes was soon asked for his views on Bardoli. In response to Irwin's assessment that Bardoli 'has been I think without doubt the most serious thing we have had to face since I came to India', and his request for his 'private opinion pretty fully about the whole thing',[65] Sykes provided an extensive analysis of the weaknesses in the land assessment procedure in Bombay. He also included recommendations for the future. Sykes identified the principal weaknesses in the land assessment system in Bombay as those relating to procedure. He pointed out that the entire assessment process took too long, at least a year; the public were only notified of the original recommendations; any changes by the Collector or other officials could cause consternation; the whole procedure was of an executive order character and there was no appeal. The Governor informed Irwin

> ...prior to the [Montford] Reforms land revenue settlement work in Bombay Presidency was carried on with little friction...A change came with the Reforms and popular representation in the Legislative Council; and more especially with recommendations of the Joint Parliamentary Committee on the Government of India Bill of 1919.[66]

In essence the Parliamentary Committee, in the context of democratic reform, had identified the unsatisfactory nature of imposing land taxation in India by executive action. It recommended that 'the main principles by which land revenue is determined, the methods of valuation, the pitch of assessment, the periods of revision, the graduation of enhancement...'[67] should be embodied in the law by statute. The Bombay Legislative Council had examined the matter in 1924, but the report of the Council Committee was not received by the Bombay Government until late 1926. Intended legislation was complicated by developments in Bardoli. Given the implications of Bardoli across India, Sykes recommended, to the Viceroy, a conference of revenue members, 'to review the situation in all its bearings and consider the possibility of introducing some kind of tribunal to which there might be recourse, and where the arguments and statistics can be carefully analysed'.[68]

The report of the re-assessment of the Bardoli Settlement was issued in April 1929 and Sykes informed Irwin:

> ...the Report, in a word, I think confirms the important general principle of rental values as the basis of settlement; but it will be claimed as a great success

> by Patel and his friends in that it reduces the enhancement of assessment in Bardoli to a quarter of its original percentage, and so also gives great stimulus to the claim for the setting up of a judicial tribunal to which reference may be made.[69]

In a later and more fulsome comment on the implications of the re-assessment, Sykes reinforced with Irwin the need to take the preparation of settlement reports 'out of the hands of inexperienced or ill-qualified officers and entrusted to a whole-time expert staff'.[70] Irwin agreed with Sykes' views and for the need for a conference to address the issues,[71] reaffirming his earlier position that a conference would allow a full examination of the issues involved.

In chapter 1 of his unpublished, incomplete and untitled autobiography,[72] Harcourt Butler outlined the importance of land revenue settlement in the peaceful administration of India and his own early experience of this work. He recalled the Viceroy Lord Curzon asking him, while working with the Government of India, 'to put in a nutshell my idea of a good land revenue settlement', and replying 'the lowest you can get through'.[73] Butler also quotes Sir Alfred Lyall[74] who once said 'that no living being could cause more harm to more people than a settlement officer who over-assessed his district'. The British in Bardoli had obviously not applied what had been long known as the most important land settlement principle of ensuring that over-assessment did not occur.

Pressure to solve the difficulties of land assessment, at least as an opportunity for Congress political activity, was further increased for Sykes in the Daskroi District of Bombay. Sykes informed Irwin, 'Congress was attempting to foment a campaign for the non-payment of arrears in land revenue there'.[75] Irwin was to respond emphatically 'I am entirely at one with you in thinking that, if any such movement shows signs of developing, it should be checked decidedly at the outset'.[76]

Lord Irwin also had detailed discussions, about the pending Land Revenue Conference, in person with Sir Malcolm Hailey. Hailey explained

> ...that we should examine the possibility of interposing some buffer between the Executive and the land revenue payers after the three principal points—of the proportion of net assets; the pitch of assessment; the duration of settlement—had been incorporated in Statute.[77]

Irwin and Hailey identified what they regarded as the best option, to provide this buffer, as an arbitral tribunal composed of a revenue expert who had not been concerned with the settlement, a judicial officer, and one non-official member, either from agriculture or business. Tactically Hailey suggested

> ...that, if Local Governments could be induced to bring in legislation dealing with the three big principles of land settlement, the Executive could have accompanied this by an announcement that, if such legislation were passed in a form that Government could accept, Government on its side would be prepared by Executive Order to create some such arbitral tribunal, to be called into operation when any unit of assessment could make out a *prima facie* case that the principles set out in legislation had been incorrectly applied.[78]

Irwin, in attaching copies of the proceedings of the Revenue Conference, attended by revenue members of the various governors' councils, held in mid-May 1929, advised the governors the main lessons identified by the Conference were:

> ...Government should concentrate on keeping the machinery of settlement up to the mark and on publicity. The need for choosing a good officer to do a settlement and for giving him ample time to do his job is greater than ever today, because of the searching and generally hostile criticism to which the actions of Government and its officers are now subjected.[79]

Irwin advised the governors also of the unanimous decision of the provincial revenue members 'that we should issue a resolution [a brief] reviewing developments in land revenue policy since 1902 when Curzon published his famous resolution and making certain general suggestions for the guidance of Local Governments...'. Irwin informed them his government would prepare a draft of a resolution for circulation and confirmed that, as under the existing constitution, Land Revenue was a reserved provincial subject, responsibility for giving effect to any suggestions the central government might make in the proposed resolution rested primarily with local governments.

The only Governor to respond by private and personal letter to Irwin's advice was Hailey.[80] He indicated that the Conference had brought home to revenue members, in a very telling manner, how widely the provinces differed in regard to essential matters of settlement procedure. Discussions with his Revenue Member, G.B. Lambert who had attended the Simla Conference, enabled Hailey to provide Irwin with further policy advice. He suggested the Government of India should ensure that its resolution clearly sets out, how much more liberal the land revenue assessment had become since 1902 across India. Hailey provided Irwin with a detailed exposition, drawn from his own experience, since Curzon's time of the evolution in developments in the area of assessment, including remissions and suspensions of revenue payment, which had become more and more lenient in the event of crop failure. Hailey believed a properly prepared resolution should serve the dual purpose of informing all the provincial legislatures of land revenue policy and practice in the various territories to enable them to benefit from comparison, and of providing the basis of an attempt 'at systems of assessment more readily explicable to the public and the assessee'.[81]

Events in Bardoli reflected the fact that the Montford Reforms required the British to rule by more democratic principles than previously, and that this was more difficult than ruling by executive action. Governor Wilson and other governors recognised this and had to contend with this factor in resolving the Bardoli campaign, and preventing similar episodes elsewhere. The next chapter will examine the British approach towards achieving constitutional outcomes in the face of the political demands of Congress, Gandhi and the Civil Disobedience Movement.

Endnotes

1. Halifax Papers, Wilson to Irwin, 14 March 1928.
2. A major administrative subdivision of a district.
3. Halifax Papers, Wilson to Irwin, 14 March 1928.
4. *Ibid.*, Wilson to Irwin, 7 April 1928.
5. Vallabhbhai, Patel (1875–1950). Born in Gujarat. Lawyer and nationalist leader. Follower of Gandhi in non-violent Civil Disobedience. Brother of Vithalbhai Patel (1871–1933), president of the Legislative Assembly in Irwin's time.
6. Halifax Papers, Wilson to Irwin, 27 April 1928.
7. *Ibid.*, Wilson to Irwin, 22 May 1928.
8. *Ibid.*, Irwin to Wilson, 8 June 1928.
9. *Ibid.*, Telegram, Viceroy to Governor of Bombay, 28 June 1928.
10. *Ibid.*, Telegram, Secretary of State to Viceroy, 4 July 1928.
11. Indian Newspaper Reports, Notes on the Press, United Provinces, for week ending 21 January 1928.
12. Halifax Papers, Telegram, Secretary of State to Viceroy, 4 July 1928.
13. *Ibid.*
14. *Ibid.*, Telegram, Viceroy to Secretary of State, 6 July 1928.
15. *Ibid.*
16. *Ibid.*
17. *Ibid.*, Telegram, Viceroy to Governor of Bombay, 7 July 1928.
18. *Ibid.*, Telegram, Viceroy to Governor of Bombay, 9 July 1928.

19. *Ibid.*, Telegram, Viceroy to Governor of Bombay, 10 July 1928.
20. *Ibid.*, Telegram, Governor of Bombay to Viceroy, 10 July 1928.
21. *Ibid.*, Telegram, Secretary of State to Viceroy, 10 July 1928.
22. *Ibid.*
23. Lord Birkenhead had suggested a policy of actively favouring British friends, or collaborators, and 'cold-shouldering' their enemies such as Congress. This approach was deemed unrealistic by India's British rulers. See Halifax Papers, Hailey to Irwin, 10 September 1928.
24. Halifax Papers, Telegram, Viceroy to Governor of Bombay, 11 July 1928.
25. *Ibid.*, Telegram, Secretary of State to Viceroy, 12 July 1928.
26. *Ibid.*, Telegram, Viceroy to Secretary of State, 16 July 1928.
27. *Ibid.*
28. *Ibid.*
29. *Ibid.*
30. *Ibid.*, Telegram, Secretary of State to Viceroy, 19 July 1928.
31. *Ibid.*, Telegram, Viceroy to Governor of Bombay, 20 July 1928.
32. *Ibid.*, Telegram, Governor of Bombay to Viceroy, 21 July 1928.
33. *Ibid.*, Telegram, Secretary of State to Viceroy, 19 July 1928.
34. *Ibid.*, Telegram, Viceroy to Secretary of State, 19 July 1928.
35. *Ibid.*, Wilson to Irwin, 24 July 1928.
36. *Ibid.*, Telegram, Governor of Bombay to Viceroy, 27 July 1928.
37. *Ibid.*, Wilson to Irwin, 28 July 1928.
38. *Ibid.*, Telegram, Governor of Bombay to Viceroy, 6 August 1928.
39. *Ibid.*, Wilson to Irwin, 7 August 1928.
40. Used in the Bardoli campaign.
41. See Bondurant, *Conquest of Violence*, pp. 53–64, for an account of the use of the *Satyagraha* philosophy by Gandhi and Patel in Bardoli. See also Hardiman, *Peasant Nationalists of Gujarat*, for an analysis of the relationship between the Indian National Congress and the peasant nationalists.
42. Halifax Papers, Wilson to Irwin, 7 August 1928.
43. See Chapter 1, for an exposition of the governors' constitutional role and Appendix 1 for the Instrument of Instructions issued to the governors.
44. Halifax Papers, Wilson to Irwin, 7 August 1928.
45. *Ibid.*, Irwin to Dawson, 21 July 1928.
46. *Ibid.*, Wilson to Irwin, 16 August 1928.
47. NAI, Home/Political, letter on file 197/1928, Irwin to various governors, August 1928 (no day date).
48. *Ibid.*, Handwritten note in margin, probably by Irwin; 'Sufficient power available under Sections 15 (i) & 16 of Criminal Law Amendment Act'.
49. *Ibid.*, Birkenhead to Irwin, August 1928 (no day date).
50. Halifax Papers, Irwin to various Governors, 8 October 1928.
51. *Ibid.*, Irwin to various Governors, 6 September 1928.
52. *Ibid.*, Hailey to Irwin, 9 September 1928.
53. Hailey Papers, Hailey to the King-Emperor, 23 August 1928.

54. *Ibid.* See also Haithcox, *Communism and Nationalism in India*, p. 10.
55. Halifax Papers, Hailey to Irwin, 18 September 1928.
56. *Ibid.*, Irwin to Wilson, 16 November 1928.
57. *Ibid.*, Irwin to several Governors, 11 January 1929.
58. *Ibid.*, Telegram, Governor of the United Provinces to Viceroy, 12 January 1929.
59. *Ibid.*, Telegram, Governor of Bombay to Viceroy, 15 January 1929.
60. *Ibid.*, Telegram, Governor of Madras to Viceroy, 13 January 1929.
61. *Ibid.*, Telegram, Governor of Central Provinces to Viceroy, 14 January 1929.
62. *Ibid.*, Wilson to Irwin, 11 October 1928.
63. *Ibid.*, Irwin to Wilson, 19 October 1928.
64. *Ibid.*, Wilson to Irwin, 23 October 1928
65. *Ibid.*, Irwin to Sykes, 19 February 1929.
66. *Ibid.*, Sykes to Irwin, 1 March 1929.
67. *Ibid.*
68. *Ibid.*
69. *Ibid.*, Sykes to Irwin, 21 April 1929.
70. *Ibid.*, Sykes to Irwin, 26 April 1929.
71. *Ibid.*, Irwin to Sykes, 4 May 1929.
72. Harcourt Butler Papers. See draft chapters of his incomplete autobiography.
73. *Ibid.*, Chapter 2, p. 12.
74. Sir A.C. Lyall (1835–1887). Senior Indian civil servant. Lieutenant-Governor of the N.W. Provinces 1882–1887. Poet.
75. Halifax Papers, Sykes to Irwin, 26 April 1929.
76. *Ibid.*, Irwin to Sykes, 3 May 1929.
77. *Ibid.*, Irwin to Habibullah, 23 April 1929. Note: The Honourable Sir Sahib Bahadur Muhammad Habibullah was a member of the Viceroy's Executive Council.
78. *Ibid.*
79. *Ibid.*, Irwin to various governors, 25 May 1929.
80. *Ibid.*, Hailey to Irwin, 30 May 1929.
81. *Ibid.*

8

The Direct Challenge of Congress, Gandhi and the Civil Disobedience Movement

The previous chapters have examined the governors' role and influence in the British response to the pressures of illegal activity placed on them by those unwilling to engage in constitutional dialogue. Irwin and the governors responded to these pressures within the existing law of India but also by introducing more stringent measures. In implementing the law, Irwin and the governors were very conscious of the need to prevent enforcement and repression complicating their attempts to conciliate and negotiate constitutional outcomes. Irwin's declaration represented a major initiative in this direction. This chapter examines the governors' role in meeting the political challenge of Congress, Gandhi and the Civil Disobedience Movement, which was complicating Irwin's goal of achieving a constitutional resolution of the problem presented to the British by India.

Surpassing Bardoli as a challenge, the matter of Gandhi's Salt March, launched on 12 March 1930, was arguably the most important and sensitive confrontation with which the governors and Lord Irwin had to contend during his viceroyalty. The Salt March was provocative in its intent and offered the British opportunities to enforce the law. Gandhi was scheduled to reach the sea at Dandi on 6 April to begin manufacturing salt in defiance of the British. As early as 2 March, Governor Hailey searching for Congress motives was offering Irwin a view that the Salt March was a ploy designed to provoke British retaliation.

> I still think that their real motive is to force us into methods of 'repression' which would bring back the Liberals and Moderates to the fold, and would deprive us of what is for the moment a potent argument against them, that they are only a minority even of the politicians.[1]

Anticipating the Salt March and reflecting Lord Irwin's penchant for close collaboration and coordination with the governors he iterated to Sykes, in Bombay Presidency, where Gandhi's march would take place, his wish

> ...to discuss precise methods by which it was proposed to deal with various possible activities of Gandhi and his followers, what were probabilities of movement attracting support of large numbers or leading to violence and whether any action was likely to be necessary against Gandhi himself.[2]

On the same day as Irwin held discussions with the Commissioner of Ahmedabad in Bombay Presidency, on these matters, Bombay was to relay the suggestion of the District Magistrate in Kaira, Bombay Presidency, that the Gandhi March should be prohibited.[3] Bombay acknowledged, however, that so long as the Salt March was conducted peacefully there was no provision in the law which permitted its prohibition. Bombay also indicated that if Gandhi was to make provocative speeches on the way, then they believed an order of prohibition should be issued by a magistrate, as had been applied to Vallabhbhai Patel, leading to his arrest on 7 March.

Irwin's response to Bombay's views set out his counter strategy to Gandhi's method. The Viceroy advised his position, in a detailed note, that nothing should be done to prevent Gandhi's march, and any action should if possible be avoided. 'The aim should be to deal with Gandhi at the end, as soon as the breach of the salt law has been committed'.[4] However, Irwin was to ask Bombay if there was any possibility of Gandhi's march being a 'fiasco', and which thereby might avoid the need for any prosecution. Irwin was, simultaneously, to advise all the governors of his approach.[5] Irwin's strategy had earlier been developed in consultation with all the local governments as advised to the King-Emperor.

> I find that they [Local Governments] are in close agreement with the view that I and my advisers take here. That is we should commit a strategic error if we allowed ourselves, as I fancy the Congress leaders desire us to do, to be pressed into launching a large number of prosecutions...at the same time we shall prosecute any speech that advocates violence...[and] strike vigorously and quickly at any attempt to introduce civil disobedience in such form, for example, as exciting the peasants not to pay their land revenue to Government.[6]

Governor Sykes met with Irwin on 26 and 27 March to discuss a possible line of action against Gandhi and the Civil Disobedience Movement.[7] The Bombay paper, the *Indian Daily Mail* reported that Sykes' visit to Irwin was because 'nation-wide Civil Disobedience is regarded as an All-India matter... the Provincial Government...consider[s] that their policy must be laid down by the Central Government in consultation with the Secretary of State'.[8] Two options were identified by Irwin and Sykes: Gandhi should be arrested and prosecuted as soon as he committed an offence. If so, questions of the length of sentence, the likelihood of a hunger strike and preparations for trying Gandhi and sending him to jail arose; the alternative policy of treating Gandhi's offence against the salt laws as trivial and unworthy of serious notice, whilst confiscating illegally made salt. After lengthy deliberations, where Sykes supported the first option and suggested Ordinances to counter intimidation, boycotting and press propaganda as well as the withdrawal of postal and telegraph facilities from offenders, Irwin opted for leaving Gandhi alone but to seek out any other leaders who broke the law. Bombay had vacillated between wishing to arrest Gandhi before his march, to arrest him before he reached the sea and to not arrest of anyone at all.[9] At least one commentator believed the Viceroy had got it wrong and an unfettered Sykes would 'have laid Gandhi by the heels'.[10]

An interesting insight into the tensions surrounding Governor Sykes in the implementation of the Gandhi policy is provided by Ashmead Bartlett, a journalist who accompanied Gandhi on his March, reporting on a visit to Sykes.

> If Gandhi in his speech and actions strongly resembles Christ, Sykes bears an even stronger resemblance to Pontius Pilate, in his weakness and vacillation. I went to see him after I returned from Dandi and found him sitting in his study...gazing out to sea, a picture of the deepest melancholy, dispair [sic] and gloom. He could not utter one single word...except to reiterate at intervals... What shall I do? What shall I do?[11]

Governor Innes' view, provided to Irwin at the beginning of Gandhi's march, which matched the applied policy, was:

> ...if he and his *jatha*[12] are going to make salt on the sea shore, I should be inclined to leave them alone...But I should be inclined at once to come to grips with the Congress and if it is possible to run in the whole of the Working Committee for conspiracy...and so to disorganise the whole movement.[13]

The British approach towards the Congress and its Committee was also to become a focus of strategic consideration for Irwin and the governors.

At this time, Irwin also had the benefit of personal and 'profound' discussions with Governor Hailey and a letter from de Montmorency on how to react to Gandhi's strategy. In reporting the governors' views to Wedgwood Benn, Irwin informed him both men, reflecting a common attitude held by people in their provinces, 'take the view that Government should go as slow as they can about arresting Gandhi on a business that the average man regards as rather ridiculous'.[14] Hailey believed, 'we should try confiscating any salt he may make, not closing our eyes however to the fact that if by this time the demonstration had assumed menacing shape in any way, or if he persists, then we will have to arrest him'. Hailey was not afraid of Gandhi hunger striking upon detention 'inasmuch as his arrest would be the signal for further activities all over the country, and he would wish to watch the progress of these before deciding that his campaign was a failure and that he must accordingly die'. Hailey felt that in his province and others 'this was only, as it were, a curtain raiser to the real business that would be no rent and no revenue campaigns. On that [Hailey] thought we should have to jump immediately and heavily'. Irwin informed the Secretary of State that he agreed with Hailey's and de Montmorency's assessments.[15] By the end of March, Hailey was already engaged in 'jumping' on members of Congress instigating non-payment of land revenue in his province.[16]

Governor Hammond had a similar view, to Innes, Hailey and de Montmorency, when he told Irwin

> ...the best thing to do with Mr Gandhi and his followers was to allow them to manufacture salt and then confiscate it and tell him to increase his output. With the salt one can confiscate the various packages and the animals and conveyances used in carrying it, under section 18 of the Indian Salt Act 1882. But I felt the Bombay Government knew their own job best.[17]

By 31 March 1930, the Government of India had received confidential information that the intention of the Congress was to initiate civil disobedience simultaneously, as far as possible, in all provinces on Gandhi's arrest or, if that was delayed, probably after his arrival at the sea on 6 April.[18] Provincial committees of Congress, however, had been requested in the first place to concentrate on breaches of the Salt Laws.[19] In pursuance of the British policy of ignoring Gandhi but prosecuting other leaders, Irwin had accepted Hailey's recommendation that Jawaharlal Nehru should be arrested if, as expected, he was to incite a formal breach of the Salt Law at Allahabad in the United Provinces to coincide with Gandhi's arrival at Dandi.[20] The arrest of Nehru, for breaking the Salt Law, was to occur on 14 April 1930.[21]

At this time Bombay continued to press Irwin for an Ordinance to cover intimidation and boycott in order to deal with the difficult security position in that presidency.[22] Irwin informed Sykes his government had prepared a draft Ordinance for consideration but, repeated a consistent theme.

> ...our general attitude is that an Ordinance should not be issued unless it is clear that rigorous exercise of powers already possessed has proved inadequate

> to cope with a serious situation ...You will I am sure realise that I could not issue an Ordinance as a gesture nor hold it out as a threat. It could only be promulgated to meet a definite and serious emergency.[23]

In pressing for extraordinary powers Sykes pointed out that while on the whole, 'our policy...seems to have been not too unsuccessful...Gandhi has scored a certain degree of success in attaining his objective, viz., to teach the masses—that the law can be defied'.[24] In this context Sykes believed the initiative in the battle still lay in the hands of their opponents. In order to wrest the initiative away, Sykes was to suggest a number of possibilities. First, he was to revisit his suggestion of taking away the privileges and protection of the law from 'a few specially selected ones of those who have openly repudiated it'. Second, he sought Ordinances to deal with intimidation, boycott and similar activities, advising 'the time seems to have come when it can no longer be postponed'.[25] Sykes indicated he would not press for Gandhi's arrest but 'it is imperative to take the initiative by concurrent steps to undermine his position and counteract his propaganda'. Third, Sykes suggested some positive news, even such as the personnel and dates for the Round Table Conference would be very helpful to provide a rallying point for the Moderates, to assist them to defend the government. Fourth, he was to suggest constructive action was necessary in the area of economic policy, covering agriculture, industry, commerce and finance. To achieve this, Sykes was to suggest setting up a Provincial Economic Council 'in order to help in consolidating commercial opinion and in concentrating attention on something constructive and useful'.[26] Sykes copied his views to the Secretary of State to 'help him understand the position in this Presidency'.[27] It was not until 30 May that an Intimidation Ordinance was issued and the Boycott Ordinance was only available several months later.[28] Sykes had to wait. The frustrated governor held, one of the difficulties of administration in the provinces was that the central government was apt to be slow to act without having secured the assent of all governors. Like Governor Lytton, Sykes believed 'On other occasions the Central Government interfered unwarrantably'.[29] Curiously, in complete contrast to his exchange with Sykes on the issuance of Ordinances, Irwin had approved, almost at the same time, the immediate issuance of an Ordinance, requested by the Governor of Bengal to meet an emergency in Chittagong involving banditry and thefts from an armoury.[30] Various other governors were also grateful for the issuance, at the end of April 1930, of a Press Ordinance against the vernacular press.[31]

By 21 April, Irwin was having doubts about the policy of no arrest being applied to Gandhi, and writing to Hailey, separately informed him he had written to all local governments seeking their advice on the matter. In setting out the various elements of the problem for Hailey's consideration, Irwin was to add, 'I should be very grateful for your considered judgment on the balance we have struck between obviously conflicting considerations'.[32] Irwin's high regard for Hailey's capacities was contained in the letter's concluding words, 'I have read your note to your Commissioners on general policy [in relation to the political situation in India] with much interest and appreciation of its wisdom'. Irwin was also to write a discrete and personal letter to de Montmorency seeking his views on the possible arrest of Gandhi.[33] Given Bombay's special situation with regard to the Mahatma, Irwin wrote a personal note to Sykes too seeking his views on an early move to arrest Gandhi pointing out, in relation to the issuance of Ordinances, the incongruity of doing so whilst the catalyst for their need remained free.[34] In the same letter Irwin was to remain sceptical about Sykes' suggestion of withdrawing civil rights but agreed with the importance of assisting the Moderates, and the importance of economic improvements but which, however, would be slow to achieve.

In his reply, Governor Hailey referring back to his experience of Gandhi's first Non-Cooperation campaign, from 1920 to 1922, identified two reasons for the Government's caution then towards arresting him.[35] The first reason was Viceroy Reading's cautious attitude towards 'binding decisions' and Sir George Lloyd's 'impulsive and individualistic' policies towards Gandhi. Second, the Government had been very conscious of the damage done by events in Amritsar and the handling of the 1919 Punjab rebellion in Amritsar and that decisive action might have precipitated violence and further damaged the British reputation. Hailey believed, as a consequence, the earlier campaign had been allowed to go on for too long. The Governor observed his main concern in the prevailing circumstances was, unless checked, it was almost inevitable the current campaign would spread from the towns to the largely unaffected countryside. In this situation

> ...my own instinct...would be to bring it as rapidly as possible to a head. If picketing and intimidation became a serious menace in the large towns, I would issue the draft Ordinance, and use it (as we have used the Salt Law) to arrest leaders. But I think it would be altogether impossible to issue such an Ordinance and to allow Gandhi to remain at liberty, breaking it daily...I am myself absolutely convinced that the arrest of Gandhi is inevitable.[36]

Hailey believed Gandhi's arrest would cause violence and protests but would not provide any support 'on which we can now effectively rely' and concluded:

> ...if I advocate bringing matters to a head by arresting him, it is in the calculated belief that we shall in the long run reduce the period of tension by

> this step...I do not want to see either him or anyone else sentenced to long term imprisonment. I should infinitely prefer to use Regulation III in his case and confine sentences to about six months in the majority of others.[37]

One can assume that Hailey's preference for short imprisonment is related to a view that a long confinement would provoke continuing agitation commensurate with its length. Irwin responded to Hailey's advice by saying 'Thank you...I feel the force of everything you say'.[38]

The next day Irwin, having taken Hailey's counsel, advised the Secretary of State:

> ...after consideration of general situation and views of Local Governments[39] we have reached a conclusion that his [Gandhi's] arrest is necessary...our conclusion...has been reached only after most anxious consideration of the various factors for and against.[40]

The factors Irwin set out for the Secretary of State largely matched those in Hailey's detailed note. Accepting Hailey's advice on the method of prosecution, Irwin informed Wedgwood Benn that Gandhi would be interned under Regulation.

> This course has certain definite advantages and it is preferred by the Bombay Government, which is primarily concerned. It gives us a free hand in regard to his period of detention: it makes the arrangements for his immediate disposal less difficult and, by eliminating a trial, reduces the danger of demonstrations: and it may, on the whole, be less wounding to Hindu feelings.[41]

Irwin had changed his mind as he had earlier indicated it would be better to proceed against Gandhi under the ordinary law, as he believed it would take a conviction to convince the public in India and in England that an offence had been committed by Gandhi.[42] Irwin hoped the Secretary of State 'approved our action' in informing the Bombay Government they could proceed to the arrest of Gandhi, then scheduled for 4 May.[43] Wedgwood Benn informed Irwin of Cabinet's approval and support for the proposed action but also that he regarded the use of a Regulation (Bombay Regulation XXV of 1827) as 'mediaevially tyrannical'.[44] Referring to the impending arrest of Gandhi, Montagu Butler informed his wife, 'I wish God had told Edw. Wood to take Patel and Motilal Nehru at the same time. He'll have to take them, so why make 2 bites at a cherry'.[45]

The close professional relationship between Irwin and Hailey was again indicated by the Viceroy's request for Hailey to 'meditate and give me your considered judgment on this general problem'.[46] Contemplating 'bad troubles in the next few weeks' over Gandhi's detention and the need to justify the British response, Irwin was to ask 'what in your view are the general principles that ought to be pursued upon the matter of enquiries? I presume that if possible they should be local, prompt and official, but I should value any general wisdom you could impart to me'. In a detailed reply Hailey, drawing on his long experience, referred back again to 1919 and Jallianwala Bagh and to the Muslim Moplah rebellion in 1921 in Madras Presidency, as background to his advice.[47] He informed Irwin, in the first case, there had been a great delay in instituting the Jallianwala Bagh enquiry because of differences over the selection of a presiding Judge. This had allowed Congress time to put together its own report which was very damaging to the government. In the case of Moplah, where the government response was very tough, involving military force, Martial Law, Ordinances and many deaths, there was very little reaction from Hindu politicians and no enquiry was held. Hailey gave these references 'because they afford some kind of guide to policy'.

Drawing from their lessons and his own personal involvement in the crisis of 1919, Hailey set out a number of principles which he hoped would be taken into consideration. First, he hoped the Government of India would not institute any form of all-India enquiry unless methods of repression were adopted which attracted a great deal of unfavourable comment, in India and England, which necessarily demanded an authoritative investigation of facts. Second, 'we should confine ourselves to *personnel* now in India,' including Indian public men, to conduct the enquiry. Third, it was essential any enquiry should be made as soon as possible after the event. Hailey pointed out this was all the more necessary now given the British would have to face an Assembly and local councils, with elected majorities, instead of the old form of imperial legislative councils. Fourth, officers from both central and local secretariats should be required to keep a full running record of daily events. Fifth, after any disturbance causing deaths or injuries, Hailey believed it was always wise for the local government to have some form of enquiry as soon as possible. Sixth, where action taken by government in repressing disorder of a political origin is likely to be attacked, the Governor thought it best to have a magisterial enquiry made as soon as possible. Where the case was really important, it was wise to have an enquiry made by a senior judicial and executive officer working together. By these measures Hailey believed not only could governments defend their own actions but also establish facts relating to the causative agents of rebellion and disorder, such as the distinct connection between the Punjab Rebellion and the Afghan War. In response Irwin thanked Hailey for his long and helpful letter about the general question of enquiries, with its enclosures. 'I am very grateful to you for your help and am taking the liberty of putting Haig and the Home Department in possession of your wisdom'.[48]

While the Governor of Bengal was able to report on 20 May 1930, that 'conditions here are quiet',[49] the Governor of Bombay had a different story. Sykes, in a succinct introduction to a long letter in which he set out a suggested policy approach to the emergency in Bombay, advised Irwin.

> It is now clear that Gandhi's personal influence was originally under-estimated, as well as the power behind the C.D.O [civil disobedience] movement, and the difficulty of dealing with the tactics of our opponents. I think it is now necessary frankly to recognise the fact that we are faced with a more or less overt rebellion, for which the term 'non-violence' is merely camouflage, and that it is supported either actively or passively by a very large section of the population. We have, for one reason or another, practically no openly active friends.[50]

Against this background Sykes suggested a principal problem was that the British had lost authority for a variety of reasons, including a historical decline in executive authority, the result of the 1919 Reforms; a reduction in visible military force, consequent upon reform of the army and an inadequate and poorly trained police force. Sykes also identified the Viceroy's policy of 'excessive impartiality' as between the various religious and sectoral groups as alienating potential friends. Sykes informed Irwin 'it is already urgent to re-establish respect for the law and to stop all this defiance of Government before the movement gets beyond us', and that 'a fresh [policy] line' was required. Sykes attached to his letter, a note 'Review of Organisation' in which he set out an approach to the problem of declining executive authority. He believed a resolution of this problem would be even more important with any new edition of constitutional reform consequent upon the Simon Commission, and the Round Table Conference. With regard to the Round Table Conference itself he was to suggest that if there was any likelihood of having to recede from the Indian Government's position on Dominion Status to save the Conference then it should be done immediately, rather than be seen to yield to pressure.

In relation to the law and order issues, Sykes contended:

> ...in my opinion the theory that it [the civil disobedience movement] can successfully be dealt with without disturbing the ordinary course of law or departing from the ordinary methods of administration must definitely be discarded. If our weakness compels us to arm ourselves with new powers or to resort to new methods, we must face it, remembering that the kind of revolution which confronts us is also novel in its tactics.[51]

Sykes suggested the military should be made more visible and pressed again for measures against limited outlawry, and Ordinances against boycott, intimidation and non-payment of taxes.[52] He called also for a 'special' Ordinance empowering district magistrates, subject to orders by the local government, to make regulations which should be enforceable by penalties and executive action. Sykes admitted the latter measure would be akin to martial law, 'but enforceable by the civil authority unless and until martial law itself became necessary'. The Governor was to stress also the need to take active measures to encourage the minority communities, the Muhammadans, Non-Brahmins, Depressed Classes and Parsis to support the government. To do this, Sykes suggested a 'clear declaration giving a definite promise to them of adequate safeguards under the new constitution'. In concluding he acknowledged:

> I am, of course, viewing these things from the thick of the conflict in Gujerat and Bombay, where I find that the Simon Report and the Round Table Conference are almost forgotten...I hope you will not think...I am unduly critical of the present policy.

Again, using his privilege, Sykes copied his letter, to Wedgwood Benn, hoping the letter 'will help you understand my view'.[53]

In a rather abrupt and matter of fact reply to Sykes, Irwin set out his thoughts on the Governor's views.[54] First of all, Irwin felt it was time Bombay dealt effectively with those 'monster processions', suggesting they should be controlled 'very severely in matters of route', as had occurred in Madras. Second, Irwin suggested to Sykes, 'If I was in your position...I should go down there [to Bombay] myself for two or three days and see people...I have seen a good deal of criticism arising during the time I have been here for that sort of thing not being done'.[55] This comment was rather pointed as Sykes had written his policy note from the Mahableshwar hills where, 'We had a delightful bungalow nestling in the forest'.[56] Irwin had had earlier experience of Governor Lytton dealing with emergencies in Calcutta, from the more comfortable circumstances of his hill station at Darjeeling. However, the Governor would have no doubt welcomed Irwin's advice that he would be discussing Sykes' suggestion for distribution of the military with the Commander-in-Chief [in the event turned down][57]. The Viceroy indicated he also hoped shortly to issue the Intimidation and Instigation Ordinances which were in the event promulgated on 27 May 1930.[58] Irwin suggested Sykes himself should do something about strengthening his police force and that he was doubtful about his proposal of arming district officers with general regulation making powers. Irwin's view was that with '*steady pressure* on those lines a good deal might be achieved in the restoration of Government authority in Gujerat'.[59] The Viceroy was sceptical also about Sykes' view that if the civil disobedience campaign was not dropped then the British should refuse any more reforms, on the basis he believed something would, in fact, come of the reform process and 'I am unwilling to utter threats that I suspect to be hollow'.[60] Irwin thought a meeting would be useful to discuss things in a more detailed manner. Wedgwood Benn's view of the appropriate response to civil disobedience had been provided to Irwin, coincidentally a day before Sykes had sent the Secretary of State his ideas. 'We are policemen who know no party so far as the maintenance of peace is concerned ...The use of force, though fully necessary, so far from being any solution of the problem, is an aggravation of it.'[61]

At this time, when the Congress Working Committee had concentrated action on Bombay, Irwin had written to Hailey asking for his advice on how to deal with Congress. 'I wish you would tell me whether you have a view about the wisdom or otherwise of proclaiming Congress itself as an illegal association, and thereby enable us to deal with any of the Working Committee we want'.[62] Against a background of relative calm in his province Hailey in his reply, in identifying what he thought was Congress' real and underlying intent in mounting civil disobedience, attempted to define the proper level of British response for Irwin. Hailey believed the Congress' talk of 'waging a war of independence...sacrificing the life-blood of our youth... bringing an iniquitous Government crashing to the ground' was hyperbole. Congress' real intent was

> ...to impress the English public with the strength of Congress organisation, to shake the Indian Government out of its fallacy that, though we can be very annoying fellows in the Legislative Assembly or the Press, we have no influence in the country at large, and generally speaking, by nagging and rattling the Englishman, to hustle him into more of those reforms which will end with his gradually retiring in disgust from the administration of the country.[63]

Hailey admitted his difficulty was to be able to predict the turning point in the agitation which had occurred, during the last civil disobedience, when extreme violence caused Gandhi to call it off. Hailey believed that these circumstances would not be repeated this time. The Governor reported a view of an interlocutor that the turning point needed to be precipitated by the Government of India exerting its authority, including by proscribing Congress. On the other hand there were views that the government had got it just about right and 'it is better to carry on for a month or so as we are doing at present; just *steady and quiet pressure*, no more'.[64] Hailey also cited opinions that Congress would call off the agitation if the right 'gesture' was given. Hailey advised the Viceroy he did not believe the first school was right. Apart from the difficulty consequent upon proscribing Congress, and of having to arrest large numbers of people, 'we should be in quite definite danger of allowing people to argue that we are fighting nationalism not civil disobedience...I would therefore only attack local committees where the case demanded it'. Hailey also believed a 'gesture' would not work as Congress was really seeking a 'bargain' which would necessarily prejudge the Round Table Conference. Hailey's advice was 'for the present the right course is to think of nothing but *steady pressure*, until one sees more definite signs of breaking away and lassitude'.[65] Irwin accepted Hailey's assessment, 'I think on the whole I am disposed to agree with you. There is always a gulf between the outward expression and the inward meaning'.[66] Irwin also advised his confidant he had just written to Sykes advising him to take a stiffer line against his processions. It is perhaps not coincidental, having absorbed Hailey's advice, that the Viceroy had used the term 'steady pressure' defining the Indian Government's fundamental policy approach towards non-cooperation, in his advice to Sykes, of 27 May, written on the same day as his letter of agreement to Hailey.

Irwin was sufficiently disturbed by developments in Bombay to inform Sykes 'it is essential for us to get into closer touch with your Government than is possible by correspondence',[67] and that he was sending Haig, his Home Member, for this purpose. Some background to this development is provided by Irwin's personal advice to Wedgwood Benn: 'Between ourselves I can't quite make Sykes out. After clamouring for my two last Ordinances... he has up to date, having had them for ten days...not applied them'.[68] After Haig's visit Irwin informed Sykes directly.

> ...it was somewhat surprising to me to find that, after they [the Ordinances] had been issued, you did not forthwith invoke their aid, and even more surprising to learn from Haig that he had gathered an impression from your Gujerat people that they did not attach any great value to them.[69]

Irwin's rather firm definition of the term 'steady pressure' was contained in his advice to Sykes that 'I feel myself at the present juncture that we ought to try and hit Congress and its works as hard as we can, and I see nothing whatever incompatible...[in being] prepared to encourage any move to peace'. In his response to the Viceroy, Sykes revealed a confusion in understanding between himself and Irwin on what Sykes called, the Government of India's 'temporary policy' to meet civil disobedience.[70]

Under the pressure of the focus of the Civil Disobedience Movement in Bombay, Sykes had informed Haig

> ...that in making use of the powers hitherto placed at our disposal we have never regarded them as effective, if the idea was really to crush the movement... We have inferred, however, from the evident reluctance of the Government of India to adopt extraordinary measures, and from the fact that no action was taken centrally against the Congress Working Committee, that the Government of India, contemplated the possibility that the Simon Report or the terms of reference to the Round Table Conference might influence the situation, and wished to leave the door open for a political remedy of this character. We have acquiesced in what we regarded as at best a temporary policy, and we have interpreted it to mean using the minimum force necessary to meet the situation from day to day.[71]

Irwin in his reply acknowledged it was out of the question to expect to crush the whole movement in any 'dramatic fashion', but did not believe that that was really the alternative to the policy

> ...of using the minimum force necessary to meet the situation from day to day. I again prefer the policy of steady pressure. We have...got to use whatever force is necessary to keep the movement under control. The ultimate settlement must be dealt with independently.[72]

And in a direct rebuttal of Sykes' reasoning and to make his policy approach quite clear, Irwin informed him:

> I do not accept your syllogism...You say, in effect, 'undiluted repression is not feasible; construction *cum* repression is not feasible; therefore we must conciliate'. It seems to me indeed that the right and only policy is conciliation *cum* so-called repression, i.e., repression where necessary, but losing no opportunity of emphasising that a happier way is open when the provoking causes of repression no longer operate.[73]

Under this approach British concession was not included as an element of negotiation.

Irwin followed his explicit advice to Sykes with a detailed exposition of his policy to all the governors 'so as to clear our minds as far as possible of any misunderstanding'.[74] In his note he stressed the importance of steady pressure, thus using and reinforcing the Hailey view, and of maintaining and encouraging the support of the Moderates. Also that it was vital not to allow any idea to prevail that the Congress would be successful, of fighting it by all available means and maximising the use of pro-Government 'propaganda'. Irwin forewarned the governors it 'may soon be necessary to attack directly the organisation that is behind them [the civil disobedience movement], i.e., not only the Central Working Committee, but also executive provincial organisations'. Irwin also sought the governors' suggestions for more effective action against the movement. Irwin indicated there would be no negotiation but, in the context of inevitable approaches to end the abnormal conditions, it might appear negotiation was occurring. In a separate note to Sykes, copying him in his letter to the other governors, Irwin informed about the beginning of settlement through approaches to him by Bikaner[75] and Jinnah, conveying a view that Gandhi might be persuaded to call off his movement 'if he could be got to believe—(a) that it was futile and damaging, and (b) that, if he did so, Government would respond in generous fashion'.[76] Irwin informed Sykes his difficulty would be if Gandhi set preconditions but he would approve of the Governor allowing an intermediary, Jayakar, to visit Gandhi in jail.

Despite the record to the contrary, Montagu Butler informed his wife:

> Edw. Wood is in no way interested in the c.d. movement, or keeping order. He regards that as the function of the Home Department and Local Governments and signs anything that is put up to him of this sort. All he cares about is the constitutional question.[77]

Along with his flawed view, perhaps Butler was unable to see any direct link between the resolution of the constitutional question leading to the possible end of civil disobedience.

In further attempts to improve the atmosphere in Bombay, Sykes suggested to Irwin an option of him meeting representative men, in his Presidency, to discuss the Simon Report and to seek their suggestions on the best way of ending the present conflict.[78] He believed this meeting would also be a useful preparation for his attendance at the forthcoming governors' conference. He was also to outline the benefits of 'some new line of conciliation' in permitting Motilal Nehru to visit Gandhi.[79] The *Indian Daily Mail* believed the ICS 'steel frame', Haig and Rainy, had influenced 'a weakly acquiescing Irwin' not to allow this to happen.[80] It is not surprising, however, that Irwin was to disapprove strongly of a meeting between Nehru and Gandhi.

> Effect on public opinion, both in India and England, would be bewildering and I am afraid, very damaging to us. The general conclusion would be that we were prepared to enter negotiations with Congress…Besides, as you will have seen since you sent your telegram, we have already decided to proceed

> against Working Committee of Congress and arrest Motilal. To permit him on eve of arrest to interview Gandhi would I consider, seem unintelligible.[81]

In addition, evidently Sykes had not taken in the added complication of the possibility, advised to Sykes only days before, of Jayakar visiting the Mahatma. Further misunderstandings, between Irwin and Sykes were revealed in the Governor's letter to the Viceroy in which he indicated:

> I was a little surprised to hear [as contained in their preceding correspondence] that you had never taken the view that we could expect Gandhi to call off the movement unconditionally...I had certainly understood that you were not prepared to encourage any attempts at negotiation unless the movement was first called off unconditionally...I note, however, that this policy has now been changed, and I will remember what you say should I again be approached in this connection.[82]

Irwin clarified Sykes' apparent misunderstanding by advising:

> I take the view that there is a substantial difference between what would generally be called negotiation on the one side and, on the other, allowing an indication to be given of what action Government would take if the movement in fact ceased...as I have already told you.[83]

Sykes was to continue to argue that Irwin misunderstood the policy, including effective repression which he, Sykes, wished to apply in Bombay.[84]

The Government of India was at this time considering further stringent action. However, Irwin informed Sykes that pending analysis of a statement which Motilal Nehru had made in the press, which could possibly be interpreted as a move towards conciliation, his arrest and the proclamation of the Central Working Committee had been postponed.[85] Setting out his views of the advantages and disadvantages of moving against Nehru and Congress for Hailey's consideration, Irwin turned, once again to him for advice on the matter. 'I know you have always been doubtful of our wisdom in proceeding against Working Committee and Motilal—and no doubt the two hang together. I should greatly value your judgment on general strategy as early as you can give it'.[86] In his same day reply, Hailey reaffirmed his earlier view that he had some doubts about proceeding against the Working Committee, 'due perhaps to a general feeling rather than to definite reasons'.[87] For consideration, he identified two points of importance: the fact the disturbances had not spread to rural areas, beyond Gujarat and that the Muslims had not joined in a 'general landslide'. Hailey reported in fact 'the majority of police and district officers alike speak of an apparent decline of interest, or at all events some lull in the general campaign'.[88] Admitting he did not fully understand why there had been this lull, Hailey pointed out that action against the Central Working Committee of Congress, followed by provincial and district committees and general arrests, would really be 'a kind of final weapon…It leaves us with very little else except something in the nature of martial law or some sort of civil equivalent'. He conceded, however, 'that if the step were proved necessary in order to counteract the growth of disaffection or mistrust among Indian troops or police, then that would be an overriding consideration to which every other must immediately give way'.[89] Hailey also did not regard Nehru's statement as an opening for negotiation, and still preferred 'steady pressure', ensuring proper preparation for the London Conference and keeping the Liberals and Moderates onside.

Irwin and his Council were to judge, soon after, that Hailey's 'overriding consideration' had in fact eventuated and, the dangers of the Working Committee's attempts at suborning troops and police had become too great. Consequently, the Working Committee of the All-India Congress was declared an unlawful association and the arrest of Motilal Nehru was ordered. The Government had decided 'the actions of the Working Committee demonstrated that they had now reached the stage of endeavouring to promote revolution through the overthrow of Government'.[90] Irwin had accepted Hailey's judgement that stern action had to be taken in the face of any attempt to undermine support for the British regime, amongst the Indian members of the army and police.

At the end of May 1930 Hailey was to receive a letter from Irwin advising him of the forthcoming governors' conference in July and of its format and attendance. Hailey was sufficiently concerned with Irwin's intentions as to write to his colleague de Montmorency, asking him for 'your own idea on the subject'.[91] Hailey's main problem was the Viceroy's intention to involve a member of each of the various governments (including the Government of India) and the governors in a 'regular day to day committee to thrash the whole matter out'. Hailey felt that apart from governors and members 'joining the general fray' they (the Governor and the member) could not 'commit their local governments; in many cases the Governor and his member might have different views and probably will do so…Surely it is better that the Governors should be left to give their personal views to the Viceroy'. De Montmorency evidently agreed[92] as Hailey then wrote to Irwin with a recommendation for the attendance of governors alone.[93] Hailey expressed his rationale in this way:

> The position of the Governor-General and of the Governors is somewhat exceptional in so far that they have both by statute and by practice a position

> of responsibility apart from that of their own Governments. To a certain extent therefore they may be assumed to have individual opinions based on their own experiences and connected with their own position, opinions which they do not necessarily share with their Cabinets; and I venture a suggestion that it is these individual opinions of Governors which are likely to be most useful to Your Excellency.

Apart from reflecting the close working relationship between the two governors,[94] these exchanges can be interpreted as demonstrating their concern not to contradict the democratic framework and conventions which had developed in the provinces to that time. There were now processes of consultation and negotiation to be followed before agreement could be achieved within 'Cabinets'. A process which included one member and excluded ministers contradicted the very basis of dyarchy. It is surprising that the Government of India and Irwin seemed not to understand this. Of course, given the sensitive implications for British India of the matters to be discussed, governors would have been able to speak more openly, unencumbered by their Cabinet colleagues. They would not, however, have been able to commit them to a policy line. Irwin was to agree with Hailey's position[95] but it must have been embarrassing for the Viceroy to reissue his invitations.

The conference had been convened to enable the Viceroy and governors to discuss and decide policy under the headings; the proper approach to the civil disobedience movement, Simon's Report and the constitutional problem.[96] The discussion on the Civil Disobedience Movement was held on the morning of 23 July. The minutes of the discussion record the Viceroy inviting the governors' views on the general situation in their provinces and them providing their consequent policy advice.[97] The Governors of Bengal, Madras, Assam, the Punjab and Bihar and Orissa all indicated, in concise presentations, that the situation in their territories was improved and all put forward some policy refinements to meet their own exigencies. It is not surprising the Governor of Bombay gave the longest description of the emergency in his presidency, which he advised had been aggravated by world and local economic conditions. Sykes had prepared himself well for the conference. He had earlier met together with a large number of Indian non-officials in Bombay seeking their input to some elements of the agenda, including the issue of consultations with Gandhi, for the governors' conference.[98] Condemnation by the non-officials of the Simon Report had been almost unanimous.[99]

In his circumstances, Sykes asked the meeting of governors whether 'a considerable development of policy is possible?'. He believed, even if the

Sapru–Jayakar negotiations[100] with Gandhi succeeded, Congress would still abstain from the Round Table Conference. If the negotiations failed

> ...or the Congress refuses to follow Gandhi, or if, as is almost inevitable, the Congress do not accept the Round Table Conference results, then the movement must be crushed, and Bombay experience shows that this cannot be done merely by 'steady pressure'.

In Sykes' view there were but two alternatives: 'to negotiate or to fight with all our strength, and at present we were unable, as far as the Bombay Presidency was concerned, to do either owing to our efforts to conform to the Government of India's policy'. Sykes argued very strongly for the granting of executive powers to relevant officers in Bombay, as had been done under the very effective Press Ordinance, which would allow for stringent action. He believed all his government's penal enactments were peace time measures and what was needed were emergency powers to override the ordinary law and procedure and to deal with situations executively, that is, peremptorily. Accordingly, Sykes recommended 'an Ordinance be prepared...on the lines of a comprehensive Defence of the Realm Act [DORA] providing all powers which seem to be necessary for dealing with revolutionary activities'.[101] He acknowledged the difficulty of promulgating an Ordinance granting such drastic powers to one province only. The Governor of the Central Provinces advised the Civil Disobedience Movement was gaining force in his province and that he was in favour of an Ordinance on the lines of a DORA The Governor of the United Provinces, Hailey, believed action needed to be taken with respect to local bodies and DORA 'should be drafted and kept in readiness, but that it is not required at the moment'. The Governor of the Punjab agreed. In summing up this part of the discussion Irwin observed the conclusions seemed to be:

> ...if the Civil Disobedience Movement were not called off... Government should continue pressure on existing lines, take up at once the question of promulgating, at an early date an Ordinance to deal effectively with local bodies, and also prepare for use, if required, an Ordinance on the lines of the DORA

Once again the Viceroy's decision reflected the advice given by Hailey and de Montmorency and Sykes' request for emergency powers had been effectively ignored. Even in the context of the governors' undoubted experience of real threat and turbulence in Bombay an all-India consideration and the Punjab Governors' judgements, had prevailed.

The discussion then turned to the question of an amnesty for prisoners regarded as political by Congress. The Viceroy noted that in reply to his personal letter to his governors of 30 June, the governors of Madras and the Punjab had raised certain objections of principle, while the other governors had agreed to the necessity at some time of release of prisoners, while expressing in some cases some differences of opinion regarding details. The Governor of the Punjab indicated in his province there were categories of prisoners who had taken part in the Civil Disobedience Movement, who were not followers of Gandhi but were Communists and revolutionaries. These prisoners would not follow Gandhi if he called the movement off and required different treatment. Also, the release from jail of Congress leaders who would then stand for election in the councils would be resented by members who had stood by government. 'On the other hand, there are many prisoners, such as picketers and members of unlawful assemblies... in regard to whom there would be no objection to their early release, if the Civil Disobedience Movement definitely ended'.[102] The Governor of Madras' view was that 'those who have been imprisoned have deliberately defied the law and deserve little consideration'.[103] The Governor of the United Provinces assumed there would be no general amnesty or release of prisoners 'until Government are satisfied that—(a) the movement has been definitely called off, and (b) the persons who give assurances to this effect can and will carry them out'.[104] Also release should be conditional on an assurance of future good behaviour. The Governor of Assam urged that the powers of the Press Ordinance should be retained but Hailey and Innes pointed out the difficulties of this. The Governor of Bombay, despite the strength of his earlier views merely indicated 'that as far as he is concerned the calling off of the movement by Gandhi would give immediate relief to the situation'.[105] Innes regarded it as 'essential that the calling off of the Civil Disobedience Movement by Gandhi should be accompanied by some kind of concessions in regard to prisoners, otherwise there would be no effective calling off'.[106] The Viceroy, in summing up agreed with Innes and observed that if Gandhi called off the movement, it would not be possible for government to remain unresponsive. Irwin noted 'the general feeling of the Conference was that there should not be any unconditional amnesty but that discretion should be left to local governments to review sentences and to release prisoners conditionally'.[107] He hoped 'Local Governments would when the time came, apply it [this formula] as liberally as conditions would permit'.

It is extraordinary, given the record of the Conference, that Montagu Butler was able to write to his wife, along with personal criticism of some of his colleagues, that

> I don't think we have reached any conclusions and the strain is considerable. The Viceroy takes us into details and the broad questions of policy are hardly touched. Hailey, backed by Innes and de Montmorency, is pushing the diehard arguments. I am backing the progressives who include Sykes and Stanley.[108]

Irwin, with little comment, sent a copy of the record of the Conference to Wedgwood Benn,[109] who circulated it to Cabinet 'because I wanted the Cabinet to know how the minds of Provincial Governors were working'.[110] Benn was to also note 'Sykes' letters, which he occasionally sends me, and the views expressed by people like Montagu Butler really troubled me'. Perhaps the Secretary of State's concern with people like Montagu Butler was drawn from a knowledge of the Governor's attitude, contained in such comments in correspondence as the Viceroy received while thanking him for the governors' conference. In advising Irwin of a deterioration 'in my absence' of the security situation, Montagu Butler was to observe 'I shall have to hit hard and may have to shoot a bit, but that is kinder, and more efficacious, than indiscriminate beating, whilst the new buckshot is most humane, so much so that I hope the mobs won't find it out'.[111] Wedgwood Benn and Irwin in developing approaches to the management of the Civil Disobedience Movement and other matters had also, as a necessary component of governance, to manage the more extreme attitudes of certain governors as part of their overall approach to the administration of India.

At the beginning of September 1930, Sykes made the observation to Irwin that 'the policy of 'steady and persistent pressure' has proved ineffective and peace negotiations lasting two months have failed'.[112] In the light of this view, Sykes suggested Bombay would take the step of encouraging the commercial world in Bombay to disown Congress, but if this failed, a new approach would be required in striking against the organisation. Sykes pressed, once again, for an 'Ordinance enabling the forfeiture [rather than just occupation] of Congress buildings, that can be brought into force immediately on my request'.[113] The Ordinance also envisaged forfeiture of funds. Hailey, at the same time as Sykes, also indicated to Irwin that, in his view, a new approach was necessary now that the 'peace overtures' had failed. 'I am considering whether it would not be well to adopt locally a more active programme than that of the "steady pressure" which we have hitherto adopted.'[114] What Hailey had in mind was to arrest all Congress 'volunteers', gradually and to extend operations until they embraced the whole province, but not to do this until 'there is a real spirit of defeatism beginning on the other side'. Hailey's current attitude to the Sapru and Jayakar negotiations being held with Gandhi he expressed in a letter to Verney, 'I do not attach any importance at all to the so-called negotiations for peace with Gandhi, etc., they seemed to me bound to failure from the first, for I do not see what it is possible to offer Gandhi and Nehru except a complete surrender of our whole position'.[115] Both Hailey and de Montmorency shared a view that the Viceroy was dealing too softly in relation to the negotiations with Gandhi.[116] Hailey duplicated Sykes' request for a special weapon, in the form of an emergency power and Local Authorities Control Ordinance, which he had first intimated was necessary at the July governors' conference.

On this occasion Irwin took up Sykes' case for an Ordinance with the Secretary of State. Irwin advised Wedgwood Benn 'the question of policy has now been considered and have reached the conclusion that the Ordinance should be promulgated. This decision is based primarily on the case of the Bombay Government...'.[117] Irwin, in setting out the reasons for his decision, indicated the Bombay Government had convinced him they now had sufficient police to implement the Ordinance. Also

> ...while we do not attach as high a value to Ordinance as Bombay Government do, we do consider that it will be of very material assistance...further if we decline in present instance to give Bombay the powers they consider necessary, we shall find it difficult to induce them to take action on other lines which future developments may in our opinion require.[118]

The Ordinance, now titled the Unlawful Association Ordinance, was originally intended to give powers to deal with the property of unlawful associations. Sykes had wished to have the power to forfeit properties rather than just occupy them and to be able to seize funds,[119] but in preparing the Ordinance for Benn's consideration Irwin had dropped property forfeiture and funds seizure as too extreme. In exchanges on Hailey's request, the Secretary of State had advised Irwin he would require the strongest justification before approving Hailey's Local Authorities Control Ordinance, as he thought the powers it sought were too drastic. Irwin had believed the powers Sykes wanted were even more so. However, Wedgwood Benn approved Sykes' Property Ordinance on the basis of Irwin's recommendations, and Irwin advised Hailey, in a rare rebuff, to make use of 'liberal legislation', in the place of his proposed Ordinance, rather than to approach Wedgwood Benn again. Irwin was 'quite sure this approach would ease the path very much for the Secretary of State vis-à-vis his own people in Parliament'.[120] Irwin's skill, in the context of his political environment, enabled him to judge how far it was practical to press strong representations on behalf of the governors to London, and to be able to temper their requests for what might be regarded as more extreme powers. Irwin's concern at the appropriate use by the governors, in particular Sykes, of their powers once obtained, was another matter.[121]

The British Indian administration even worked on New Year's Day, and 1931 opened with dissension between Irwin and Sykes on the question of the use of water cannon rather than *lathi*[122] charges to break up demonstrations. Irwin was rather attracted to the idea of water cannon because the use of *lathis* 'give the Congress people exactly the advertisement they want'.[123] Sykes disagreed preferring effective police action rather than armoured cars with water cannon which scheme would 'require the most careful examination before adoption'.[124] Sykes and Irwin had also disagreed over the holding of a population census in India which Sykes wished to postpone because he believed it would break down in places of Congress activity such as Gujarat. Irwin was of the view that if the census was called off it would be seen as a surrender to Congress.[125]

In Bengal and in Burma the situation was such, at the beginning of 1931, that the Viceroy was already seeking special powers from the Secretary of State to assist Bengal with detenus and in the case of Burma to counter rebellion.[126] In Madras, Governor Stanley had reported a 'recrudescence' of the Civil Disobedience Movement due to a rumour that a general amnesty for political prisoners was pending. This was attracting large numbers of people to deliberately court arrest.[127] Irwin advised Stanley of the policy he had agreed with the Secretary of State towards any amnesty.

> The line which I have taken with the Secretary of State, and in which I think he agrees, has been that any amnesty must be consequential on the abandonment of the civil disobedience movement. The only consideration which might lead me to modify this attitude is the necessity of giving some of the leaders an opportunity to talk among themselves.[128]

At the end of January 1931, Irwin had decided on the unconditional release of Gandhi and the members of the Working Committee of the All-India Congress to allow 'full liberty of discussion' of the Prime Minister's statement.[129] He had circulated a possible draft announcement to governors which included reference to its being prepared in consultation with local governments, that is, with their agreement. Illustrating the trust placed in Governor Hailey's diplomatic skills, Irwin had telegraphed him requesting that he should alert the Congress Working Committee to what was happening and 'get a hint conveyed to them that they should go slow. I must leave matter entirely to your discretion and it may already be too late'.[130]

In the light of the action proposed in relation to the release of Gandhi and the Congress Working Committee, Innes, in Burma, had been requested by the Secretary of State to defer using his new Ordinance for a few days.[131] Innes had agreed but had indicated there might be some difficulty in passing the subsequent Bill without certification. Again, in a revealing message to the Secretary of State, supportive of his Governor in the practicality of his local situation, Irwin advised:

> I feel very strongly that, within the limits of the general policy agreed upon with you, we ought to give the Governor liberty of action when confronted with a difficult parliamentary situation. He has to shoulder the responsibility for the tranquility of his Province, and I think he ought to have full discretion to use his extraordinary powers on a matter of agreed policy if he considers that the situation is of such gravity as to make this necessary for the discharge of his responsibilities.

In an endorsement of the confidence placed in Innes, which Irwin had conveyed, the Secretary of State agreed that the Governor could use his extraordinary powers if necessary.[132]

The governors had varying attitudes to Irwin's intention to release Gandhi and members of the Congress Committee and to his draft announcement of the releases. De Montmorency felt immediate release might result in the Committee making some undesirable declaration and 'I must confess I feel rather pessimistic about the eventual situation'.[133] He believed the pressure for a general amnesty would be great and should be resisted until the Disobedience Movement was called off. Sykes agreed, counseling 'that no further concession be granted until Congress have called off civil disobedience in all its forms'.[134] Governor Stephenson asked 'that we shall have ample opportunity to represent our views before any extensions are made to list of releases, and that it is clearly understood that there will be no relaxation in fighting civil disobedience'.[135] Bengal urged that, due to the threatening situation in Calcutta, the statement and releases be postponed until after Independence Day on 26 January.[136] The governors of the United Provinces and Burma had no comments.[137] Governor Stanley urged the need to include advice that release of members of the Congress Committee would not involve a general amnesty to prevent people trying 'to earn cheap martyrdom within the next few days'.[138] In the most acerbic response of all, Montagu Butler commented:

> ...your telegram...has reached me too late to consult colleagues or give a considered opinion. Accordingly, if you decide to issue statement by tomorrow as indicated, I suggest omission of the words 'in consultation with Local Governments'.[139]

Taking his governors' views into account Irwin made his announcement, and released Gandhi and the Congress Committee on 25 January 1931.[140]

On 1 February 1931, Gandhi wrote to the Viceroy in relation to what he saw as police excesses during the Civil Disobedience Movement thereby, in effect, opening the period of negotiations between himself and Lord Irwin which led to the Irwin/Gandhi Settlement of 4 March 1931. The terms of the Settlement were agreed by the Secretary of State and Irwin.[141] In the period leading up to the Settlement, the Government of India was to ask local governments their views on certain matters connected with an amnesty towards political prisoners if developments were to make one possible.[142] These matters included, the question of a general amnesty; the withdrawal of Ordinances; the withdrawal of notifications declaring associations unlawful under the CLAA; demands for clemency and the possible extension of the scope of releases before the stage of general amnesty was reached. All local governments, and by inference governors, opposed such broad concessions, preferring 'abandonment of civil disobedience followed by an amnesty to simultaneity of action'.[143] In a consideration of the issues, Irwin was to defer to local governments' objections to his proposal that High Court judges should have the authority to define whether those convicted of violent crime or incitement to commit such crimes might be released under the amnesty.[144] The governors wished to keep such decisions within their own jurisdictions.

On 5 March 1931, the Governor-General in Council published the text of the Settlement with Gandhi,[145] and on 6 March Irwin wrote to all the governors elucidating the terms of the Settlement for them.[146] Irwin wrote separately to Sykes, essentially in the same terms but making additional reference to how the matter of forfeited lands, sold to third parties during the Bardoli crisis, might be handled.[147] Irwin had discussed the issue earlier with Sykes in New Delhi and had told Gandhi, 'Government would be entirely neutral in the matter and that, if they could through third parties get the land back, Government would not interfere'.[148] Irwin informed Sykes that Gandhi had 'felt more strongly about this [the issue of forfeited lands] than anything else...I hope you will be satisfied with the way in which I have, as I hope, preserved your position in this very difficult matter'.[149]

Responding to Irwin's success, and while describing the application of the terms of the Settlement in their provinces and some of their difficulties, the governors were to give clear acknowledgement of the Viceroy's central and pivotal role in achieving the Settlement. Governor Stanley was to congratulate the Viceroy and to comment 'I look upon it as a very great triumph and it is entirely due to you personally'.[150] Governor Hammond in similar terms wrote 'you must be needing a rest, which has been thoroughly well earned if I may say so'.[151] Innes conveyed his thought 'that it was quite wonderful that you got a settlement at all', and added 'I have never met Gandhi'.[152]

Lambert congratulated Irwin on his 'historic achievement'.[153] Jackson, who had been in New Delhi at the time of the Viceroy's negotiations with Gandhi, observed, 'you have every reason for personal satisfaction with the results, so far, of your great endeavour…'.[154] Montagu Butler responded flatly advising only of progress on prisoner releases.[155] Sykes was to make reference to his disappointment that his agreement, with the Viceroy, reached New Delhi, 'that picketing of any sort cannot possibly be peaceful, could not be adhered to'.[156] Sykes was also to reinforce the importance of maintaining their agreed position on land in Bardoli. Stephenson in a most pessimistic response was to advise Irwin candidly.

> I cannot say that, except so far as outward demonstrations go, there is any real enthusiasm here about the agreement. I think it is the fact of the agreement rather than its terms that is objected to…civil disobedience was on the verge of collapse. The result of the agreement is to restore its [Congress's] prestige and power and weaken those of Government.[157]

This view was reinforced by Hailey in a letter to Dawson, editor of *The Times* of London.

> There is great depression both in the Civil Service and among officers of the Indian Army at the results of the recent Delhi Settlement. I am not of course at the moment questioning the wisdom of that step, but merely looking objectively at the reactions which we will have to face.[158]

Congress had been given a much needed boost. The Viceroy had indeed placed Gandhi and the Congress as equal partners with the British in the negotiating process which would lead to Indian independence, and future viceroys and governors would have to deal with this reality.

Irwin had had a long pattern of close consultation on important all-India matters with the governors, including taking advice on appropriate responses to the Non-cooperation Movement. However, no record can be found in the Viceroy's or governors' private papers of him seeking advice from them in relation to the policy decision he took to actually meet with Gandhi, or on the elements and detail of the actual conduct of his negotiations with him. No Governor was present to support Irwin in his negotiations. Irwin had informed Goschen of his judgement that 'once he [Gandhi] had asked to see me, it seemed to me quite impossible to refuse without placing oneself quite hopelessly wrong'.[159] This was a personal decision with which the Secretary of State had agreed.[160] Nor did the Viceroy use any of the governors as emissaries to Gandhi, including while in Yeravda jail, but had allowed others to do so. With the exceptions of acting Governor Sir Henry Lawrence[161] of Bombay and Sir Frederick Sykes, the governors do not seem to have met Gandhi, during the Irwin era. Lawrence met Gandhi on 18 and 19 May 1926, in relation to the Agricultural Commission.[162] Sykes met with Gandhi on 16 April 1931, two days before Irwin departed, to discuss the question of land revenue and the return of the confiscated property of the Gujerat peasants.[163] Hailey did not meet Gandhi until 18 May 1931, and after Irwin had left India, to discuss the economic crisis, that year, in the United Provinces.[164] Montagu Butler had met Gandhi in 1919 to discuss terms of a Commission into the events that had occurred at Amritsar.[165]

Additionally, Irwin does not appear to have received unsolicited advice from the governors on how the negotiations with Gandhi might be approached, as had happened, not infrequently, on other matters of importance in India. Irwin, at the time of his meetings with Gandhi had consulted personally with Sykes, of Bombay where the main focus of the Non-cooperation Movement had occurred to determine the presidency's requirements. However, the Viceroy had been selective in adhering to any understanding of what Sykes advised were the immutable requirements for Bombay, such as the abandonment of picketing. The Viceroy had also interpreted, selectively, advice received from other local governments and his own administration on what were to become the essential elements of his Settlement, such as the components of an amnesty.

Whilst this volume has set out to highlight the role of the governors of British India in supporting the Viceroy in his decision making process, it must be acknowledged Irwin himself defined the detail of the parameters of his own personal and policy approach towards Gandhi and their negotiations, which reached settlement so late in Irwin's viceroyalty. Amongst a number of possibilities this might be explained by a view that Irwin was uncertain whether the governors would provide full support for the nature of his complex and fast moving discussions with Gandhi. Stephenson's attitude towards the Settlement may have been the common and underlying view held by the governors. It may be Irwin recalled the flawed advice given by the governors on the membership of the Simon Commission and wished to control the process of negotiation himself, and, of course, Hailey was in England at this time.[166] Interestingly, Gandhi had also overcome the counsel of Congress against continuing negotiations with Irwin. The Irwin/Gandhi Settlement was, to a very large degree, founded on the willingness of both individuals to have confidence in their own personal judgement of what was achievable. This element of confidence in personal judgement was only possible in the context of the trust Irwin and Gandhi had developed in each other, which factor Irwin himself had recognised. 'As he [Irwin] explained to...[Benn], he gathered 'that it [the negotiations] is going to be a question of personal appeal and conviction, rather than of any argument'.[167] This factor was unparalleled, thus far, in British Indian history. Sapru made the observation:

> The task [the settlement with Congress] was one of stupendous difficulty and if we succeeded it is particularly wholly due to the courteous statesmanship of Lord Irwin on the one side which enabled him to rise above narrow administrative considerations and the spirit of reasonableness on the part of Mr Gandhi and others.[168]

There was no room for the governors to make a contribution in these circumstances. Nevertheless, Sapru as well as Gandhi were well aware of the strength and influence of the governors, including relating to the matter of influencing the honouring of the Irwin/Gandhi Pact.

> He [Gandhi] is afraid that Hailey being a strong man will prevail...he [Gandhi] still believes in the good intentions of the Viceroy, though he doubts his strength to overrule the Governors, more particularly Hailey who presides over a Province where the situation is most acute.[169]

Of significance in the context of the history of Irwin's relationship, of active policy consultation, with the governors during his viceroyalty is that he did not seek or receive their contribution to this most important achievement. With this exception, the British administration's policy approach towards Congress, Gandhi and the Civil Disobedience Movement was again notable for the very close level of cooperation between the Viceroy and the governors of British India, and the degree of contribution by them. It is interesting to note that the governors and Viceroy recognised that, as a result of the Montford Reforms, they had lost a considerable degree of autocratic authority, which would have been previously available, to deal with Congress, Gandhi and their adherents. They now found it necessary to respond to these challenges within the more democratic framework presented by the Reforms. Some governors would have preferred more executive authority.

Endnotes

1. Halifax Papers, Hailey to Irwin, 2 March 1930.
2. *Ibid.*, Telegram, Viceroy to Secretary of State, 10 March 1930.
3. *Ibid.*

4. *Ibid.*
5. *Ibid.*, Viceroy to various governors, 10 March 1930.
6. *Ibid.*, Irwin to the King-Emperor, 29 January 1930.
7. NAI, Home/Political, file 257/IV, 1930, memorandum of discussions on 26 and 27 March by H.E. the Viceroy with H.E. the Governor of Bombay, Sir James Crerar and Mr H. Haig in regard to the policy to be adopted in connection with the Civil Disobedience Movement.
8. *Indian Daily Mail,* 26 March 1930.
9. Gopal, *Irwin*, p. 60; Halifax Papers, Telegram, Viceroy to Secretary of State, 12 March 1930; Telegram, Viceroy to Governor of Bombay, 4 April 1930.
10. London *Daily Mail,* 10 April 1930.
11. Hailey Papers, Note on file written by Ashmead Bartlett on 12 April 1930. Bartlett's reputation for truthful reporting was not entirely sound. De Montmorency had informed Hailey, 'I wrote to the Government of India about him. Some of the stuff he proposed to send home was disgracefully untrue'. Hailey Papers, de Montmorency to Hailey, 24 April 1930.
12. Companion supporters.
13. Halifax Papers, Innes to Irwin, 10 March 1930.
14. *Ibid.*, Telegram, Viceroy to Secretary of State, 19 March 1930.
15. *Ibid.*
16. *Ibid.*, Irwin to Innes, 31 March 1930.
17. *Ibid.*, Hammond to Irwin, 26 March 1930.
18. This British intelligence was correct as widespread civil disobedience was launched on Gandhi's arrival at Dandi.
19. Halifax Papers., Telegram, Viceroy to Secretary of State, 31 March 1930.
20. *Ibid.*, Telegram, Viceroy to Governor of Bombay, 5 April 1930.
21. *Ibid.*, Telegram, Viceroy to Secretary of State, 14 April 1930.
22. *Ibid.*, Telegram, Governor of Bombay to Viceroy, 9 April 1930.
23. *Ibid.*, Telegram, Viceroy to Governor of Bombay, 12 April 1930.
24. *Ibid.*, Sykes to Irwin, 15 April 1930.
25. *Ibid.*
26. *Ibid.*
27. *Ibid.*
28. Sykes, *From Many Angles*, p. 385.
29. *Ibid.*
30. Halifax Papers, Telegram, Viceroy to Governor of Bengal, 19 April 1930.
31. *Ibid.*, Telegram, Governor of United Provinces to Viceroy, 27 April 1930; de Montmorency to Irwin, 27 April 1930; Jackson to Irwin, 28 April 1930.
32. *Ibid.*, Irwin to Hailey, 21 April 1930.
33. *Ibid.*, Irwin to de Montmorency, 22 April 1930.
34. *Ibid.*, Irwin to Sykes, 21 April 1930.
35. *Ibid.*, Hailey to Irwin, 25 April 1930.
36. *Ibid.*
37. *Ibid.*

38. *Ibid.*, Irwin to Hailey, 28 April 1930.
39. According to Gopal, not all local governments, including the United Provinces, agreed with the appropriateness of the arrest of Gandhi at this time. The Governor of the United Provinces, Hailey certainly did. See Gopal, *Irwin*, pp. 69, 70.
40. Halifax Papers, Telegram, Viceroy to Secretary of State, 29 April 1930.
41. *Ibid.*
42. *Ibid.*, Sykes to Irwin, 22 April 1930.
43. *Ibid.*, Telegram, Viceroy to Secretary of State, 29 April 1929. Gandhi's actual arrest occurred on 5 May.
44. *Ibid.*, Telegram, Secretary of State to Viceroy, 1 May 1930.
45. Montagu Butler Papers, Butler to his wife, 2 May 1930.
46. Halifax Papers, Irwin to Hailey, 3 May 1930.
47. *Ibid.*, Hailey to Irwin, 8 May 1930. Jallianwala Bagh was the site, in Amritsar in the Punjab, of an infamous killing of civilians by British troops led by General Dyer on 13 April 1919. See Wolpert, *A New History of India*, p. 299.
48. Halifax Papers, Irwin to Hailey, 12 May 1930.
49. *Ibid.*, Jackson to Irwin, 20 May 1930.
50. *Ibid.*, Sykes to Irwin, 21 May 1930.
51. *Ibid.*
52. *Ibid.*
53. *Ibid.*, Sykes to Irwin, 23 May 1930.
54. *Ibid.*, Irwin to Sykes, 27 May 1930.
55. *Ibid.*
56. Sykes, *From Many Angles*, p. 367.
57. Halifax Papers, Irwin to Sykes, 11 June 1930.
58. *Ibid.*, Telegram, Secretary of State to Viceroy, 27 May 1930.
59. *Ibid.*, Irwin to Sykes, 27 May 1930. My italics.
60. *Ibid.*
61. *Ibid.*, Wedgwood Benn to Irwin, 22 May 1930.
62. Halifax Papers, Irwin to Hailey, 20 May 1930.
63. *Ibid.*, Hailey to Irwin, 23 May 1930.
64. *Ibid.*, My italics. The policy of 'steady pressure' and the use of the term was evidently inculcated into the senior ICS approach to nationalism. Both Muddiman and Innes see the need for the steady and fair enforcement of the law. See p. 113, Chapter 5 when they referred, in 1926, to the Malaviya incident. NAI, Home/Political, note on file 209/26, 12 August 1926.
65. Halifax Papers. My italics. See also Cell, *Hailey*, pp. 171–172.
66. *Ibid.*, Irwin to Hailey, 27 May 1930.
67. *Ibid.*, Telegram, Viceroy to Governor of Bombay, 6 June 1930.
68. *Ibid.*, Irwin to Wedgwood Benn, 12 June 1930.
69. *Ibid.*, Irwin to Sykes, 17 June 1930.
70. *Ibid.*, Sykes to Irwin, 20 June 1930.
71. *Ibid.*

72. *Ibid.*, Irwin to Sykes 24 June 1930.
73. *Ibid.*
74. *Ibid.*, Irwin to various Governors, 22 June 1930.
75. Maharaja of Bikaner (1880–1943). The Maharaja was regarded as a progressive ruler. He put his resources at Britain's disposal in 1914. First Chancellor of the Indian Chamber of Princes from 1921 to 1926. He attended the Round Table Conferences in London in 1930 and 1931.
76. Halifax Papers, Irwin to Sykes, 22 June 1930.
77. Montagu Butler Papers, Butler to his wife, 14 September 1930.
78. Halifax Papers, Telegram, Governor of Bombay to Viceroy, 23 June 1930. A meeting of representative Indian non-officials, organised by Sykes, occurred on 16 July 1930. See reference in commentary, relating to governors' conference in this chapter at p. X.
79. *Ibid.*
80. *Indian Daily Mail,* 18 July 1930.
81. Halifax Papers, Telegram, Viceroy to Governor of Bombay, 24 June 1930.
82. *Ibid.*, Sykes to Irwin, 23 June 1930.
83. *Ibid.*, Irwin to Sykes, 27 June 1930.
84. *Ibid.*, Sykes to Irwin, 4 July 1930.
85. *Ibid.*, Telegram, Viceroy to Governor of Bombay, 25 June 1930.
86. *Ibid.*, Telegram, Viceroy to Governor of the United Provinces, 25 June 1930.
87. *Ibid.*, Hailey to Irwin, 25 June 1930.
88. *Ibid.*
89. *Ibid.*
90. *Ibid.*, Telegram, Viceroy to Secretary of State, 30 June 1930; Irwin to Hailey, 1 July 1930.
91. Hailey Papers, Hailey to de Montmorency, 26 May 1930.
92. No reply from de Montmorency on file (Hailey or Halifax Papers).
93. Hailey Papers, Hailey to Irwin, 30 May 1930.
94. *Ibid.,* Hailey to de Montmorency, 11 July 1930; de Montmorency to Hailey, 14 July 1930. The governors had agreed a prior position on the Simon Report for the governors' conference.
95. *Ibid.,* Hailey to de Montmorency, 5 June 1930.
96. *Ibid.,* Irwin to Wedgwood Benn, 25 July 1930.
97. Sykes Papers, 2(b), Folios 244–247.
98. *Ibid.,* Note on file, 16 July 1930.
99. *Times of India,* 18 July 1930.
100. Halifax Papers, Telegram, Viceroy to Governors of Bombay and United Provinces, 14 July 1930.
101. Sykes Papers, 2(b), Folios 244–247.
102. *Ibid.*
103. *Ibid.*
104. *Ibid.*
105. *Ibid.*

106. *Ibid.*
107. *Ibid.*
108. Montagu Butler Papers, Butler to his wife, 23 July 1930.
109. Halifax Papers, Irwin to Wedgwood Benn, 25 July 1930.
110. *Ibid.*, Telegram, Secretary of State to Viceroy, 19 September 1930.
111. *Ibid.*, Montagu Butler to Irwin, 30 July 1930.
112. *Ibid.*, Sykes to Irwin, 8 September 1930.
113. *Ibid.*
114. *Ibid.*, Hailey to Irwin, 9 September, 1930.
115. Hailey Papers, Hailey to Verney, 14 August 1930.
116. *Ibid.*, de Montmorency to Hailey 3 September 1930; Hailey to de Montmorency, 6 September 1930.
117. Halifax Papers, Telegram, Viceroy to Secretary of State, 12 September 1930.
118. *Ibid.*
119. *Ibid.*, Sykes to Irwin, 18 September 1930.
120. *Ibid.*, Irwin to Hailey, 8 October 1930.
121. *Ibid.*, Telegram, Viceroy to Governor of Bombay, 13 October 1930.
122. Long heavy iron-bound bamboo stick used as a weapon.
123. Halifax Papers, Irwin to Sykes, 1 January 1931.
124. *Ibid.*, Sykes to Irwin, 2 January 1931.
125. *Ibid.*, Irwin to Sykes, 4 January 1931.
126. *Ibid.*, Telegrams, Viceroy to Secretary of State, 6, 8 and 11 January 1931.
127. *Ibid.*, Stanley to Irwin, 16 January 1931.
128. *Ibid.*, Irwin to Stanley, 20 January 1931.
129. *Ibid.*, Telegram, Irwin to various governors, 23 January 1931.
130. *Ibid.*, Telegram, Viceroy to Governor of the United Provinces, 22 January 1931.
131. *Ibid.*, Telegram, Viceroy to Secretary of State, 24 January 1931.
132. *Ibid.*, Telegram, Secretary of State to Viceroy, 4 February 1931.
133. *Ibid.*, de Montmorency to Irwin, 24 January 1931.
134. *Ibid.*, Telegram, Governor of Bombay to Viceroy, 23 January 1931.
135. *Ibid.*, Telegram, Governor of Bihar and Orissa to Viceroy, 23 January 1931.
136. *Ibid.*, Telegram, Private Secretary to Governor of Bengal to Private Secretary to Viceroy, 23 January 1931.
137. *Ibid.*, Telegram, Governor of United Provinces to Viceroy, 23 January 1931; Telegram, Governor of Burma to Viceroy, 23 January 1931.
138. *Ibid.*, Telegram, Governor of Madras to Viceroy, 23 January 1931.
139. *Ibid.*, Telegram, Governor of Central Provinces to Viceroy, 23 January 1931.
140. *Ibid.*, Telegram, Viceroy to Secretary of State, 25 January 1931.
141. *Ibid.*, Telegram, Secretary of State to Viceroy, 4 March 1931.
142. *Ibid.*, Telegram, Viceroy to Secretary of State, 1 February 1931.
143. Gopal, *Irwin*, replies of local governments, 30 January to 7 February 1931, p. 102.
144. *Ibid.*

145. *Ibid.*, See full text of the Settlement, which ran to 21 paragraphs, in Appendix to Gopal's *Irwin*.
146. Halifax Papers, Irwin to various governors, 6 March 1931.
147. *Ibid.*, Irwin to Sykes, 6 March 1931.
148. *Ibid.*
149. *Ibid.*
150. *Ibid.*, Stanley to Irwin, 6 March 1931.
151. *Ibid.*, Hammond to Irwin, 6 March 1931.
152. *Ibid.*, Innes to Irwin, 14 March 1931.
153. *Ibid.*, Lambert to Irwin, 16 March 1931.
154. *Ibid.*, Jackson to Irwin, 8 March 1931.
155. *Ibid.*, Montagu Butler to Irwin, 10 March 1931.
156. *Ibid.*, Sykes to Irwin, 11 March 1931.
157. *Ibid.*, Stephenson to Irwin, 16 March 1931.
158. Hailey Papers, Hailey to Dawson, 13 November 1930.
159. Halifax Papers, Irwin to Goschen, 30 March 1931.
160. *Ibid.*, Telegram, Secretary of State to Viceroy, 4 March 1931.
161. Sir H.S. Lawrence. ICS, 1888. Acting Governor of Bombay from March to July 1926.
162. www.gandhiserve.org/information/chronology-1926/chronology-1926.html/, accessed 13 September 2007.
163. www.gandhiserve.org/information/chronology-1931/chronology-1931.html/, accessed 13 September 2007.
164. Cell, *Hailey*, p. 182; NAI. Home/Political, note on file 33/11, 1931. No day/month reference.
165. Montagu Butler Papers, Butler to his wife, 25 October 1919.
166. Hailey was re-appointed Governor of the United Provinces on 19 April 1931, after returning from his work with the first Round Table Conference.
167. Brown, *Gandhi*, p. 248.
168. Sapru Papers, Sapru to Benn, 14 March 1931
169. *Ibid.*, Sapru to Kaitis [*sic*], 16 July 1931. Letter written from 'Rookwood', Simla.

Conclusion

I have set out to explore the influence and contribution of the British governors in administering and governing India, during Lord Irwin's viceroyalty, in order to fill a gap in the historical record and analysis. The study confirms a suspicion that the governors have been given too little credit for their contribution and their impact has not really been measured or analysed. A similar situation may exist in the case of other viceroyalties. However, Lord Irwin's time was chosen not only because it could be taken as an exemplar of general gubernatorial function and activity, particularly since the Montford Reforms, but also because of the critical all-India policy matters that concerned the Viceroy and governors during the period 1926 to early 1931. While my primary objective became an attempt to define the manner and nature of the governors' contribution to the governing of India in a practical and direct sense, an important element was the opportunity to identify their underlying intent and attitude towards rising and nascent Indian nationalism.

The pro-consuls were the centre of social activity and ambitions in their provinces. They dealt out sought after largesse to the collaborating classes and actively engaged in encouraging friends to support the British regime. This active collaboration was a factor contributing towards an essentially non-violent relationship between India and Britain. The governors were also the most obvious display of the panoply and pomp of empire, but one which needed the acquiescence of the Indian population. An important element in the nature of the governors', and also Irwin's, connection with an increasingly nationalist India was the personal relationship established with some of its leadership. This factor engendered a certain mutual respect and together with Gandhi's principles, also played some part in preventing large scale, violent revolution or a war of liberation. The governors were seen in their 'nation building' activities opening hospitals, irrigation works and railways. They administered and ruled vast territories within which they exercised considerable power.

It cannot be surprising that the research has revealed the respective governors as men of different capacity, character and Indian experience.

This differentiation can be defined to a high degree by their professional origins, either in the Indian Civil Service, selected for office on the basis of high ability, or as men of political and often aristocratic origin in Britain. Lord Irwin, himself, brought no experience and a restricted knowledge of India to his important position as Viceroy. In this sense he mirrored the presidency governors. This circumstance required Irwin to seek advice and counsel to support him in his decision making capacity, particularly in the early stages of his administration. In New Delhi and Simla, Irwin had a well qualified and competent bureaucracy to provide him with advice and briefing on the intricacy and multitude of governmental affairs, both at the central as well as provincial levels. However, I have revealed quite definitively that the Viceroy sought out and relied upon another important layer of advice, namely that of the nine governors of the provinces and presidencies. The governors were in effect a higher cadre of administrative elite, a 'super' Indian Civil Service. Not only did Irwin seek the advice of the governors on individual provincial matters to meet his requirements, but he also actively sought the governors' expertise and perspectives as a crucial contribution to all-India policy development. In this practice, Irwin grew to rely more on certain governors than others. The governors could be described as Irwin's policy intimates in the nature of their professional relationship with him.

Provincial politics and that of the Centre were linked through the governors both at the imperial and nationalist levels. As the most senior members of the ICS the provincial governors were able to provide expert advice and support based on their abilities and long experience of India and her peoples. The presidency based governors brought other levels of expertise to their sometimes difficult environment, often based on earlier successful political and administrative careers in Britain. Irwin required all governors to bring to their decision making an awareness of all-India considerations and performed a role as policy coordinator. This is not to say that Irwin sought advice on all aspects of his administration, as under dyarchy significant areas of the government were entirely the responsibility of the Centre, and were highly technical and required specialised expertise. External affairs and national economic policy were some examples. The process of decision making by the governors and Irwin in India was constrained by British Parliamentary and public opinion most often expressed by the Secretary of State. Indian public opinion, the political position taken by the various nascent legislative bodies and the nationalist opposition were also critical influences on them.

As a result of the Montford Reforms and the *Government of India Act* of 1919, involving the introduction of dyarchy, there had been a deliberate shift of political and administrative power to the provinces from the central government. The very nature of dyarchy meant that the administration of those portfolios and issues of most relevance to the populace was at the provincial level. This shift in power magnified the importance of the respective governors within their provinces, increased their responsibilities and their workload, in contrast to their pre-reform equivalents. They were the heads of their governments, power brokers between the various Indian political factions, dispensers of favours to Indian collaborators and also mentors to the rising political classes. The governors were the 'key stone' in the complex dyarchic system, holding the transferred and reserved portfolios together within the provincial governments. The legal and constitutional powers of the governors were defined by the 1919 *Government of India Act,* and were significant. Some aspects of the governors' authority were limited by the oversight of the Viceroy and Secretary of State. In the case of Irwin this, often informal, oversight was conducted in a collaborative way and was very rarely directive. An important restraint on the exercise of the governors' power and authority was in fact their own morality and personal standards, which were an important element of the application of colonial governance, further adumbrated more formally by their Instrument of Instructions.

This work has revealed that, particularly, the ICS governors of Irwin's time understood the implications for the British in India of the Montford Reforms and of the Preamble of the *Government of India Act*, and to a very large extent pursued their progressive objectives. It can be argued that, while dyarchy was not a truly democratic system, the Montford Reforms required the governors to adopt a more liberal and progressive approach to government, than had previously existed. The governors recognised this requirement. Indeed they had, to a significant degree, been selected for high office, as governors, on the basis of their support for the Reform measures. Some of the governors had in fact contributed to the development of policy which established the Reforms. The governors themselves had used the term 'liberal' in describing their own intentions towards Indian constitutional development and India's future. With little exception the governors' record does not reveal reactionary attitudes to India's constitutional goals. They knew what forces had been set in train and that they would have to deal lawfully with this new element of legitimate and evolving challenge to their rule. While the governors were actively engaged in the process of imparting the parliamentary skills which they believed were necessary for self-government, they were very conscious of their perceived responsibility towards the vast politically uneducated Indian population. They believed this circumstance limited their ability to hand over political power which can be seen as a rationale for continuing imperial rule. However, the record shows this position was not taken cynically by the governors in order to delay independence. Even so the absence of a time frame, identified by the British to give India its Independence qualifies to some degree the progressive intent of the Montagu Declaration. The 'liberal' governors worked towards the objectives set by the Reforms but the British had not yet come to terms with the measure's logical conclusion—that there had to be an identified end-point to British rule. As history records imperial rule ultimately ended largely as an outcome of economic and military weakness. The fact that the governors had not identified a definite end-point to the British presence is not surprising given the significance of what this step would mean in terms of Britain's global political and economic policy. It was not the governors' role to set an end-point but it was their function to engage in the process of constitutional evolution, which they did with a high degree of success. This latter point does not contradict the view put forward by Bridge, Low, Moore and Hyam that the trend of British policy, developed within the tensions of labour and conservative politics, was to resist nationalist aspirations, and independence only occurred under a complexity of great pressures.

Irwin's fundamentally progressive and positive approach to the goals of Indian nationalism complemented, to a high degree, those of the ICS governors, and was strongly influenced by them. If Irwin and the governors had adopted a hard line approach to the challenge of Congress it is likely this would have provoked an equally hard line response, and even revolution. Reactionary measures were not appropriate to the age and Irwin and the governors knew this. The ICS governors, particularly, and Irwin were at one end of the 1920s political spectrum, defining British intent towards India and the conservative 'diehards' at the other. This is not to say the governors were not inherently conservative in personal, social and political outlook but they, in comparison to many of their British compatriots in the Indian army, commerce and even in the British administration, had entered into the spirit of the Montford Reforms and dyarchy.

The governors' role in the development and implementation of the Montford Reforms and the working of dyarchy has enabled an identification of their intent and attitudes towards Indian nationalist aspirations. Their participation and active support of the Reforms and dyarchy establishes that the ICS governors recognised the trend of a more progressive age. This factor underpinned their approach and attitudes to the other policy issues examined. They did not attempt to complicate or qualify the spirit of the Reforms. Again the term 'liberal' could be applied more fully to some governors than others. For example it might be argued that of the 'liberal' ICS governors Hailey was the most 'conservative' and more so than Irwin. Also, it must be said that the presidency governors, Lytton, Sykes and Jackson, did little to allow the evolution of the political aspirations identified by Indian nationalists. Montagu Butler, of all the ICS governors, would also have to be included in this category. Also, governors could be liberal in one respect and 'diehard' in others, for example, in relation to counter-terrorism measures. Furthermore, political liberalism may be difficult to judge on a British basis: conservative governors favoured broadening the franchise, but their objective may have been in order to undermine the educated elite. However, it must be said that this work has not been able to identify any overt intention or conspiracy to do so. But, in analysing the underlying attitudes of the presidency governors towards the growth of Indian democracy one does sense a more conservative position. The attitudes of most of the presidency governors, under study, towards the implementation of a process which would lead to Indian Independence, significantly contrast with their provincial colleagues. This difference can be explained in terms of their respective pedigrees, importantly, as none of the presidential governors had served in the ICS, and thus were denied the service's skills and experience in Indian affairs. It is also relevant in this regard, that the presidency governors were political appointments and their attitudes would have been reinforced by increasingly Conservative political control from Westminster in the 1920s. Also, that the presidencies faced the most acute difficulties with the nationalist movement and social unrest and, in a sense, the presidency governors may have been, as has been noted in the case of Lord Lytton, 'die-hardened' by their experiences. But their difference in attitude did work to complicate their relationship with Irwin, and their effective contribution to the British response to nationalism and emergency in the presidencies.

In an examination of an important policy area, this work confirms the high degree to which the governors contributed to and influenced important policy decisions relating to the Simon Commission, and its constitutional objectives. Given Irwin's inexperience in Indian matters, at that time, he naturally deferred to the governors on the range of matters relating to the Commission. The most important issue, as it transpired, was the composition of the Commission itself. Here Irwin took advice from Hailey and Muddiman in particular, and other governors that the membership of the Commission should be derived from the British Parliament, and thus exclude Indians. They believed it would not be possible to obtain an impartial and representative Indian contribution. In effect the governors' advice was so persuasive as to even alter Birkenhead's misgivings on the omission of Indians. This error of judgement has been regarded by history as Irwin's greatest mistake in

India, but in fact it can be sheeted home to the governors. This episode demonstrates most fully the degree of influence the governors exercised in the process of decision making at the all-India level. That the governors' seriously flawed advice to Irwin and Birkenhead, and judgement of Indian reaction, was accepted reinforces the fact of the governors' influence. Even though inexperienced, Irwin must have wondered about the validity of the governors' views, but deferred to their assumed collective wisdom in convincing Birkenhead that his preference for an inclusive Royal Commission was wrong. It is most unlikely the governors' advice was mischievous in intention, and really designed to complicate Indian constitutional evolution. This viewpoint is reinforced by their surprise at the level of Indian hostility towards the British decision. The governors' misjudged advice on membership of the Commission can be seen as reflecting a degree of complacency and insensitivity. On this one issue the governors severely damaged the British relationship with nationalist India, compromising and complicating the work they were doing to further the objectives of the Reforms including administering dyarchy.

The governors' substantial influence is also reflected in their advice to Irwin on a range of aspects relating to preparing for the Commission. This included ideas on how to achieve the inclusion of Indian opinion in the Commission's consideration, on aspects of the announcement of the Commission and the timing of its visit to India. Hailey was Irwin's key adviser on the Simon Commission and on a range of other policy areas, and the Viceroy consistently conveyed Hailey's advice to the Secretary of State, openly acknowledging its provenance. Three governors, in particular Hailey, Innes and de Montmorency, provided significant input into a policy paper the Viceroy had written, on reform in the central government, for Simon Commission purposes. The governors provided comprehensive responses commenting on and refining the Viceroy's ideas. The governors also submitted their views on reform of the constitution at the provincial level, with the ideas of Hailey and de Montmorency, on this matter, greatly influencing the final Simon Commission Report itself. The governors were also to provide their advice directly to Simon and his Commission in India. The fact of these exchanges demonstrates the nature of the professional relationship between Irwin and the governors and the reliance and value he placed on their advice, which he most often accepted. The chapter on the Simon Commission provides an overarching theme of the governors providing consistent liaison, cooperation and support to Irwin. It also reveals their fallibility, but despite this episode, Irwin continued to seek the governors' full collaboration during his term.

In common with a number of Lord Irwin's apparent initiatives little credit is given, by his biographers and historians, to the governors of India for their role in the development of the proposal for his Dominion Status Declaration and the first Round Table. My research corrects this omission. An examination of the available material reveals quite unequivocally the role of Governor Stephenson, in particular, in seeding and developing these ideas with Irwin. The Governor alerted Irwin to the dangers of a defective Simon Commission Report, and hence the imperative of a declaration of constitutional intent by the Viceroy to maintain some degree of Indian nationalist cooperation. He also, advised on the usefulness of a conference in England to win back the support of moderate Indian politicians. In addition Hailey was involved in refining the plans for Irwin's announcement and put forward a proposal attempting to synchronise the Declaration with the issuance of the Simon Report. He also participated in the drafting of the Declaration itself and attempted to clarify the term 'Dominion Status' for Irwin. Most governors indicated support to Irwin for his joint initiative, which was to a significant degree developed in India by their cadre and approved in England at the highest political level. This is a key finding which alters the historiography. No reference can be found in the secondary sources that gives this credit to the governors, and all credit is given to Irwin. The importance of the governors' experience and expertise is further reflected in Hailey's and Innes' participation in the Round Table Conference as advisors. Hailey, in particular, provided significant support to the Conference and was able to influence outcomes. He participated largely as a free agent and put forward his own ideas.

These references provide proof of the governors' extensive participation and contribution to all-India policy development at the most senior levels in India and Britain. Their policy advice was integral to the progression of important government initiatives. Chapters 2–4 thus confirm the governors' intimate involvement in a full range of all-India policy issues related to British attempts to meet the demands of rising Indian nationalism within a constitutional framework. Chapters 5–8 examine the governors' responses to a number of extreme challenges, working outside and complicating the preferred British constitutional framework. To a significant extent the main challenges were centred in the presidencies where Irwin and the governors had to contend with communalism, communism, labour disputes and terrorism. Communalism, while not specifically directed at the British, destabilised and distracted their focus on peaceful administration, opening them up to criticism as not being effective rulers or being somewhat devious. The policy pursued by Irwin and the governors of attempting to resolve communal tensions as a matter of high importance, contradicts a view that the British fomented communal differences in order to *divide et impera.* While some of the governors could see a benefit for them of adopting this approach, the policy of Irwin, and of the governors whose advice he accepted on the matter, was to attempt to resolve this perennial Indian problem. As a consequence Irwin was to give addresses on the matter in Simla and Delhi. While attempts to resolve communalism were to prove unsuccessful, once again Irwin had sought, taken into account, and agreed with the views of his governors on an important policy issue. The fact the governors had not put forward a policy recommending 'divide and rule' reinforces the balance and objectivity of their judgement in achieving British objectives.

Even under the direct pressure of emergency, in the provinces, the responses of the local rulers had to be tempered by the expectations of the British Parliament and British public opinion, expressed directly to the governors by the Viceroy and Secretary of State, and by sensitivity to nationalist criticism and opinion in India. This caused considerable tension within the governmental hierarchy, with the governors expected to keep the peace in the face of often violent challenge and to be as moderate as possible in their response. Nevertheless, the resolution of these difficulties was conducted within an extensive dialogue and exchange of views in order to reach mutually acceptable outcomes. The extension of the Viceroy's and Secretary of State's policy on dealing with the infiltration of communism, and its influence on labour disputes, mainly into Bengal and Bombay, but also Madras, produced tensions for their gubernatorial colleagues. The Viceroy carried forward a policy of developing approaches to the threat of emergency in consultation with all the governors and indicated a willingness, only in extreme circumstances, to use Ordinances and new legislation. ICS governors consistently provided advice which preferred action within the existing law. Irwin's support or otherwise of the governors, to the Secretary of State, could depend on his view of their respective judgement, and his papers provide a clear impression of the governors' relative competence, which is a definite element in their ability to have influenced Indian history. Irwin's attitude to Lytton, Sykes and Jackson contrasts significantly with the views he held of Harcourt Butler, Hailey, Innes, de Montmorency and Stephenson, all ICS men. Some governors such as Hammond in Assam and Montagu Butler in the Central Provinces kept themselves distant from controversy as far as was possible, contrasting with Hailey, in particular who often volunteered his advice and participation.

In addition, the governors were faced with the problem of terrorism, not only in terms of how to suppress it, but also of how to deal with the terrorists once imprisoned. This was an issue discussed between the governors and Irwin alongside that of communal tension which aided the terrorists. In the case of the terrorists, who were sometimes Communists, the governors and Irwin were presented with a dilemma. As the terrorists could only be seen as violent and extreme it might be expected that stringent responses were appropriate, including the manner of imprisonment. However, even in this case, an overriding consideration was a British Parliamentary and public view that it was unacceptable to have Bengal's prisons filled with so-called detenus, even if they were terrorists. Secretaries of state, therefore, insisted on a policy of the overall population of prisoners not being increased. In Bengal, Lytton, in particular, resisted this approach but his successor actively complied. Lytton's and Sykes' governorships were characterised by the nature of their robust, and sometimes ill-considered, exchanges with the Government of India and the Viceroy in the policy development process. To some extent this reflected personalities but certainly compromised the acceptance of their advice at more senior levels. Governor Jackson, replacing Lytton in Bengal, was more inclined to cooperate with the policy of the Viceroy and Secretary of State on detenus, particularly following their advice to him of their expectations of his performance and their view that Lytton had been a failure. In these circumstances, Jackson's approach to the detenu problem generated tension between him and his police and officials. Lytton and Sykes had tended to reduce themselves to conduits of information and thus to functionaries. The Viceroy and his ICS advisers remained concerned about the need to nurture allies. This policy produced tensions with some governors needing to address the practical question of keeping peace. Some governors had developed special relationships with leading nationalist figures and also worked with them in the legislatures.

The various secretaries of state and the Viceroy were very sensitive to attracting accusations of repression, in response to emergency, further complicating their dialogue with the nationalists in attempts to draw them into the constitutional process contained in the Round Table Conference initiative. The presidency governors were most concerned to deal with the circumstances of local challenge directly and stringently, rather than cater to all-India considerations. In this context, consistent themes were Irwin's wish to deal with emergency within the existing laws of the presidencies and India, and particularly the Labour Secretary of State's unwillingness to allow governors to introduce new and more harsh measures by overriding their respective legislatures by certification. The Viceroy preferred not to issue Ordinances or use his powers under Regulation III of 1818. This approach by the Government of India generated significant tensions in the relationship with, in particular, Bengal and Bombay. However, both the Viceroy and the secretaries of state were willing to provide increased powers to the governors once convinced of a real need, and that they were not draconian. More moderate advice was provided by the ICS governors, and accepted, on how to approach these difficulties.

An analysis of events in Bardoli, in Bombay Presidency, surrounding resistance by farmers to the paying of an increased land tax assessment reinforces our understanding of the nature of the practice of Indian government. Initially, Wilson had been left alone to resolve the matter and his primary responsibility was acknowledged by Irwin. However, as the situation escalated both the Viceroy and Secretary of State and then the British Cabinet became involved. Birkenhead, on this occasion, wished British authorities in India to take more active measures than they were willing to apply, that could have led to military intervention. Irwin supported Wilson's preference to negotiate an outcome with the farmers and their leaders, which Birkenhead was compelled to accept. In the event Birkenhead, Irwin and Wilson, between themselves, in effect, negotiated an approach to resolve Bardoli before applying it successfully. All governors were asked to provide their analysis of the catalyst for the Bardoli campaign and how it might be nullified in the future. Thus their collective experience and expertise were sought on the matter, and assimilated in order to guard against the threat of misjudged land tax assessment, in the context of nationalist challenge. The Bardoli circumstance was a further important example of how the hierarchy of British rulers worked together, drawing on their experience and expertise, to resolve challenges. Bardoli also provides an example of the advantage the governors had in working with a cooperative, competent and courteous Viceroy, particularly when he had confidence in their abilities.

Further reinforcement of the significance of the governors in the development and application of all-India policy is provided conclusively by their comprehensive participation, with the Viceroy, in developing and applying strategies to deal with Congress and Mahatma Gandhi, from the beginning of 1930. Again, some governors feature more prominently than others. As Gandhi's Salt March proceeded Irwin sought the governors' advice on whether to change their policy, which they had developed together, of no arrest. Receiving Hailey's detailed advice, that it was then necessary to arrest Gandhi and on the manner of arrest and also the length of imprisonment, Irwin sought approval for that action, of significant consequence, from the Secretary of State. Irwin had also received the advice of the majority of governors supporting this approach. Hailey's views on how to conduct an effective enquiry into the circumstances of the arrest was also provided. His comprehensive and strategic response encapsulating elements of his long experience in India and his personal expertise, combined to produce the level of advice so highly valued by the Viceroy. Both Irwin and Hailey tended to match each other in seeking moderate strategic approaches towards their problems in India, rather than repressive or provocative measures. Irwin agreed with Hailey's suggestion of steady, quiet pressure against Congress, which was a consistent policy approach developed within the ICS. Sykes, the Governor most immediately concerned with the Gandhi crisis, continued to be exasperated by Irwin's and, by implication Hailey's position on how the emergency in Bombay and elsewhere should be handled and continued to press for Ordinances. The Viceroy's views of Sykes' performance in Bombay compromised his willingness to accede to the Governor's request for increased powers.

The outcome of the July 1930 governors' conference, which endorsed a continued moderate policy towards Congress, whilst discussions with Gandhi continued, reinforces a view of the significant influence of most of the ICS governors. Given the conciliatory intentions surrounding the first Round Table Conference, Irwin decided to release Gandhi and Congress leaders to create a more positive attitude towards reconciliation with them. The governors had differing attitudes towards the release, including on the matter of a general amnesty regarding political prisoners. The release of Gandhi enabled Irwin to meet with him to negotiate a political settlement. Irwin's decision to meet Gandhi, and the terms of their settlement, do not appear to have involved the governors. Some governors held a view that British prestige had been compromised. With these exceptions the governors were an intimate component of the Viceroy's and Secretary of State's decision making process on all-India affairs, and they heavily depended on them. Interestingly, Irwin's conciliatory approach to Indian nationalism and Gandhi, which as has been seen was so strongly influenced by the Governor cadre, in some senses matched his later attempts, when as Chamberlain's Foreign Minister, he attempted to appease Nazi Germany before the Second World War.

A study of the role and effectiveness of other governors during other viceroyalties would complement and provide a useful comparison to this work. In this respect a similar analysis of Lord Willingdon's period as Viceroy, given his reactionary style, would usefully contrast the role, influence and attitude of the governors of his period, with those governors who ruled during the progressive time of Irwin. Given that a number of those governors who served with Irwin also worked with Willingdon, it would be possible to establish if their relationship with the two viceroys was consistent. If these governors continued their progressive and steadying attitudes, towards

Indian nationalism in their relationship with Willingdon, in the face of his conservatism, it would further reinforce the high degree of influence they had exercised with Irwin.

A superficial examination, that did not incorporate recourse to original sources, of the nature of all-India administration and government in Lord Irwin's time, would not reveal the significant extent to which the various governors of the presidencies and provinces were involved in a most comprehensive and vital contribution to the development and implementation of policies required to administer the Indian Empire, in the demanding circumstances of 1926 to 1931. While the Viceroy contributed to, and was the final arbiter on all-India policy development the Raj could not have functioned without the participation of the governors. They were a key and integral component of the government, administration and political structure of British India. Even though a minority of mainly presidential governors did, to some extent, act as a brake on constitutional advance, it can be claimed the Indian administration was dominated by the best elements of the ICS who understood, and implemented, the liberal trends of their era, defined by the Montford Reforms. The decision making process of the Viceroy is most often seen as discrete, and any credit or otherwise is thus most often ascribed in history to him alone. Analysts of Indian history have indeed given too much credit to Lord Irwin and the secretaries of state in their administration of India, and too little to the *Satraps*. The governors were critical contributors to the making of Indian history but, as in the nature of the civil service they have been given too little credit for their contributions. This detailed exploration and exposition of the governors' roles has corrected this misconception and confirmed that, in fact, the steel framework of British India was provided by a governors' Raj.

Appendix 1

Instrument of Instructions Issued to Governors[1]

'The Governor is responsible to Parliament for doing his utmost, consistently with the general purposes of the Government of India Act, 1919, to maintain the standards of good administration and to further all changes tending to make India fitted for self-government. He is required to encourage religious toleration, cooperation and good-will among all creeds and classes, to protect the interests of all minorities, to maintain the standards of conduct of the public service and the probity of public finance, and to promote all measures making for the moral, social and industrial welfare of the people and tending to fit all classes of the population without distinction to take their due share in the public life and government of the country.

In particular and without prejudice to the generality of the foregoing:

I. The Governor is responsible for maintaining the safety and tranquility of his province and for using his influence to compose religious and racial animosities, and to prevent religious and racial conflicts.

II. The Governor has a general responsibility for seeing that the administration of the transferred subjects by ministers is properly conducted. He will assist his ministers by all the means in his power with information and advice. He will restrict the exercise of the power to act in opposition to his ministers' advice, to cases in which he considers that the consequences of acquiescence would be serious.

III. The Governor is required to advise his ministers in regard to their relations with the provincial legislative council, to support them generally in difficulties so far as possible, and in the event of an adverse vote in the legislative council to require the resignation of a minister only when it seems to him that the minister has lost the confidence of the council.

IV. The Governor is responsible for due compliance with any orders affecting the administration of transferred subjects which may be issued by the Secretary of State or the Government of India.

V. The Governor is responsible for bringing to the notice of the minister concerned any observations on the administration of a transferred subject which may be communicated to him by the Government of India.

VI. In the case of any provincial Bill which appears to the Governor likely to affect any matter hereby specially committed to his charge, or any all-India subject, or any general principles laid down by the Secretary of State or the Government of India for the administration of a reserved subject, the Governor shall, before assenting to such Bill, consider whether he should reserve it for the consideration of the Governor-General.

VII. The Governor is required to see that no monopoly or special privilege which is inconsistent with the public interest is granted to any private undertaking and that no unfair discrimination in matters affecting commercial or industrial interests is permitted.

VIII. The Governor is responsible for the safeguarding of the legitimate interests of the European and Anglo-Indian community.

IX. The Governor is responsible for the protection of all members of the public services in the legitimate exercise of their functions, and in the enjoyment of all recognised rights and privileges.

X. The Governor is required to secure that in all extensions of educational facilities adequate provision is made for the special needs of the Muslim and other minority community.

XI. The Governor is required to secure that the interests of existing educational institutions maintained and controlled by religious bodies are duly protected in the event of any changes of educational policy affecting them adversely.

XII. The Governor is required to secure that due provision is made for the advancement and social protection of depressed and backward classes and aboriginal tribes'.

Endnote

1. Mukherji, *The Indian Constitution*, pp. 216–218.

Appendix 2

Preamble to: *The Consolidated Government of India Act, 1919*[1]

'Whereas it is the declared policy of Parliament to provide for the increasing association of Indians in every branch of Indian administration, and for the gradual development of self governing institutions, with a view to the progressive realisation of responsible government in British India as an integral part of the empire:

And whereas progress in giving effect to this policy can only be achieved by successive stages, and it is expedient that substantial steps in this direction should now be taken:

And whereas the time and manner of each advance can be determined only by Parliament, upon whom responsibility lies for the welfare and advancement of the Indian peoples:

And whereas the action of Parliament in such matters must be guided by co-operation received from those on whom new opportunities of service will be conferred, and by the extent to which it is found that confidence can be reposed in their sense of responsibility:

And whereas concurrently with the gradual development of self-governing institutions in the provinces of India it is expedient to give to those provinces in provincial matters the largest measure of independence of the Government of India, which is compatible with the due discharge by the latter of its own responsibilities'...

Endnote

1. Mukherji, *The Indian Constitution,* pp. 13–14.

Appendix 3

The Governors of British India and Secretaries of State During Lord Irwin's Viceroyalty: 3 April 1926–18 April 1931

(Drawn from The India Office List)

Edward Frederick Lindley Wood (1881–1959) 1st Earl of Halifax, British Conservative politician; as Lord Irwin, Viceroy of India from 1926 to 1931; foreign secretary during the period of appeasement of Germany.

Assam

Sir John Henry Kerr, KCSI, KCIE (1871–1934).

Educated at Clare College, Cambridge. In 1890 appointed to the Indian Civil Service (ICS). Served in Bengal, Bihar, Midnapore. Governor of Assam: 10 October 1922–27 June 1927.

Sir Egbert Laurie Lucas Hammond, KCSI, CBE (1873–1939).

Educated at Keble College, Oxford. In 1895 appointed to ICS. Served in Bengal, Cooch Behar District, Bihar and Orissa. Governor of Assam: 28 June 1927–10 May 1932.

Bengal

Victor Alexander George Robert Bulwer-Lytton, Earl of Lytton, PC, KG, GCSI, GCIE (1876–1947).

Born at Simla. Educated at Trinity College, Cambridge. Filled various posts in the admiralty and The India Office. Governor of Bengal: 28 March

1922–27 March 1927. Acting Viceroy in 1925. In 1927 and 1928 led Indian delegations to 8th and 9th Assembly of the League of Nations.

Sir Francis Stanley Jackson, PC, GCSI, GCIE, KStJ (1870–1947).

Educated at Trinity College, Cambridge. Soldier. Unionist MP for Howdenshire. Financial Secretary to the War Office. Governor of Bengal: 28 March 1927–28 March 1932.

Note: Both Lytton and Jackson attended the same college at Cambridge and served as governors of Bengal.

Bihar and Orissa

Sir Henry Wheeler, KCSI, KCIE (1870–1950).

Educated at Christ's College, Cambridge. In 1889 appointed to ICS. Served in Bengal. Governor of Bihar and Orissa: 12 April 1922–6 April 1927. Council of India: 1927–1937.

Sir Hugh Lansdown Stephenson, GCIE, KCSI (1871–1941).

Educated at Christ Church, Oxford. In1894 appointed to ICS. Served in Bengal. Governor of Bihar and Orissa: 7 April 1927–6 April 1932. Acting Governor of Bengal in 1926 and 1930.

Bombay

Lieutenant-Colonel, the Right Honourable Sir Leslie Orme Wilson, PC, GCSI, GCMG, GCIE, DSO (1876–1955).

Educated at St Michaels, Westgate, and St Paul's School. Soldier. ADC to the Governor of NSW 1903–1909. Various positions as Parliamentary Secretary. Unionist MP for Reading 1913–1922. MP for South Portsmouth 1922–1923. Governor of Bombay: 10 December 1923–7 December 1928. Governor of Queensland, 1932.

Major-General, the Right Honourable Sir Frederick Hugh Sykes, PC, GCSI, GCIE, GBE, KCB, CMG, KJStJ (1877–1954).

Educated in Paris. Soldier. Commanded the Military Wing of the Royal Flying Corps, Controller-General of Civil Aviation. Unionist MP for Hallam. Governor of Bombay: 8 December 1928–9 December 1933.

Burma

Sir Spencer Harcourt Butler, GCSI, GCIE, FRSA, FRAS, FZS (1869–1938).

Educated at Balliol College, Oxford. In 1888 appointed to the ICS. Served in the North-Western Provinces and Oudh, Lucknow. Governor-General's Council, 1910–1915. Lieutenant-Governor of the United Provinces of Agra and Oudh: 15 February 1918 – 2 January 1921. Governor of the United Provinces of Agra and Oudh: 3 January 1921–20 December 1922. Lieutenant-Governor of Burma: 28 October 1915–22 September 1917. Governor of Burma: 2 January 1923–19 December 1927. Chair of Indian States Committee, January 1928.

Sir Charles Alexander Innes, KCSI, CIE (1874–1959).

Educated at St John's College, Oxford. In 1897 appointed to the ICS. Served in Madras, Malabar. Governor-General's Council, 1921–1927. Governor of Burma: 20 December 1927–19 December 1932.

Central Provinces and Berar

Sir Montagu Sherard Dawes Butler, KCSI, CB, CVO, CBE (1873–1952).

Educated at Pembroke College, Cambridge. In 1895 appointed to ICS. Served in various positions in the Punjab, Kotah State, Lahore, Attock. Governor of the Central Provinces and Berar: 26 January 1925–28 November 1929; and again from 29 March 1930 to 14 September 1933.

Madras

The Right Honourable George Joachim Goschen, 2nd Viscount Goschen of Hawkhurst, PC, GCSI, GCIE, CBE (1866–1952).

Educated at Balliol College, Oxford. Private Secretary to Governor of NSW. Conservative MP for East Grinstead, 1895–1906. Parliamentary Secretary, 1918. Governor of Madras: 14 April 1924–11 November 1929. Acting Viceroy from 29 June to 24 October 1929.

Lieutenant-Colonel, the Right Honourable Sir George Frederick Stanley, PC, GCSI, GCIE, CMG (1872–1938).

Educated at Wellington and RMA Woolwich. Soldier. Financial Secretary to the War Office. Conservative MP for Preston and Willesden East. Held various positions as Parliamentary Secretary. Governor of Madras: 12 November 1929–14 November 1934.

Punjab

William Malcolm Hailey, Lord Hailey of Shahpur, PC, OM, GCSI, GCIE, GCMG (1872–1969).

Educated at Corpus Christie College, Oxford. In 1894 appointed to ICS. Served in the Punjab and as Chief Commissioner of Delhi, 1912. Governor-General's Council, 1919. Governor of the Punjab: 31 May 1924–8 August 1928.

Sir Geoffrey Fitzhervey de Montmorency, GCIE, KCSI, KCVO, CBE (1876–1955).

Educated at Pembroke College, Cambridge. In 1899 appointed to ICS. Served in the Punjab and as Personal Assistant to the Chief Commissioner of Delhi, 1912–1917. Deputy Commissioner, Lyallpur, Punjab, 1918–1920. Private Secretary to the Viceroy, 1922. Governor-General's Council, 1926. Governor of the Punjab: 9 August 1928–11 April 1933.

United Provinces of Agra and Oudh

Sir William Sinclair Marris, KCSI, KCIE (1873–1945).

Educated at Christ Church, Oxford. In 1895 appointed to the ICS. Served in the North- Western Provinces and Oudh, United Provinces, 1917. Joint Secretary at the Home Department to assist Edwin Montagu on reforms programme, 1919. Collector of Aligarh. Governor of Assam: 3 April 1921–10 October 1922. Governor of the United Provinces: 24 December 1922–13 January 1928. Council of India: 1928–1929.

Sir Alexander Phillips Muddiman, KCSI, CIE (1875–1928).

Educated at Wimborne, University College, London. In 1897 appointed to the ICS. Served in: Bihar, Bengal, Calcutta. Governor of the United Provinces, 14 January 1928–17 June 1928. He died while in office.

William Malcolm Hailey, Lord Hailey of Shahpur, OM, GCSI, GCMG, GCIE, PC (15 February 1872 – 1 June 1969).

Governor of the United Provinces: 9 August 1928–15 October 1930, and again from 19 April 1931–5 December 1934.

The Secretaries of State For India During Lord Irwin's Viceroyalty

The Right Honourable, the Earl of Birkenhead (1872–1930), 7 November 1924–31 October 1928.

The Right Honourable, the Viscount Peel (1867–1937), 21 March 1922–22 January 1924 and 1 November 1928–7 June 1929.

The Right Honourable, W. Wedgwood Benn (1877–1960), 8 June 1929–25 August 1931.

The Right Honourable, Sir Samuel John Gurney Hoare (1880–1959), 26 August 1931–6 June 1935.

Glossary

Brahmin:	Member of Hindu upper (priestly) class
Detenus:	Persons detained in custody
Dyarchy:	A dual system of government
Goondas:	Criminals
Gordian Knot:	Difficult problem or task
Izzat:	Concept of honour in the culture of India
Jatha:	Armed Sikh band
Kalaaza:	Black fever
Lathi:	Long bamboo stick used as a weapon
Mahatma:	Person regarded with special reverence—great soul
Montford:	Combination of the names Montagu and Chelmsford
Mufussil:	The boundaries of original British settlement in India
Raj:	Sovereignty in India
Ryots:	Farmers or agriculturalists
Sajjada nishin:	Hereditary custodians of the *sufi* shrines
Satrap:	Persian term for provincial governor
Satyagraha:	Passive resistance; truth force
Sufi:	Muslim ascetic mystic
Swaraj:	Independence for India
Taluka:	Administrative subdivision of a district
Taluqdurs:	Great landowners
Zamindar:	Land proprietor paying land-tax to British Government
a priori:	Valid independently of experience
divide et impera:	Divide and rule
in camera:	Privately not in public
literati:	The learned class
pax Britannica:	British peace, law and order
prima facie:	On the first impression

Bibliography

Primary Sources

Documentary Authorities

India Office Library, London.

MSS EUR D703 - Birkenhead Papers; E252 - Clague Papers; C359 - Gandhi Papers; C429 & D595 - Goschen Papers; F115 - Haig Papers; E220 - Hailey Papers; C152 - Halifax Papers; F116 - Harcourt_Butler Papers; F160 - Lytton Papers; C279 - Marris Papers; F226 - Memoirs_of_Indian_Political_Officers; F225 & C286 - Montagu_Butler Papers; D528 - Peel Papers; D714 - Permanent_Under Secretaries_of_State - Private Papers; E238 - Reading Papers; D961 - Royal Empire_Society (Sir John Kerr); F77 - Simon Papers; F 150 - Sykes Papers; F137 - Thompson Papers; D601 - Willingdon Papers; D601 (b) - Wilson Papers.

National Library of Australia, Canberra.

Indian National Congress Reports, 1925–1931, Microform, MFM G24144.

Sapru Papers, Microform, MFM G2137–2153.

National Archives of India, New Delhi.

Proceedings of the Home and Political Departments for the years 1926–1931, Government of India Press, New Delhi.

Memoirs, Autobiographies, Publications, Contemporary Journal Articles, Speeches/Lectures —written by Irwin and the Governors

Memoirs, Autobiographies, Publications

Butler, Sir H.S. *India Insistent*. London: William Heinemann, 1931.

———. *Unpublished and Incomplete Autobiography*, Harcourt Butler Papers, MSS EUR F116, India Office Library.

———. *Political Department Manual*, 1910. This manual provided advice to British political officers (residents) on how to treat with the Princes. (See Copland, *The Princes of India in the Endgame of Empire*, p. 31.)

de Montmorency, Sir G. *The Indian States and Indian Federation*. Cambridge: Cambridge University Press, 1942.

———. *India Today and Tomorrow*. London: The Signpost Press, 1944.

Hailey, Lord. *The Future of Colonial Peoples*. Oxford: Oxford University Press, 1944.

Halifax, Lord. *Fullness of Days*. New York: Dodd, Mead, 1957.

Halifax, Viscount. *The Indian Problem*. New York: Oxford University Press, 1942.

Kerr, Sir J.H. *Rampini's Bengal Tenancy Act 1913 and 1918*. Calcutta: Government of India, 1913 and 1918.

———. *Settlement Reports of Saran and Darbanga* (Land Districts in Bihar), Government of India (no date but circa 1900).

Lytton, Earl of. *Pundits and Elephants*. London: Peter Davies, 1942.

Marris, Sir W.S. *Civil Government for Indian Students*. Shillong: Government of India., 1921.

Muddiman, Sir A. *Memoirs*. Allahabad: Government Press, 1930. (Published after his death in 1928. For private circulation only.)

Sykes, Sir F. *From Many Angles: An Autobiography*. London: Harrap & Co, 1942.

Wheeler, Sir H. *A Chaukidari Manual, with the Village Chaukidari (Amendment) Act*. Calcutta: Government of Bengal, 1922.

Contemporary Journal Articles

Hailey, Sir M. 'India', *Round Table* 12 (September 1922): 844–855.

———. 'India—1983', *Asiatic Review* 100 (1933): 620–632.

Hailey, Lord. 'India in the Modern World: A British View', *Foreign Affairs* 21 (April 1943): 401–412.

———. 'The Future of Colonial Peoples', *International Affairs (Royal Institute of International Affairs)* 20, no. 2 (April 1944): 277–278.

Halifax, Viscount. 'The Political Future of India', *Foreign Affairs* 13 (April 1935): 420–430.

———. 'India: Two Hundred Years', *Foreign Affairs* 26 (October 1947): 104–115.

———. 'Indian Constitutional Reform', *International Affairs (Royal Institute of International Affairs)* 14, no. 2 (March–April, 1935): 198–216.

Muddiman, A. 'British India', citations list, *Comparative Legislation and International Law*, 3rd Series, 6, no. 3 (1924): 135–145.

Sykes, Sir F. 'The Indian States and the Reforms', *International Affairs (Royal Institute of International Affairs)* 14, no. 1 (January–February 1935): 48–68.

Contemporary Speeches/Lectures

Butler, Sir H. *Collection of Speeches*. Rangoon: Government Press, 1927.

———. *Speeches of His Excellency Sir M. Butler*, Volume 1, 1925 to 1929. Nagpur: Nagpur Government Printing, 1931, 1933.

Irwin, Lord. *Speeches, 1926–1931*, Volumes 1 and 2. Simla: Government of India Press, 1930, 1931.
———. *Indian Problems: Speeches by Lord Irwin*. London: Allen and Unwin, 1932.
———. *Some Aspects of the Indian Problem*. Massey Lecture, Toronto: Oxford University Press, 1932.
Marris, Sir W.S. *Speeches*. United Provinces: Government Press, 1928.
———. *India: The Political Problem*. Nottingham: Cust Foundation Lecture, University College, 1930.

Papers, Publications —sourced in the India Office Library and the National Archives of India

Reports of the Native Newspapers of Bombay, MFM × 286.
Reports of the Native Newspapers of Madras, MFM × 286.
Reports of the Native Newspapers of Bengal, MFM × 286.
Indian Newspaper Reports (Vernacular). Notes on the Press, United Provinces. Printed and Published by the Government Press, United Provinces. Allahabad.

Indian Newspapers

Amrita Bazar Patrika, Calcutta. *Behar Herald*, Patna. *Bengalee*, Calcutta. *Calcutta Municipal Gazette*. *Capital*, Calcutta. *Englishman*, Calcutta. *Forward*, Calcutta. *Hindu*, Madras. *Hindustan Times*, Delhi. *Indian Daily Mail*, Bombay. *Indian National Herald*. *Leader*, Allahabad. *Madras Mail*. New India, Madras. *Pioneer*. *Rangoon Times*. *Star*, Allahabad. *The Statesman*, Calcutta. *Times of India*. *Tribune*, Lahore, Simla, Ambala, Chandigarh.

English Newspapers

London Daily Mail. *The Times of London*.

Contemporary Reports

Report of the Reforms Enquiry Committee, London, 1924. (Muddiman Report).
Report of the Committee; All Parties Conference, 1928. (Nehru Report).
Report of the Indian States Committee, 1928–1929. (Butler Report).

Report of the Royal Commission on Agriculture in India, London, 1928. (Linlithgow Report).

Report of the Indian Statutory Commission, Volumes 1 to 3, London, 1930. (Simon Commission Report).

Report of the First Round Table Conference, London, 1931.

Report of the Royal Commission on Labour in India, London, 1931. (Whitley Report).

Report on the Constitutional Problem in India, London: Oxford University Press, 1942–1943.

Parliamentary Papers

Cmd No 3700 Government of India's Despatch, 20 September 1930 on Proposals for Constitutional Reforms.

Reference Works

District Gazetteers of the United Provinces of Agra and Oudh, edited by H.R. Nevill. Allahabad: Government Press, 1903–1936.

The Gazette of India (commenced 1912).

The India Office List. Published annually until 1947. Harrison and Sons, Ltd, London.

The Indian Annual Register, Calcutta.

The Indian Quarterly Register, Calcutta, 1926. (See Vol I pp.70 ff., for report of riots in April 1926.)

Hansard, United Kingdom Parliament.

Consolidated Government of India Act, 1915–1919, London, 1919.

Secondary Works

Book References

Anderson, B. *Imagined Communities*. London: Verso, 1991.

Andrews, C.F. *Mahatma Gandhi's Ideas*. New York: Macmillan, 1930.

Appadorai, A. *Dyarchy in Practice*. Madras: Longmans Green, 1937.

Argov, D. *Moderates and Extremists in the Indian Nationalist Movement*. New York: Asia Publishing House, 1967.

Arnold, A. *The Congress in Tamilnad: Nationalist Politics in South India, 1919–1937.* Canberra: South Asian History Section, Australian National University, 1977.

Awasthi, D. *Administrative History of Modern India: Sir Spencer Harcourt Butler's Idea, Policies, and Activities in the United Provinces of Agra and Awadh, 1918–1922.* Delhi: National Publishing House, 1973.

Baker, C.J. *South India: Political Institutions and Political Change, 1880–1940.* Delhi: Macmillan Co. of India, 1975.

———. *Politics of South India, 1920–1937.* Cambridge: Cambridge University Press, 1976.

Bakshi, S.R. *The Simon Commission and Indian Nationalism.* New Delhi: Munshiran Monoharlal Publishers, 1977.

Bayly, C.A. *The Local Roots of Indian Politics: Allahabad 1880–1920.* Oxford: Clarendon Press, 1975.

———. *Indian Society and the Making of the British Empire*, Melbourne, Cambridge University Press, 1988.

Bayly, C. and Harper, T. *Forgotten Armies: The Fall of British Asia, 1941–1945.* London: Allen Lane, 2004.

Besant, A.W. *World Problems of Today.* London: Theosophical Publishing House, 1926.

Bevan, E. *Indian Nationalism: An Independent Estimate.* London: Macmillan, 1914.

———. *Thoughts on Indian Discontents.* London: Macmillan, 1929.

Birdwood, Field-Marshall, Lord. *Khaki and Gown.* London: Ward Lock, 1942.

———. *In My Time.* London: Skeffington, 1946.

Birdwood, Lord. *A Continent Decides.* London: Robert Hale, 1953.

Birkenhead, Second Earl. *Halifax: The Life of Lord Halifax.* London: Hamish Hamilton, 1965.

———. *The Life of F.E. Smith: First Earl of Birkenhead.* London: Eyre and Spottiswoode, 1965.

Bondurant, J.V. *Conquest of Violence: The Gandhian Philosophy of Conflict.* Berkeley: University of California Press, 1958.

Bose, S. *The Indian Struggle: 1920–1942.* Bombay: Asia Publishing House, 1964.

Brasted, H. *Reflections on History Today and the Appearance of a New World Disorder.* Armidale: University of New England, 2005.

Bridge, C. *Holding India to the Empire: The British Conservative Party and the 1935 Constitution.* New Delhi: Sterling Publishers, 1986.

Broomfield, J.H. *Elite Conflict in a Plural Society: Twentieth Century Bengal.* Berkeley and Los Angeles: University of California Press, 1968.

———. *Mostly About Bengal.* New Delhi: Manohar Publications, 1982.

Brown, J.M. *Gandhi's Rise to Power, Indian Politics 1915–1922.* Cambridge: Cambridge University Press, 1972.

———. *Gandhi: Prisoner of Hope.* Oxford: Oxford University Press, 1990.

———. *Nehru: A Political Life.* New Haven: Yale University Press, 2003.

Butler, J.R.M. *Lord Lothian: 1882–1940.* London: Macmillan, 1960.

Butler, Lord. *The Art of the Possible: The Memoirs of Lord Butler*. Boston: Gambit, 1971.

Cain, P.J. and Hopkins, A.G. *British Imperialism 1688–2000*. New York: Longman Publishing Group, 2001.

Campbell Johnson, A. *Viscount Halifax*. London: Hale, 1941.

Carr, E.H. *What is History?* New York: Knopf, 1962.

Cell, J.W. *Hailey: A Study in British Imperialism: 1872–1969*. New York: Cambridge University Press, 1992.

Chakrabarty, B. *Subhas Chandra Bose and Middle Class Radicalism: A Study in Middle Class Nationalism 1928–1940*. London: London School of Economics and Political Science, 1990.

Chakrabarty, D. *Rethinking Working Class History: Bengal 1890–1946*. Princeton: Princeton University Press, 1989.

———. *Habitations of Modernity: Essays in the Wake of Subaltern Studies*. Chicago: University of Chicago Press, 2002.

Chatterji, Basidev. *Trade, Tariffs and Empire: Lancashire and British Policy in India 1919–1939*. New Delhi: Oxford University Press, 1992.

Chatterji, Bhola. *Aspects of Bengal Politics in the Early Nineteen-Thirties*. Calcutta: World Press, 1969.

Chaturvedi, B. and Sykes, M. *C.F. Andrews*. London: Allen and Unwin, 1949.

Chirol, Sir V. *India: Old and New*. London: Macmillan, 1924.

Coatman, J. *Years of Destiny: India 1926–1932*. London: Jonathan Cape, 1932.

Colley, L. *Captives: Britain, Empire and the World*. London: Pimlico, 2003.

Comming, Sir J. *Political India: 1832–1932*. Delhi: S. Chand, 1968.

Cooper, D. *Old Men Forget*. New York: Dutton, 1954.

Copland, I. *The Princes of India in the Endgame of Empire, 1917–1947*. Cambridge: Cambridge University Press, 1997.

Coupland, R. *The Indian Problem 1833–1935*. Oxford: Oxford University Press, 1968.

Craddock, Sir R. *The Dilemma in India*. London: Constable, 1929.

Curtis, L. *Dyarchy*. New York: Hesperides Press, 2006.

Darwin, J. *Britain, Egypt, and the Middle East: Imperial Policy in the Aftermath of War, 1918–1922*. London: Macmillan, 1981.

———. *Britain and Decolonisation: The Retreat from Empire in the Post-war World*. London: Macmillan, 1988.

———. *The End of the British Empire: The Historical Debate*. Oxford: Basel Blackwell, 1991.

———. *The Empire Project: The Rise and Fall of the British World System, 1830–1970*. Cambridge: Cambridge University Press, 1990.

———. *Unfinished Empire: The Global Expansion of Britain*. London: Allen Lane, 2012.

Davis, L.E. and Huttenback, R.A. *Mammon and the Pursuit of Empire: The Political Economy of British Imperialism 1860–1912*. Cambridge: Cambridge University Press, 1986.

Directorate of the Chamber's Special Organisation. *The British Crown and the Indian States*. London: P.S. King, 1929.

Dobbin, C. *Basic Documents in the Development of Modern India and Pakistan 1830–1947*. London: Van Nostrand Reinhold, 1970.

———. *Urban Leadership in Western India: Politics and Communities in Bombay City, 1840–1885*. London: Oxford University Press, 1972.

Edelstein, M. 'Imperialism: Cost and Benefit', in R. Floud and D. McCloskey (eds), *The Economic History of Britain since 1700*, Volume 2, 1860–1939, pp. 197–216. Cambridge: Cambridge University Press, 1994.

Ferguson, N. *Empire: How Britain Made the Modern World*. London: Penguin, 2004.

———. *Colossus: The Price of America's Empire*. New York: Penguin, 2004.

———. *Empire: The Rise and Demise of the British World Order and the Lessons for Global Power*. London: Penguin, 2004.

Fischer, L. *The Life of Mahatma Gandhi*. New York: Vintage Books, 1962.

Forster, E.M. *The Hill of Devi*. London: Edward Arnold and Company, 1953.

Freeman, J. and Nearing, S. *Dollar Diplomacy: A Study in American Imperialism*. New York: Heubsch and Viking, 1928.

Gallagher, J. 'Congress in Decline: Bengal 1930–1939', in Anil Seal (ed.), *The Decline, Revival and Fall of the British Empire: The Ford Lectures and Other Essays*, pp. 155–211. Cambridge: Cambridge University Press, 1982.

Gallagher, J., Seal, A. and Johnson, G. (eds), *Locality, Province and Nation: Essays on Indian Politics, 1870–1940*. Cambridge: Cambridge University Press, 1973.

Gandhi, M.K. *The Collected Works of Mahatma Gandhi*. New Delhi: Government of India, Ministry of Information, Publications Division, 1964–1968.

———. *The Story of My Experiments with Truth*. Ahmedabad: Navajivan Press, 2nd edn, 1940.

Gehlat, N.S. *The Office of the Governor, its Constitutional Image and Reality*. Allahabad: Chugh, 1977.

Gilbert, M. and Gott, R.G. *The Appeasers*. London: Weidenfeld and Nicolson, 1963.

Gilmartin, D. *Empire and Islam: Punjab and the Making of Pakistan*. London: I.B. Taurus & Co Ltd, 1988.

Goldsmith, R.W. *The Financial Development of India: 1860–1977*. London: New Haven, 1983.

Gopal, S. *The Viceroyalty of Lord Irwin, 1926–1931*. Oxford: Clarendon Press, 1957.

Haithcox, J.P. *Communism and Nationalism in India: M.N. Roy and Comintern Policy, 1920–1939*. Princeton: N.J. Princeton University Press, 1971.

Hanson, J. *The Decline of the American Empire*. Westport Conn.: Praeger, 1993.

Hardiman, D. *Peasant Nationalists of Gujarat: Kheda District, 1917–1934*. New Delhi: Oxford University Press, 1981.

Hartog, Lady. *India: New Pattern*, foreword by Lord Hailey. London: George Allen, 1955.

Hoare, Sir S. (Viscount Templewood). *The Unbroken Thread*. London: Collins, 1949.

———. *Nine Troubled Years*. London: Collins, 1954.

Hodgson, S. *Lord Halifax: An Appreciation*. London: Christophers, 1941.

Husain, A. *Fazl-i-Husain: A Political Biography*. Bombay: Longmans, 1946.

Hutchins, F.G. *The Illusion of Permanence: British Imperialism in India*. Princeton: Princeton University Press, 1967.

Hyam, R. *Britain's Declining Empire: The Road to Decolonisation 1918–1968*. Cambridge: Cambridge University Press, 2006.

Iggers, G.G. *Historiography in the Twentieth Century: From Scientific Objectivity to the Postmodern Challenge*. London: Wesleyan University Press, 1997.

Irani, C.R. *Bengal: The Communist Challenge*. Bombay: Lalvani Publishing House, 1968.

Irschick, E.F. *Politics and Social Conflict in South India: The Non-Brahmin Movement and Tamil Separatism, 1916–1929*. Berkeley and Los Angeles: University of California Press, 1969.

———. *Tamil Revivalism in the 1930s*. Madras: CRE-A, 1986.

Jalal, A. and Bose, S. (eds). *Nationalism, Democracy and Development: State and Politics in India*. New Delhi: Oxford University Press, 1997.

———. (eds). *Modern South Asia: History, Culture, Political Economy*. New York: Routledge, 2004.

James, L. *Raj: The Making and Unmaking of British India*. London: Little, Brown and Co., 1998.

Johnson, G. *New Cambridge History of India*, edited by Gordon Johnson, C.A. Bayly and J.F. Richards. Cambridge: Cambridge University Press, 1987.

———. *Provincial Politics and Indian Nationalism: Bombay and the Indian National Congress 1880–1915*. Cambridge: Cambridge University Press, 1973.

Jones, E.S. *Mahatma Gandhi: An Interpretation*. London: Hodder and Stoughton, 1948.

Joshi, S. *Struggle for Hegemony in India 1920–1947: The Colonial States, the Left and the National Movement*. New Delhi: SAGE Publications, 1992.

Judd, D. *Empire*. 1996. *The British Imperial Experience from 1765 to the Present*. London: HarperCollins Publication.

Kanwar, P. *Imperial Simla: The Political Culture of the Raj*. New Delhi: Oxford University Press, 2nd edn, 2003.

Keith, A.B. *A Constitutional History of India 1600–1935*. London: Methuen and Co., 1936.

Kennedy, P. *The Rise and Fall of the Great Powers: Economic Change and Military Conflict from 1500 to 2000*. New York: Random House, 1989.

Kincaid, D.C. *British Social Life in India 1608–1937*. London: Routledge, 1939.

Kirk-Greene, A. *On Crown Service: A History of H.M. Colonial and Overseas Civil Services, 1837–1997*. London: I.B. Taurus, 1999.

Laushey, D.M. *Bengal Terrorism and the Marxist Left: Aspects of Regional Nationalism in India 1905–1942*. Calcutta: Firma K.L. Mukhopadhyay, 1975.

Lawrence, Sir W.R. *The India We Served*. Boston: Houghton Miffin, 1929.

Lockhart, J.G. *Viscount Halifax*. London: Geoffrey Bles, 1935, 1936.

Louis Roger, W.M. (ed.). *Imperialism: The Robinson and Gallagher Controversy*. London: New Viewpoints, 1976.

Louis, W.R. *Imperialism at Bay: The United States and the Decolonisation of the British Empire 1941–1945*. New York, Oxford: Clarendon Press, 1978.

Low, D.A. *Soundings in Modern South Asian History*. Berkeley: University of California Press, 1968.

———. *Lion Rampart: Essays in the Study of British Imperialism*. London: Cass, 1973.

———. *Eclipse of Empire*. Cambridge: Cambridge University Press, 1991.

———. *Rearguard Action: Selected Essays on Late Colonial Indian History*. New Delhi: Sterling Publishers, 1996.

———. *Britain and Indian Nationalism: The Imprint of Ambiguity 1929–1942*. London: Cambridge University Press, 1997.

Low, D.A. and Brasted, H. (eds), *Freedom, Trauma, Continuities: Northern India and Independence*. New Delhi: SAGE Publications, 1998.

Low, D.A. (ed.), *Congress and the Raj: Facets of the Indian Struggle 1917–1947*. New Delhi: Oxford University Press, 2004.

Mackonochie, Sir E. *Life in the Indian Civil Service*. London: Unknown Publisher, 1926.

Markovits, C. *Indian Business and Nationalist Politics 1931–1939: The Indigenous Capitalist Class and the Rise of the Congress Party*. Cambridge: Cambridge University Press, 1985.

Marlowe, J. *The Late Victorian Empire*. London: Macmillan, 1967.

Mason, P. *A Matter of Honour*. New York: Holt, Rinehart and Winston, 1974.

Masselos, J. *Nationalism on the Indian Subcontinent*. Melbourne: Thomas Nelson, 1972.

———. (ed.). *India: Creating a Modern Nation*. New Delhi: Sterling Publishers, 1990.

———. *Indian Nationalism: An History*. New Delhi: Sterling, 1991.

———. *The City in Action: Bombay Struggles for Power*. New Delhi: Oxford University Press, 2007.

May, E.R. *American Imperialism: A Speculative Essay*. Chicago: Atheneum, 1991.

Mayhew, A. *Education of India*. London: Faber and Gwyer, 1926.

Mayo, K. *Mother India*. London: Cape, 1927.

McGuire, J., Reeves, P. and Brasted, H. (eds). *Politics of Violence: From Ayodhya to Behrampada*. New Delhi: Thousand Oaks: SAGE Publications, 1996.

Mehta, S.D. *The Cotton Mills of India 1854–1954*. Bombay: The Textile Association, 1954.

Menon, D.M. *Caste, Nationalism and Communism in South India: Malabar, 1900–1948*. Cambridge: Cambridge University Press, 1994.

Mersey, C.B. 2nd Viscount. *The Viceroys and Governors General of India 1757–1947*. London: Murray, 1949.

Misra, A.K. *The Administration of the United Provinces of Agra and Oudh under Sir William Malcolm Hailey, 1928–1934*. Lucknow: Gyan Deep Prakashan, 1994.

Misra, B.B. *The Administrative History of India 1834–1947*. London: Oxford University Press, 1970.

———. *The Bureaucracy in India: An Historical Analysis of Development up to 1947*. New Delhi: Oxford University Press, 1977.

Montagu, E.S. *An Indian Diary*. London: Heinemann, Ltd., 1930.

———. *Liberalism and Indian Politics, 1872–1922*. London: Edward Arnold, 1966.

Moore, R.J. *The Crisis of Indian Unity: 1917–1940*. Oxford: Clarendon, 1974.

———. *Endgames of Empire: Studies of Britain's Indian Problem*. New Delhi: Oxford University Press, 1988.

Moraes, F. *Jawaharlal Nehru*. New York: Macmillan, 1957.

———. *Witness to an Era*. New Delhi: Vikas Publishing, 1973.

Morris, J. *Pax Brittanica: The Climax of an Empire*. London: Faber and Faber, 1968.

Mukherji, P. *The Indian Constitution*. Calcutta and Simla: Thacker, Spink and Co., 1920.

Nanda, B.R. *Mahatma Gandhi*. London: George Allen and Unwin Ltd, 1958.

———. *Gokhale: The Indian Moderates and the British Raj*. New Delhi: Oxford University Press, 1977.

———. *Three Statesmen: Gokhale, Gandhi and Nehru*. New Delhi: Oxford University Press, 2004.

Nehru, J. *Autobiography*. New Delhi: Oxford University Press, 1982.

O'Dwyer, Sir M. *India as I Knew It: 1885–1925*. London: Constable and Company Ltd., 1925.

O'Malley, L.S.S. *The Indian Civil Service: 1601–1930*. London: Frank Cass & Co. Ltd, 2nd edn, 1965.

O'Rourke, K.H. and Williamson, J.G. *Globalisation and History: The Evolution of a Nineteenth Century Atlantic Economy*. London: The MIT Press, 1999.

Page, D. *Prelude to Partition: The Indian Muslims and the Imperial System of Control, 1920–1932*. New Delhi: Oxford University Press, 1999.

Pandey, B.N. *Nehru*. London: Macmillan, 1977.

———. (ed.). *The Indian Nationalist Movement, 1885–1947*. London: Macmillan, 1979.

Pandey, D. *The Arya Samaj and Indian Nationalism*. New Delhi: Chand, 1972.

Pandey, G. *The Ascendancy of the Congress in Uttar Pradesh 1926–34: A Study in Imperfect Mobilisation*. New Delhi: Oxford Uiversity Press, 1978.

Panikkar, K.M. *Indian States and the Government of India*. London: Martin Hopkinson Ltd., 1932.

———. *The Working of Dyarchy in India: 1919–1928*. Bombay: Keralputra, 1928.

Potter, D.C. *India's Political Administrators 1919–1983*. Oxford: Oxford University Press, 1986.

Rai Chowduri, S. *Leftism in India, 1917–1947*. Basingstoke: Palgrave Macmillan, 2007.

Ramusack, B.N. *The Princes of India in the Twilight of Empire*. Columbus: Ohio State University, 1978.

Ray, Rajat. *Urban Roots of Indian Nationalism: Pressure Groups and Conflicts of Interests in Calcutta City Politics, 1875–1939*. New Delhi: Vikas Publishing House Pvt Ltd, 1979.

Raychaudhuri, T. 'British Rule in India: An Assessment', in P.J. Marshall (ed.), *The Cambridge Illustrated History of the British Empire*, pp. 357–369. Cambridge: Cambridge University Press 1996.

Reed, Sir S. *The India I Knew, 1897–1947*. London: Odhams, 1952.

Riddick, J.F. *Who Was Who in British India.* Westport: Greenwood Publishing Group, 1998. (Note this book is inconsistent with the biographical information contained in *The India Office List.*)

Robinson, R. and Gallagher, J. *Africa and the Victorians: The Official Mind of Imperialism*, 2nd edn. London: Macmillan Press, 1981.

Robb, P.G. *The Government of India and Reform: Policies towards Politics and the Constitution, 1916–1921.* Oxford: Oxford University Press, 1976.

———. 'The Bureaucrat as Reformer: Two Indian Civil Servants and the Constitution of 1919', in P.G. Robb and D. Taylor (eds), *Rule, Protest, Identity: Aspects of Modern South Asia*, pp. 49–82. London: Curzon Press, 1978.

———. (ed.). *Rural India: Land, Power and Society under British Rule.* London: Curzon Press, 1983.

———. *History of India.* Basingstoke, Hampshire: Houndmills, 2002.

———. *Liberalism, Modernity and the Nation: Empire, Identity and India.* New Delhi: Oxford University Press, 2007.

———. *Peasants Political Economy and Law: Empire, Identity and India.* New Delhi: Oxford University Press, 2007.

Roberts, A. *Holy Fox.* London: Phoenix Press, 1997.

Roberts, Earl of Kandahar. *Forty-One Years in India.* London: Macmillan, 1897.

Robinson. F. *Separation among Indian Muslims: The Politics of the United Provinces Muslims, 1860–1923.* London: Cambridge University Press, 1974.

Robinson, F. and Brass, P.R. (eds). *The Indian National Congress and Indian Society, 1885–1985: Ideology, Social Structure and Political Dominance.* Delhi: Chanakya Publications, 1987.

Rothermund, D. *An Economic History of India.* London: Routledge, 1991.

Roy, T. *The Economic History of India, 1857–1947.* New Delhi: Oxford University Press, 2002.

Rumbold, A. *Watershed in India.* London: Athlone Press, 1979.

Rutherford, V.H. *Modern India: Its Problems and Their Solutions.* London: Labour Publishing Co, 1927.

Sachs, B. *Ramsay Macdonald in Thought and Action.* New York: Macmillan, 1952.

Seal, A. *The Emergence of Indian Nationalism.* Cambridge: Cambridge University Press, 1971.

Seton, Sir M. *India Office.* London: G.P. Putnam and Son, 1927.

Simon, J.A.S. 1st Viscount. *The Memoirs of the Rt Hon Viscount Simon.* London: Hutchinson, 1952.

Smith, V.A. *The Oxford History of India.* New Delhi: Oxford University Press, 1974.

Smythies, O. *Ten Thousand Miles on Elephants* (foreword by Lord Hailey). London: Seeley Service, 1961.

Stein, B. *A History of India.* Oxford: Blackwell, 1998.

Stone, I. *The Global Export of Capital from Great Britain, 1865–1914.* London: Macmillan, 1999.

Symonds, R. *Oxford and Empire.* Oxford: Clarendon Press, 1986.

Swinton, Earl of. *I Remember.* London: Hutchinson and Co, 1940.

Taylor, H.A. *Smith of Birkenhead.* London: Stanley Paul, 1931.

Tendulkar, D.G. and Jhaveri, V.K. *Mahatma.* Delhi: Publication Division, Government of India, 8 volumes, 1953–1954.

Thomas, I. *Our Lord Birkenhead: An Oxford Appreciation.* London: Putnam, 1930.

Thompson, E.J. *The Making of the Indian Princes.* New York: Oxford University Press, 1943.

Thompson, E.J. and Garrett, G.T. *Rise and Fulfillment of British Rule in India.* Allahabad: Central Book Depot, 1969.

Tinker, H. *The Foundations of Local Self Government in India, Pakistan and Burma* (foreword by Lord Hailey). London: Pall Mall Press, 1954.

———. *Viceroy: Curzon to Mountbatten.* Karachi: Oxford University Press, 1997.

Tomlinson, B.R. *The Indian National Congress and the Raj, 1929–1942: The Penultimate Phase.* London: Macmillan, 1976.

———. *The Political Economy of the Raj, 1914–1947.* London: Macmillan Press, 1979.

Vidal, G. *The Decline and Fall of the American Empire.* Berkeley: California, 1992.

Wakefield, Sir E. *Past Imperative: My Life in India, 1927–1947.* London: Chatto and Windus, 1966.

Washbrook, D. and Baker, C.J. *South India: Political Institutions and Political Change 1880–1940.* Delhi: Macmillan Co of India, 1975.

Washbrook, D. *Emergence of Provincial Politics: The Madras Presidency, 1870–1920.* Cambridge: Cambridge University Press, 1976.

Woods, P. *Roots of Parliamentary Democracy in India: Montagu Chelmsford Reforms, 1917–1923.* Delhi: Chanakya Publications, 1996.

Whyte, Sir F. *India, a Federation.* New Delhi: Government of India, 1930.

Wilberforce-Bell, Major. *Kathiawad.* New Delhi: Ajay Book Service, 1980.

Wolpert, S. *A New History of India*, 6th edn. Oxford: Oxford University Press, 2000.

Woodruff, P. *The Men Who Ruled India*, Volume 2. London: Jonathan Cape, 1963.

Wrench, E. *Dawson and Our Times.* London: Hutchinson, 1955.

Yang, A.A. *The Limited Raj: Agrarian Relations in Colonial India, Saran District, 1793–1920.* Oakland: University of California Press, 1989.

———. *Bazaar India: Markets, Society and the Colonial State in Gangetic Bihar.* Oakland: University of California Press, 1998.

Young, G.M. *Stanley Baldwin.* London: Hart Davis, 1952.

Journal Articles

Aitken, J. 'Official Regulation of British Overseas Investment, 1914–1931', *Economic History Review,* New Series 23, no. 2 (August 1970): 324–335.

Awasthi, D. 'Sir Spencer Harcourt Butler and his Eastern Oxford', *Asiatic Society of Pakistan* 10 (June 1965): 159–666.

———. 'Sir Spencer Harcourt Butler and the University Education in India', *Indian History* 43 (December 1965): 855–865.

Bayly, C.A. 'Returning the British to South Asian History: The Limits of Colonial Hegemony', *South Asia* 17, no. 2 (December 1994): 1–25.

Benn, Wedgwood. 'The War and India's Freedom', *Contemporary Review*—New York 156 (December 1939): 652–659.

Carr, C.T. 'Introduction to the Review of Legislation 1922', *Comparative Legislation and International Law,* 3rd Ser., 6, no. 3 (1924): 29–36.

Crawley, W.F. 'Kisan Sabhas and Agrarian Revolt in the United Provinces 1920 to 1921', *Modern Asian Studies* 5, no. 2 (1971): 95–109.

Danzig, R. 'The Announcement of August 20th, 1917', *The Journal of Asian Studies* 28, no. 1 (November 1968): 19–37.

———. 'The Many-layered Cake: A Case Study in the Reform of the Indian Empire', *Modern Asian Studies* 3, no. 1 (1969): 57–74.

Darwin, J. 'Imperial Policy between the Wars', *Historical Journal* 23, no. 3 (1980): 657–665.

Dolobran, Lord Lloyd of, 'The Problem of Constitutional Reform in India', *International Affairs (Royal Institute of International Affairs)* 12, no. 5 (September 1933): 593–610.

Dutt, A.K. 'The Origins of Uneven Development: The Indian Subcontinent', *American Economic Review* 82, no. 2 (May 1992): 146–150.

Epstein, S. 'District Officers in Decline: The Erosion of British Authority in the Bombay countryside 1919 to 1947', *Modern Asian Studies* 16 (1982): 493–528.

Ewing, A. 'The Indian Civil Service 1919–1924: Discontent and the Response in London and in New Delhi', *Modern Asian Studies* 18, no. 1 (1984): 33–53.

Gallagher, J. 'Congress in Decline: Bengal 1930–1939', *Modern Asian Studies* 7, no. 3 (1973): 589–645.

Gallagher, J. and Seal, A. 'Britain and India between the Wars', *Modern Asian Studies* 15, no. 3 (1981): 387–414.

Guha, R. 'Subaltern Studies and its Critics: Debates over Indian History', *History and Theory* 40, no. 1 (February 2000): 135–148.

Holdsworth, W. 'The Indian States', *New York University Law Quarterly Review* VII, no. 1 (September 1929): 1–16.

Louis, W.R. and Robinson, R. 'The Imperialism of Decolonisation', *Imperial and Commonwealth History* 22, no. 3 (1994): 462–511.

Low, D.A. 'The Government of India and the First Non-cooperation Movement 1920–1922', *The Journal of Asian Studies* 25, no. 2 (February 1966): 241–259.

MacLeod, R.M. 'Scientific Advice for British India: Imperial Perceptions and Administrative Goals, 1898–1923', *Modern Asian Studies* 9, no. 3 (1975): 343–384.

Maheshwari, S. 'The All-India Services', *Public Administration* 49 (1971): 291–308.

Minault, G. and Lelyveld, D. 'The Campaign for a Muslim University, 1898–1920', *Modern Asian Studies* 8, no. 2 (1974): 145–189.

Murray-Hogben, W. 'An Imperial Dilemma: The Reluctant Indianisation of the Indian Political Service', *Modern Asian Studies* 15, no. 4 (1981): 751–769.

Newman, R.K. 'India and the Anglo-Chinese Opium Agreements, 1907–1914', *Modern Asian Studies* 23, no. 3 (1989): 525–560.

O'Dwyer, M.F. 'Present Conditions in India', *Fortnightly Review* 115 (July–December 1921): 177–193.

———. 'Three Years of Reform in India', *Fortnightly Review* 115 (January–June 1924): 352–369.

Olivier, Lord. 'The Disease of Indian Dyarchy', *Contemporary Review*—New York 127 (May 1925): 554–562.

Patiala, The Maharajah of. 'The Problem of the Indian States', *International Affairs (Royal Institute of International Affairs)* 7, no. 6 (November 1928): 389–406.

Potter, D.C. 'Manpower Shortage and the End of Colonialism: The Case of the INDIAN civil Service', *Modern Asian Studies* 7, no. 1 (1973): 47–73.

Razi, W.S. 'Sir H. Butler on the Indian Educational and Political Situation in the Early Twentieth Century'. *Asiatic Society of Pakistan* 7 (December 1962): 349–355.

Reeves, P.D. 'Anti-non-cooperation in the United Provinces 1921', *The Journal of Asian Studies* 25, no. 2 (February 1966): 261–274.

Richter, W.L. and Ramusack, B. 'The Chamber and the Consultation: Changing Forms of Princely Association in India', *The Journal of Asian Studies* 34, no. 3 (May 1975): 755–776.

Robb, P. 'The Government of India and Annie Besant', *Modern Asian Studies* 10, no. 1 (1976): 107–130.

Rothermund, D. 'The Great Depression and British Financial Policy in India, 1929–1934', *Indian Economic and Social History Review* 18, no. 1 (1981): 1–17.

Seal, A. 'Imperialism and Nationalism in India', *Modern Asian Studies* 7, no. 3 (1973): 321–347.

Singh, R.P. 'The India Office and its Attitude towards Constitutional Advance at the Centre, 1921–1925', *Indian History* 30 (1971): 341–360.

Spinner, T.J. Jr, 'George Joachim Goschen: The Man Lord Randolph Churchill Forgot', *Modern History* 39, no. 4 (December 1967): 405–424.

Tai, Y.T. 'Assuaging the Sikhs: Government Responses to the Akali Movement, 1920–1925', *Modern Asian Studies* 29, no. 3 (July 1995): 655–703.

Editorial Summary (India). 'The British Empire', *Political Science Quarterly,* 41 (1) (March 1926): 80–96.

Tomlinson, B.R. 'India and the British Empire, 1880–1935', *Indian Economic and Social History Review* 12 (1975): 337–380.

Washbrook, D. 'South Asia, the World System and World Capitalism', *The Journal of Asian Studies* 49, no. 3 (August 1990): 479–508.

Watson, S. 'Gandhi and the Viceroys', *History Today* 8, no. 2 (1958): 88–97.

Watts, S. 1999. 'British Development Policies and Malaria in India, 1897–1929', *Past and Present,* 165 (November 1999): 145–189.

Windschuttle, K. 'Lengthened Shadows: The Burdens of Empire', *New Criterion* 22, no. 1 (September 2003): 4–15.

Woods, P. 'The Montagu–Chelmsford Reforms (1919): A Re-assessment', *South Asia* 17, no. 1 (June 1994): 25–42.

Unpublished Theses

Ayres, R.G. 'The Impact of Viceregal Attitudes towards Gandhi on Imperial Policy, 1929–1934'. Unpublished B.A. thesis, University of New England, 1984.

Macnamara, M.F. 'Lords Willingdon and Lytton: A Study in Gubernatorial Attitudes to Rising Indian Nationalism, 1913–1927'. Unpublished M. Litt. thesis, University of New England, 1986.

———. 'The Governors of British India during Lord Irwin's Viceroyalty: 1926–1931'. Doctoral thesis, University of New England, 2009

Reeves, P.D. 'The Landlord's Response to Political Change in the United Provinces of Agra and Oudh, India, 1921–1937'. Unpublished PhD thesis, ANU, 1963.

Watts, J.F.C. 'The Viceroyalty of Lord Irwin 1926–1931: With Special Reference to the Political and Constitutional Developments'. D.Phil. thesis, Oxon. Oct.,1973.

Author Index

Subject Index

About the Author

Michael Fenwick Macnamara retired as a senior official from the Australian Civil Service in 2005. His career provided him perspectives into the working principles and practices of an administrative system inherited from the British, as in India. This allowed an insightful understanding and interpretation of the system practised by the administrators of British India.

He has a personal connection and deep interest in the history of India. He is a member of the Kipling Society, the Indian Military Historical Society and is a life member of the British Association for Cemeteries in South Asia.

He is currently an independent scholar and Honorary Associate, School of Humanities, University of New England, Australia.

About the Author